高等院校旅游专业系列教材
旅游企业岗位培训系列教材

Practical English for Tourism

实用旅游英语

（第2版）

黄中军　李秀霞　王乃换　编著

清华大学出版社
北京

内 容 简 介

本书根据国际旅游业发展的新形势和新特点，结合旅游服务所涉及的业务范围，按照旅游服务操作规程与要求，对照"吃、住、行、游、购、娱"等板块逐一进行具体介绍，并通过创设旅游真实情境指导学生实训，强化应用技能与能力培养。

本书内容翔实、案例丰富，强化实战演练，实用性强，并注重旅游全过程服务与实践能力培养，因此既适用于大学本科旅游管理专业的教学，也可以作为专升本及高职高专院校旅游管理专业的教材，还可用于旅游企业从业者的职业教育与培训。

本书封面贴有清华大学出版社防伪标签，无标签者不得销售。
版权所有，侵权必究。举报：010-62782989，beiqinquan@tup.tsinghua.edu.cn。

图书在版编目（CIP）数据

实用旅游英语/黄中军，李秀霞，王乃换编著. —2版. —北京：清华大学出版社，2023.3（2024.8重印）
高等院校旅游专业系列教材　旅游企业岗位培训系列教材
ISBN 978-7-302-42760-5

Ⅰ. ①实… Ⅱ. ①黄… ②李… ③王… Ⅲ. ①旅游–英语–自学参考资料 Ⅳ. ①H31

中国版本图书馆 CIP 数据核字（2016）第 021239 号

责任编辑：杜　星
封面设计：常雪影
责任校对：王凤芝
责任印制：曹婉颖

出版发行：清华大学出版社
网　　　址：https://www.tup.com.cn, https://www.wqxuetang.com
地　　　址：北京清华大学学研大厦 A 座　　邮　编：100084
社　总　机：010-83470000　　邮　购：010-62786544
投稿与读者服务：010-62776969，c-service@tup.tsinghua.edu.cn
质　量　反　馈：010-62772015，zhiliang@tup.tsinghua.edu.cn

印 装 者：三河市东方印刷有限公司
经　　销：全国新华书店
开　　本：185mm×230mm　　印　张：19.25　　字　数：387 千字
版　　次：2010 年 8 月第 1 版　2023 年 3 月第 2 版　印　次：2024 年 8 月第 3 次印刷
定　　价：56.00 元

产品编号：065058-01

旅游系列教材编审委员会

主　　任：牟惟仲
副 主 任：林　征　　冀俊杰　　张昌连　　武裕生　　张建国
　　　　　车亚军　　田小梅　　吕亚非　　钟丽娟　　李大军
编审委员：黄中军　　时永春　　马继兴　　王春艳　　李爱华
　　　　　杨　昆　　赵立群　　吕亚非　　蔡洪胜　　梁艳智
　　　　　张冬冬　　钟丽娟　　童　俊　　巩玉环　　高　歌
　　　　　郑强国　　张凤霞　　段云鹏　　张冠男　　张百菊
　　　　　王瑞春　　叶杰琳　　王　锐　　郑转玲　　王丽飞
总　　编：李大军
副 主 编：杨　昆　　李爱华　　赵立群　　梁艳智　　王春艳
专 家 组：武裕生　　马继兴　　黄中军　　时永春　　吕亚非

序　言

随着我国改革开放进程加快和国民经济的高速发展,交通与通信技术的不断进步,旅游景区(点)维护、旅游文化挖掘及宾馆酒店设施设备的不断完善,居民收入和闲暇时间的增多,旅游正日益成为现代社会人们主要的生活方式和社会经济活动,大众化旅游时代已经快速到来。

旅游作为文化创意产业的核心支柱,在国际交往、文化交流、扶贫脱贫、拉动内需、解决就业、丰富社会生活、促进经济发展、构建和谐社会、弘扬中华文化等方面发挥着巨大作用,旅游已成为当今世界经济发展最快的"绿色朝阳产业"。

2021年5月,文化和旅游部印发《"十四五"文化和旅游市场发展规划》,规划确定了"十四五"时期旅游业发展的总体思路、基本目标、主要任务和保障措施,是未来我国旅游业发展的行动纲领和基本遵循,为我国的旅游业发展指明了方向。

随着全球旅游业的飞速发展,旅游观念、产品、营销方式、运营方式及管理手段等都发生了巨大变化,面对国际旅游业激烈的市场竞争,旅游行业的从业员工急需更新观念、提高服务技能、提升业务与道德素质,旅游行业和企业也在呼唤"有知识、懂管理、会操作、能执行"的专业实用型人才。加强旅游经营管理模式的创新、加速旅游经营管理专业技能型人才培养已成为当前亟待解决的问题。

针对我国高等职业教育旅游管理专业知识老化、教材陈旧、重理论轻实践、缺乏实际操作技能训练等问题,为满足社会就业发展和日益增长的旅游市场需求,我们组织多年从事旅游教学实践的国内知名专家教授及旅游企业经理共同精心编撰了本套教材,旨在迅速提高大学生和旅游从业者专业素质,更好地服务于我国旅游事业。

本套教材根据大学旅游管理专业教学大纲和课程设置,融入旅游管理的最新实践教学理念,坚持以习近平新时代中国特色社会主义思想为指导,力求严谨,注重新发展理念,依照旅游活动的基本过程和规律,全面贯彻国家新近颁布实施的旅游法规及各项管理规定,按照旅游企业用人需求,结合解决学生就业,注重校企结合,贴近行业企业业务实际,强化理论与实践的紧密结合,注重管理方法、实践技能与岗位应用的培养,并注重教学内容和教材结构的创新。

本套教材的出版,对帮助学生尽快熟悉旅游操作规程与业务管理,毕业后能够顺利走上社会就业具有特殊意义。

牟惟仲

2022年10月

第 2 版 前 言

旅游业作为文化创意产业的核心支柱,在国际交往、文化交流、拉动内需、解决就业、丰富社会生活、促进经济发展、构建和谐社会、弘扬中华文化等方面发挥着越来越大的作用,旅游业已成为我国服务经济发展的重要产业,在我国经济发展中占有极其重要的位置。为了加快推动旅游业的发展,国务院发布了《关于加快发展旅游业的意见》,这是党中央和中国政府的一项重大决策。

外语是涉外服务工具,也是对外交流的重要手段,英语作为国际旅行的通用语言和主要交际工具,旅游从业人员的英语应用水平直接影响着我国旅游业的发展速度与服务质量;为了满足日益增长的旅游市场需求,为了培养社会急需的既有丰富旅游专业知识、又有过硬外语水平的专业人才,我们组织多年在一线从事旅游英语教学和旅游实践活动的专家教授,共同精心编写了此教材,旨在迅速提高大学生和旅游从业者的专业英语应用水平,更好地服务于我国的旅游事业。

本书作为普通高等教育旅游管理专业的特色教材,自 2010 年出版以来,因写作质量好、实用性强而多次重印,很受全国各高等院校师生欢迎。此次再版,以科学发展观为指导,严格按照教育部"加强职业教育、突出实践技能培养"的要求,针对大学旅游英语教学要求和职业能力培养目标,结合模块化组合和实例教学,注重强化听力、口语、阅读、翻译训练;作者审慎地对教材内容进行了反复论证、精心设计、深入推敲、悉心写作;本书再版对帮助学生尽快熟悉旅游服务业务要求、走上社会顺利就业、从事旅游职业岗位工作具有特殊意义。

全书共分 7 大部分,以培养学习者应用能力为主线,依照旅游服务实际业务的基本过程和规律,结合旅游咨询、名胜古迹游览、饮食、购物、娱乐等活动,具体介绍自然景观、人文景观、历史名城、宗教圣殿、饮食文化、社会习俗、旅游购物、节日假日等旅游热点内容,并注重把传统教材的以理论为中心转变为以实际工作需要为中心,充分体现实用性、互动性、交际性、趣味性原则。为了方便教师教学和学生学习,本书还配有听力音频,读者可先扫描书后的防盗码,获取权限后,再扫描书中二维码,即可听取。

由于本书融入了旅游英语的最新实践教学理念,力求严谨,注重与时俱进,具有理论适中、知识系统、案例鲜活、贴近实际、突出实用性的特点,因此,本书既适用于大学本科旅游管理专业的教学,也可作为专升本及高职高专院校旅游英语课程选用教材,并可用于旅游企业从业者的职业教育与岗位培训。

本书由李大军总体筹划并具体组织,由留英旅游专家杨昆教授审定,由留美旅游专家蔡丽伟教授复审。作者编写分工:牟惟仲(序言),黄中军(第一部分、第三部分),黄晶晶(第二部分),王乃换(第四部分),李秀霞(第五部分),宋改娟(第六部分),巩玉环(第七部分),高炯、李峥、张翠玲(附录),华燕萍、李晓新(文字修改、版式调整、制作课件)。

  在修订再版过程中,我们参阅了大量旅游英语方面的最新书刊和网站资料,精选了优质案例和图片,并得到有关专家教授的具体指导,在此一并致谢。为方便教学,本书配有电子课件,读者可以扫描书后二维码免费下载。由于作者水平有限,书中难免存在疏漏和不足,因此恳请专家和广大读者给予批评指正。

编　者
2022 年 11 月

目 录

Part I   Arrival ··· 1
    Unit 1   At the Airport ··· 1
    Unit 2   At the Immigration & Customs ······················· 10
    Unit 3   At the Hotel ·· 19
    Unit 4   At the Restaurant ·· 28
    Unit 5   Traffic ··· 37

Part II   Tourism Consultation ··· 47
    Unit 1   Asking About Scenic Spots ······························· 47
    Unit 2   At the Travel Agency ······································· 56
    Unit 3   At the Bank ··· 64
    Unit 4   Emergency Cases When Traveling ···················· 72

Part III   Beauty Spots ·· 80
    Unit 1   Natural Scenery ··· 80
    Unit 2   Historical Sites ·· 88
    Unit 3   Religious Shrines ··· 97
    Unit 4   Holiday Resorts ··· 106

Part IV   Festivals and City Tours ································· 114
    Unit 1   Festivals ·· 114
    Unit 2   Famous Cities ··· 122
    Unit 3   Museums and Palaces ····································· 130
    Unit 4   Parks ··· 139

Part V   Food & Drinks ·· 148
    Unit 1   Chinese Cuisine ·· 148
    Unit 2   French Cuisine ·· 157
    Unit 3   Muslim Cuisine ··· 165
    Unit 4   Tea and Coffee ··· 173

  Unit 5 Wine ··· 183

Part VI Shopping ·· 192
  Unit 1 Tourist Souvenirs ·· 192
  Unit 2 Jewelry ··· 200
  Unit 3 Clothing ·· 209
  Unit 4 Perfume and Makeup ··· 217
  Unit 5 Antiques ·· 226

Part VII Entertainment ··· 235
  Unit 1 Peking Opera ·· 235
  Unit 2 Acrobatics and Chinese Martial Arts ··························· 243
  Unit 3 Movies ·· 252
  Unit 4 Sports ··· 260
  Unit 5 Bars ·· 268

附录一：本书专有名词列表 ·· 277

附录二：明清两朝皇帝 ·· 281

附录三：东西方主要节日 ··· 283

附录四：应用文样本 ·· 285

附录五：世界七大奇迹 ·· 289

附录六：十二属相与十二星宿表 ·· 291

附录七：肢体语言 ·· 292

附录八：出入境检疫检验申明卡 ·· 294

参考文献 ·· 297

Part I

Arrival

Unit 1 At the Airport

Section 1 Listening and Speaking

Ⅰ. Listen and Repeat

Dialogue 1 Getting Plane Tickets
Brant is a ticket agent at John F. Kennedy International Airport and Annie is a tourist who needs a return ticket to Beijing.
Brant: Good morning, ma'am. What can I do for you?
Annie: I'd like to have a round-way ticket to Beijing, please.
Brant: Do you want to fly first class or economy class?
Annie: Economy class, please. How much is it?
Brant: It's $820. It is cheap but non-refundable.
Annie: I see. Can I get a discount?
Brant: Sorry, you can't. To get a discount, you'll have to book tickets a few days in advance.
Annie: Do I need to change planes?
Brant: Yes, you need to change planes in Detroit.
Annie: Oh, I see. What is the departure time of the next flight?
Brant: 3 p.m..
Annie: OK, please get me an economy class round-way ticket for the next flight. I'd like an aisle seat.

Brant: Okay. By the way, would you like to sign up for our frequent flyer program? If you do, you'll be entitled to one free round trip to Thailand or Egypt when you accumulate certain miles of air travel.

Annie: Wow, that's really good! I'd like to sign up for it.

Brant: Then you can go to Window 9 to go through the formalities.

Annie: Okay. Thank you very much.

Brant: You are welcome.

Dialogue 2   Checking in

Bruce is going back to San Francisco by air and he has just arrived at Beijing Capital International Airport. Ms. Wang is the clerk at the check-in zone.

Announcer: Air China announces the departure of Flight CA983 nonstop to San Francisco. Passengers please proceed through security clearance to Gate 6.

Wang: Good afternoon.

Bruce: Good afternoon. Is this the right gate to check in for Flight CA983 to San Francisco?

Wang: Yes, may I see your ticket and passport, please?

Bruce: Here you are.

Wang: Please put your bag on the conveyor belt and step through the metal detector.

Bruce: Okay. How many items of carry-on luggage are permitted?

Wang: According to our regulations, you are allowed to carry on only two items of luggage. So you have to check that big suitcase.

Bruce: I see.

Wang: Here are your tags. Please put them on your luggage.

Bruce: Thank you. By the way, will the flight depart on time?

Wang: I'm not sure. It's rainy today and the flight might be delayed owing to bad weather.

Bruce: Oh, that's too bad. My wife is expecting me in San Francisco. It will be our 20th wedding anniversary tomorrow.

Wang: In that case you'd better call your wife in advance.

Bruce: Thank you very much.

Wang: You are welcome.

Ⅱ. Act Out

1. Listen to the dialogue. Then practice it with your partners using the words and expressions below to help you.

Part I
Arrival

> **Air hostess**: help, show, boarding pass, seat 15D, aisle, non-smoking, ensure, operation, navigation, communication, take-off, landing, electronic, device, mobile phone, remote-controlled toy, cosmetics, cigarette, model plane, doll, delicious, sandwich, sausages, coffee, tea, lemon juice.
> **James**: find, seat, smoke, laptop, sell, duty-free goods, offer, meal, serve, drink, wonderful.

2. **Study the following sample dialogue. Then strike up a conversation with your partners using the sentences listed in the chart.**

A: Good morning, sir. **I'd like to apply for refund of my ticket.**
B: Okay, but you have to pay a service charge of 500 yuan.
A: No problem.

1. I'd like to apply for refund of my ticket.
2. I'd like to reconfirm my flight from Beijing to London.
3. What's the purpose of your visit?
4. Is it direct or do I need to change planes?
5. Could you get me some airsickness pills? I feel sick.
6. How long will you be staying in the United States?
7. Can I change my flight schedule?
8. How much is tourist class?
9. We may have lost some baggage, so we'd like to make a lost baggage report.
10. I need to be in Chicago by 2 this afternoon, but my flight has been canceled.

III. Focus Listening

A. **Listen to the recording and choose the correct answer for each question.**

1. What is the number of the flight?
   A. 105   B. 115   C. 125   D. 135
2. It will take the plane _____ to arrive at the destination.
   A. 8 hours and 45 minutes   B. 9 hours and 25 minutes
   C. 10 hours and 35 minutes   D. 11 hours and 55 minutes
3. What is the speed of the plane on the average?

A. 800 kilometers per hour   B. 880 kilometers per hour
   C. 900 kilometers per hour   D. 1 800 kilometers per hour
4. Passengers can put their carry-on luggage _____.
   A. in the overhead bin   B. under the seat in front of them
   C. on the tray table   D. Both A and B
5. Which of the following statements is true?
   A. Laptop computers can't be used throughout the flight.
   B. Mobile phones can't be used throughout the flight.
   C. The plane will be flying at an altitude of 8 000 meters.
   D. The flying distance between Beijing and London is 10 000 kilometers.

B. Listen to the recording and complete the sentences below.

1. The destination airport is _____.
2. The temperature outside the plane is _____ degrees Fahrenheit.
3. For your safety, please _____ for the time being.
4. You may claim your checked baggage in the _____.
5. The transit passengers should go to the _____ to complete the procedures.

Section 2　Reading

Beijing Capital International Airport

Beijing Capital International Airport (BCIA), formally put to use on March 2, 1958, is known as the premier international hub for Beijing, the capital of the People's Republic of China and is ranked as the world's ninth busiest airport by Airports Council International. BCIA lies in the northeast of Beijing and handles both domestic and international flights. The Distance from the airport to Tian'anmen Square, the heart of Beijing, is approximately 25 kilometers. Passengers can easily reach downtown areas by airport express, airport shuttle or taxi.

Airport Terminals

The terminal can be defined as that part of the airport where passengers wait to board their planes. The facilities at the terminal may comprise lounges, shops, restaurants, cafés, left-luggage counters, clinics, bathrooms, public telephones, self-service banks, etc. Before the construction of Terminal 3 or T3, the airport has two terminals and two runways with a combined annual transport capacity of 36 million passengers. But such a capacity can no longer satisfy the needs of present-day China's development of economy and tourism. The airport, therefore, embarked on its massive program of expansion in 2004—the construction of Terminal 3 including a new terminal building, a new runway and some auxiliary facilities.

As one of the most important projects for the Beijing 2008 Olympic Games, Terminal 3, which commenced to be built on March 28, 2004, has been completed by now after four years of painstaking effort. The new terminal, seen from the air, looks like a huge dragon, the symbol of the Chinese nation. The newly built T3 runway is 3800 meters in length and 60 meters in width. Even the world's biggest passenger plane, the superjumbo Airbus A380 can safely take off and land there.

T3 was officially put to use on February 29, 2008. It consists of three concourses, T3C, T3D and T3E. T3C is used for domestic and international check-in, domestic departures, and domestic and international baggage claim. T3D is temporarily dedicated to charter flights during the Olympic and the Paralympic Games. T3E is designed for international departures and arrivals.

T3 is so far the largest single aviation project in the world. With the total scale of 1 000 000 square meters T3 equals the size of 170 soccer fields and is twice as big as Terminal 1 and Terminal 2 combined. Up till now BCIA has altogether 3 runways, 137 taxiways and 314 aircraft stands, and the total passenger handling capacity has increased from 36 million to 76 million annually.

Departures

For domestic departures, passengers with check-in luggage shall go to the check-in counter with their plane tickets and valid identity cards to have their luggage checked and obtain their boarding passes. For travelers without check-in luggage they shall simply proceed to the counter marked "Check-in Without Luggage".

For international departures, passengers shall make a factual declaration to the Customs at airports by completing a Declaration Form except that they are exempted from Customs inspection and control in accordance with relevant regulations. Passengers who select "No" in all the items on the form may choose to go through "Nothing to Declare" Channel or Green Channel for Customs procedures. Those who tick "Yes" in the items shall have to fill out the form with such details as description, quantity, model, etc. and then choose to go through the "Goods to Declare" Channel or the "Red Channel".

Arrivals

For domestic arrivals, passengers can go to the Luggage Claim Hall of the terminal building to claim their luggage. To find out the carousel of their luggage, they can see the Luggage Claim Carousel Screen installed at the entrance of the hall. For passengers with too much luggage, the airport trolley can be a great help. To prevent luggage from being mistakenly taken, the airport personnel will check passengers' luggage tag at the entrance.

For international arrivals, overseas passengers are required to show their valid passport and entry visa and complete the Entry Health Quarantine Declaration Card according to the requirement of inspection and quarantine authorities while Chinese passengers should possess valid passport.

Security Check

Security is of great significance for every airport in view of the deluge of various crimes and terrorism. At the security check passengers are required to show their boarding passes, airline tickets and valid ID cards to the security personnel before they get through the detection passage and have their hand-carry articles examined by an X-ray.

Items Prohibited in Both Carry-on and Check-in Luggage

According to the applicable provisions of China Customs, the prohibited items include such items as firearms, explosive objects, controlled cutters, combustible or detonable objects, toxic or harmful objects, corrosive objects, radioactive objects and any other objects harmful to aviation safety, such as ferromagnetic objects and objects with strong pungent odor.

Vocabulary

applicable /'æplikəbl/ adj. 可应用的,可适用的
authority /ɔː'θɔriti/ n. 权威,权威人士
carousel /ˌkærə'zel/ n. 行李传送带
combustible /kəm'bʌstəbl/ adj. 易燃的
comprise /kəm'praiz/ v. 包含,由……组成
corrosive /kə'rəusiv/ adj. 腐蚀的,腐蚀性的
deluge /'deljuːdʒ/ n. v. 大洪水,泛滥,困扰
detonable /'detənəbl/ adj. 可爆炸的
embark /im'bɑːk/ v. 从事,着手
exempt /ig'zempt/ v. 免除
facility /fə'siliti/ n. 工具,设备
identity /ai'dentiti/ n. 身份
massive /'mæsiv/ adj. 大规模的,宏伟的
premier /'premjə/ adj. 第一的,首要的
proceed /prə'siːd/ vi. 进行,继续下去
provision /prə'viʒən/ n. 条款,规定
pungent /'pʌndʒənt/ adj. 刺激性的,辛辣的
quarantine /'kwɔrəntiːn/ n. vt. 检疫,隔离
radioactive /'reidiəu'æktiv/ adj. 放射性的,有辐射能的
terminal /'təːminl/ n. 终点站,总站,航空集散站

Phrases & Expressions

put to use 使用,利用
consist of 由……组成
embark on 开始;从事
owing to 因为,由于
take off 脱下;(飞机)起飞

Notes to the Text

1. Passengers can easily reach downtown areas by airport express, airport shuttle or taxi. 乘客乘坐机场快线、机场大巴或出租车可以很容易地抵达市中心。Airport express 是机场快线,从东直门到首都机场三号航站楼,全程只需要 16 分钟。
2. For domestic departures, passengers with check-in luggage shall go to the check-in counter. 作为国内航班乘客启程,携带需托运的行李的乘客要到机场行李托运登记处。这里的 check-in luggage 是指需要托运的行李。

Exercise 1   Reading Comprehension

Answer the following Questions according to the text

1. What do the facilities at the terminal include?
2. Would you give some detailed information about the expansion program of the airport?
3. If you want to go abroad and have nothing to declare at the Customs, what channel should you choose?
4. For departures, what are passengers required to do at Security Check?
5. What items are prohibited in carry-on and check-in luggage?

Exercise 2   Word Training

Fill in the blanks with the words given below. Change the form where necessary.

| massive | facility | comprise | embark | proceed |
| provision | exempt | authority | identity | applicable |

1. The offer is only _____ for journeys made during this week.
2. In the movie Bruce was chased and shot by the police in a case of mistaken _____.
3. The prime minister promised to get to work on the state's _____ deficit.
4. They had a detailed discussion of the _____ contained in the contract.
5. Our company deals in various kinds of airport _____.
6. The city's population is largely _____ of Asians and Europeans.

7. China has _____ on its massive program of developing the west.
8. His identity of a foreign official _____ him from the customs duties for these basic necessities.
9. None of us questioned the _____ of the American aviation expert.
10. Passengers for the New York flight should _____ to Gate 38.

Section 3   Translation

Ⅰ. *Translate the following sentences into Chinese.*
1. How long is the layover in Chicago?
2. We'd like to pre-board those passengers with young children.
3. The flight has been delayed, but all connecting flights can be made.
4. How many days in advance do I have to book tickets in order to get a discount?
5. For those who are going on to New York, your connecting flight will depart from Gate 8.

Ⅱ. *Translate the following sentences into English.*
1. 对不起,这次航班的机票已预订完。
2. 从北京到美国的最低票价是多少?
3. 请问今天有哪些航班从上海飞往加拿大?
4. 我打电话是想问一下 UA2121 是否能够准时起飞。
5. 我想要一张去纽约的往返票。

Section 4   Classified Word Bank

Read the following words and expressions aloud and then learn them by heart.

1.	airport terminal	机场候机楼
2.	airports shuttle	机场班车
3.	boarding pass	登机牌
4.	currency exchange	货币兑换处
5.	customs declaration	海关报关处
6.	departure gate	登机口
7.	departure lounge	候机室
8.	departure time	起飞时间

9.	domestic departure	国内航班出港
10.	duty-free shop	免税店
11.	flight connections	转机处
12.	flight number	航班号
13.	goods to declare	报关物品
14.	international departure	国际航班出港
15.	left luggage	行李寄存处
16.	left-luggage counters	行李寄存处
17.	lost property	失物招领
18.	luggage claim	行李领取处
19.	nothing to declare	不需报关
20.	transfer passengers	中转旅客

Unit 2 At the Immigration & Customs

Section 1 Listening and Speaking

I. Listen and Repeat

Dialogue 1 Going Through the Immigration

Jack has just arrived at Beijing Capital International Airport from the United States. He is now going through the immigration. Ms. Zhang, an immigration officer, is carrying out the inspection.

Zhang: Good morning, sir. May I see your passport, please?

Jack: Here you are.

Zhang: So you come from the United States?

Jack: Yes, I do.

Zhang: What's the purpose of your visit?

Jack: I'm here to brush up my Chinese. I have been admitted by Peking University.

Zhang: Oh, really? Peking University is one of the first-class universities in China.
Jack: Yes, it is.
Zhang: How long do you plan on staying?
Jack: For six months.
Zhang: And do you have a return ticket to the States?
Jack: No.
Zhang: Where are you staying?
Jack: I'm not sure. But the Office of International Students of Peking University will make arrangements for my board and lodging.
Zhang: That's good. What do you do in the United States?
Jack: I'm a business manager in an import & export corporation.
Zhang: I see. Thank you very much.
Jack: You are welcome.

Dialogue 2 At the Customs

After going through the immigration, Jack comes to the Customs Declaration. Miss Chen, another customs officer is talking with him.

Chen: Good morning, sir.
Jack: Good morning.
Chen: Do you have anything to declare?
Jack: Yes, I have 5 bottles of whisky.
Chen: Do you have any foodstuff in your bag?
Jack: Only some baked beef and chicken I bought at the JFK International Airport.
Chen: I'm sorry, you won't be able to take them through the customs. They're forbidden for entry by the People's Republic of China.
Jack: Oh, what a shame!
Chen: Would you open that big bag, please? What are these?
Jack: They are laser disks for adults.
Chen: I'm sorry, such pornography is strictly forbidden in China. We have to detain and destroy them.
Jack: I see. By the way, can I carry a little dog with me next time when I come to China?
Chen: Yes, but you must obtain the Hydrophobia Immunity Certificate and Quarantine Certificate issued by the departing country or local Quarantine Authority.
Jack: Oh, thank you very much.
Chen: You are welcome.

Ⅱ. Act Out

1. Listen to the dialogue. Then practice it with your partners using the words and expressions below to help you.

> **Mary**: suitcase, missing, check, where, luggage tag, bad, important article, medium-sized, dark blue, brand, Queen, deliver, China World Hotel, address, cell phone number.
>
> **Officer**: wait, moment, flight, arrive, maybe, mistake, fault, passenger, wrong luggage, return, office, lost luggage, report, describe, fill in, inform, immediately, sorry, inconvenience, bring.

2. Study the following sample dialogue. Then strike up a conversation with your partners using the sentences listed in the chart.

A: Good morning, sir. **Do you have anything to declare**?

B: No, nothing to declare.

A: Then please go through "Nothing to Declare" Channel for Customs procedures.

B: Okay, thank you.

1. **Do you have anything to declare**?
2. Are there any cigarettes or liquor in your bag?
3. Where can I go through the customs formalities?
4. Could you fill in this Customs Declaration Form, please?
5. Imitative weapons are forbidden for entry by People's Republic of China.
6. Please put your bags on the conveyor belt and step through the metal detector.
7. You'll have to pay duty on this.
8. Please fill out this Departure and Arrival Card for immigration clearance.
9. Please give this declaration card to the officer at the exit.
10. I need to examine the contents of your purse.

Ⅲ. Focus Listening

A. Listen to the recording and choose the correct answer for each question.

1. Overseas passengers need to go through _____ checks before leaving Beijing Capital

Part I Arrival

International Airport.

    A. 3   B. 4   C. 5   D. 6

2. If you suffer from _____, you should report to the quarantine staff.

    A. the flu   B. a fever   C. AIDs   D. diabetes

3. What will you have to show when going through the Immigration?

    A. Valid passport

    B. Entry visa

    C. The filled-in Entry Registration Card

    D. All of the above.

4. Where is the luggage claim hall of Terminal 3?

    A. On the first floor

    B. On the second floor

    C. On the third floor

    D. On the fourth floor

5. When going through the Customs, you are required to fill out _____.

    A. a Declaration Form

    B. an Entry Registration Card

    C. an Entry Health Quarantine Declaration Card

    D. a Lost-luggage Registration Form

B. Listen to the recording and complete the sentences below.

1. A 54-year-old woman has been caught at _____.
2. The woman was arrested when she got off a flight from Jakarta on _____.
3. Her luggage was X-rayed because the Quarantine and Inspection Service officers notice her backpack seemed to have been _____.
4. Australian Customs officers found _____ of heroin in her backpack.
5. The woman was charged with _____.

Section 2   Reading

Drug Smuggling Through Airport Customs

    Drug smuggling is a cancer sweeping across the world and so much has it hurt our body and society that we must take a stand against it. The situation, as everybody can see, has never been so severe as today. Various kinds of drugs are routinely smuggled through customs into such countries as the United States, Russia, Japan, China, some western European countries and so on. Worst of all, some customs employees have also been involved in the crime. The following news just uncovers the corruption within the customs service at the airport.

Federal agents yesterday arrested 20 airport baggage and cargo handlers and charged them with running a decade-long drug smuggling operation that brought hundreds of pounds of cocaine and marijuana a year through Kennedy International Airport under the noses of customs officials.

The arrests unveiled a criminal conspiracy of stunning duration, prosecutors said, in which the baggage handlers moved drug shipments worth tens of millions of dollars through the airport with virtual impunity. The smuggling operation also showed what federal officials called vulnerability in the nation's airline security system. Unlike baggage screeners, who became federal employees subject to more stringent federal regulations in the wake of the Sept. 11, 2001, terrorist attacks, baggage and cargo handlers are often employed by private contractors working for airlines.

"A network of corrupt airport employees, motivated by greed, might just as well have been collaborating with terrorists as with drug smugglers," Michael J. Garcia, the acting assistant secretary of U.S. Immigration and Customs Enforcement, said at a news conference to announce the arrests.

The arrests concluded a 14-month investigation during which federal agents seized more than 400 kilograms of cocaine and hundreds of pounds of marijuana arriving at Kennedy on international flights, almost all of them from Guyana and Jamaica, officials said. One of the shipments, a 185-kilogram package of cocaine worth $23 million found in the cargo section of a passenger flight in September, is the largest intercepted at Kennedy, officials said.

The baggage handlers and their supervisors, who had unrestricted access to the tarmac and airplanes, worked together to unload the drug shipments, prosecutors said. They would then move them to safe areas for pickup and distribution, carefully avoiding surveillance cameras and all forms of border inspection and security, prosecutors said.

The drugs were hidden in luggage, cargo boxes and, in at least one instance, buried under bags of ice in the galley of a passenger flight, said Roslynn R. Mauskopf, the U. S. attorney for the Eastern District, whose office worked with customs officials and the Port Authority of New York and New Jersey on the investigation.

"This was a classic inside job," Mauskopf said.

The conspiracy came to light in late 2002, Mauskopf said, after customs officials intercepted several shipments of cocaine on Universal Airlines flights from Guyana. Agents began doing surveillance of the airline and soon arrested an airport employee diverting a suitcase containing 17 kilograms of cocaine.

The employee began cooperating with investigators, who recorded him discussing drug shipments with a number of the principals in the smuggling operation.

After working undetected for years, the baggage handlers seemed to think they were invincible, a law enforcement official said.

"This was a joke to them," he said.

Prosecutors declined to comment yesterday on who supplied and distributed the drugs, saying their investigation was continuing.

Vocabulary

charge /tʃɑ:dʒ/ v. 起诉
collaborate /kəˈlæbəreit/ vi. 勾结,通敌;合作
conspiracy /kənˈspirəsi/ n. 共谋
contractor /kənˈtræktə/ n. 承包人
corruption /kəˈrʌpʃən/ n. 腐败,贪污
decline /diˈklain/ v. 谢绝,婉拒
enforcement /inˈfɔ:smənt/ n. 执行,强制
impunity /imˈpju:niti/ n. 不受惩罚
intercept /ˌintəˈsept/ vt. 截获,中途截取
invincible /inˈvinsəbl/ adj. 不能征服的,无敌的
involve /inˈvɔlv/ vt. 包括,使陷于
marijuana /ˌmæriˈhwɑ:nə/ n. 大麻
prosecutor /ˈprɔsikju:tə/ n. 原告,检举人
stringent /ˈstrindʒənt/ adj. 严厉的
stunning /ˈstʌniŋ/ adj. 令人吃惊的,极好的

supervisor /ˈsjuːpəvaizə/ *n.* 管理人,主管
surveillance /səˈveiləns/ *n.* 监视,监督
tarmac /ˈtɑːmæk/ *n.* 停机坪
unveil /ʌnˈveil/ *vt.* 使公诸于众,揭开
vulnerability /ˌvʌlnərəˈbiləti/ *n.* 弱点

Phrases & Expressions

be involved in 卷入……,参与……
charge sb. with sth. 起诉;指控
be subject to 受制于某物;易受……的影响
in the wake of 作为……的结果;因为……的缘故
have access to 具有使用某物的能力、机会或权利
come to light 披露;(使)为人所知

Notes to the Text

1. Drug smuggling is a cancer sweeping across the world. 毒品走私已经成为横扫世界的毒瘤。a cancer 在这里是一种暗喻(metaphor),指社会恶习,社会毒瘤。又如：Financial problems have been a constant headache for the real estate company. 资金问题一直是令这家房地产公司头疼的事情。headache 是指那些令人头疼难办的事情。
2. This was a classic inside job. 这是非常典型的监守自盗。an inside job 内贼作案;监守自盗。
3. …under the noses of customs officials. 就在海关官员的眼皮底下。又如：The thief escaped right under the noses of the police. 这个贼就在警察的眼皮底下逃跑了。

Exercise 1 Reading Comprehension

Answer the following Questions according to the text.
1. What were the twenty baggage and cargo handlers accused of by federal agents?
2. Generally speaking what do cargo and baggage handlers differ from baggage screeners?
3. With whom might the corrupt airport employees collude?
4. Who provided substantial assistance for the baggage handlers involved in the drug smuggling?

5. When and how was the criminal conspiracy exposed?

Exercise 2 Word Training

Fill in the blanks with the words given below. Change the form where necessary.

| corruption | unveil | invincible | stunning | decline |
| involve | charge | collaborate | enforcement | intercept |

1. Her phone calls were _____ by the agents of FBI.
2. I'm afraid that your husband was _____ in a drug smuggling.
3. The investigation uncovered widespread _____ within the local authorities.
4. The CEO of the corporation _____ plans to explore the international market.
5. These customs officers were accused of _____ with drug smugglers.
6. The football team was once reputed to be _____.
7. You look absolutely _____ in that blue dress.
8. Alison had been invited to the costume ball but _____ on the grounds that she had other plans.
9. Various crimes are a real challenge to law _____ agencies in many countries.
10. The man the police arrested last night has been _____ with armed robbery.

Section 3 Translation

I. *Translate the following sentences into Chinese.*
1. Each passenger is allowed only one camera duty-free.
2. Photos, disks, movies, tapes, videotapes, laser disks and other objects which are harmful to Chinese politics, economy, culture and morality are forbidden for entry by the People's Republic of China.
3. When going through the immigration, overseas passengers should possess valid passport and entry visa.
4. After getting off the airplane and entering the Terminal Building at the Beijing Capital International Airport, you can go to the first floor to claim your luggage.
5. If you have something to declare, you may choose to go through the Red Channel for

customs procedures.

Ⅱ. *Translate the following sentences into English.*
1. 请把你的行李拿到这边来检查。
2. 如遇紧急情况,请拨打110寻求警察的帮助。
3. 你有多少现金要带入这个国家?
4. 你有什么东西要带进这个国家吗?
5. 你的旅行是属于哪一类的?

Section 4　Classified Word Bank

Read the following words and expressions aloud and then learn them by heart.

1.	business visa	商务签证
2.	country of origin	原住地
3.	customs declaration	海关申报单
4.	date of expiration	失效日期
5.	date of validity	期限
6.	destination country	目的地国家
7.	diplomatic passport	外交护照
8.	duration of status	身份有效期
9.	dutiable articles	纳税物品
10.	duty-free articles	免税物品
11.	entry visa	入境签证
12.	exit visa	出境签证
13.	official passport	官员护照
14.	passport number	护照号
15.	resident visa	居留签证
16.	service passport	公务护照
17.	student visa	留学生签证
18.	tourist visa	旅游签证
19.	transit visa	过境签证
20.	visa type	签证种类

Part I Arrival

Unit 3 At the Hotel

Section 1 Listening and Speaking

I. Listen and Repeat

Dialogue 1 Reserving a Room by Telephone

Jean Brick is visiting Beijing in summer. She intends to stay at Beijing Hotel and now she is calling from Chicago to make a reservation. Mr. Wang is the operator at the Reception Desk.

Wang: Beijing Hotel. May I help you?

Jean: Yes, please. I'm calling from Chicago. I'd like to make a reservation at your hotel.

Wang: OK, may I have your name, please?

Jean: Jean Brick.

Wang: I see. What kind of room would you like? We have single rooms, double rooms, deluxe rooms, presidential suite, etc.

Jean: I'd like a deluxe room with a double bed. What's the rate per night?

Wang: RMB 3,800 yuan or U.S. $ 475. How long will you be staying?

Jean: Four nights from July 2nd to 5th.

Wang: OK. A deluxe room with a double bed from July 2nd to 5th.

Jean: That's right. By the way, I'd like to have a quiet room, please.

Wang: There is no problem, madam.

Jean: Do I need to pay a deposit?

Wang: It's not necessary, but you have to check in before 2 p.m. on July 2nd. Otherwise your reservation will be automatically cancelled.

Jean: I see. Thank you very much. Bye.

Wang: Bye.

Dialogue 2 Checking in

Ms. Jean Brick has just arrived in Beijing and she is checking in at Beijing Hotel. Mr. Zhang, the receptionist, is receiving her.

Zhang: Good afternoon, madam. Welcome to Beijing Hotel.

Jean: Good afternoon. My name's Jean Brick from Chicago. I reserved a deluxe room at your hotel on June 15th.

Zhang: Just a moment, please. Let me check. Oh, yes, Ms. Brick. We do have your reservation. You booked a deluxe room with a double bed for four nights. And you asked for a quiet room.

Jean: Exactly.

Zhang: May I see your passport, please?

Jean: Okay. Here you are.

Zhang: Thank you. Could you fill out this registration form, please?

Jean: Certainly. (*Filling out the form*) Here you are.

Zhang: Thank you, Ms. Brick. Your room number is 2526. Here is the key. Do you need a bellboy?

Jean: Yes, please.

Zhang: Then I'll have someone bring your baggage up.

Jean: Thank you. Do you serve meals now? I'd like something to eat.

Zhang: Yes, we have very good restaurants here, which serve both Chinese and Western food.

Jean: Good. What are the hours of the restaurants?

Zhang: They are open from 7 a.m. to 11 p.m. every day.

Jean: I see. By the way, could I have a wake-up call at 6 tomorrow morning?

Zhang: No problem. Enjoy your stay!

Jean: Thank you very much.

Zhang: It's my pleasure.

Ⅱ. Act Out

1. **Listen to the dialogue. Then practice it with your partners using the words and expressions below to help you.**

> **Jean**: good morning, Jean, check out, Room 2526, 2 morning calls, 3 meals, pay by credit card, receipt, have my baggage, brought down, by the way, book, plane ticket, thank.
>
> **Zhao**: room number, Jean Brick, use, hotel service, during your stay, total, including service charge, 15 500 yuan, in cash, by credit card, no problem, certainly, bellboy, lobby, no problem, welcome.

2. **Study the following sample dialogue. Then strike up a conversation with your partners using the sentences listed in the chart.**

A: Good afternoon. What can I do for you?

B: Good afternoon. **Can I have a sea view room**?

A: I'm sorry. We haven't got any sea view room left. How about a garden view room? It's equally nice.

B: That's ok.

1. Can I have a sea view room?
2. Do you have any vacancies?
3. I'd like a room for a week.
4. I'd like a room with a king-sized bed.
5. I'd like a wake-up morning call, please.
6. May I change my room? It's too noisy.
7. I need to check out. Please have my luggage brought down.
8. Are pets allowed?
9. How do I get room service?
10. I think I'll have to extend my stay here by about three days.

III. Focus Listening

A. **Listen to the recording and choose the correct answer for each question.**

1. The feature service of the Grand View Garden is _____.
   A. Red Chamber Banquet
   B. organized performances
   C. Chinese massage
   D. hot springs

2. The local snack mentioned in the passage is _____.
   A. sesame paste noodles.
   B. steamed rice cakes with sweet stuffing
   C. cross-bridge rice noodles
   D. spring rolls

3. What kind of massage do you hear from the passage?

    A. Japanese massage

    B. American massage

    C. Asian massage

    D. Thai massage

4. One of the aims of some guests coming to China is to enjoy _____.

    A. Beijing snacks

    B. soybean milk

    C. Peking Opera

    D. Red Chamber Wine

5. What does green-oriented management mean?

    A. green food

    B. energy conservation

    C. environmental protection

    D. all of the above

B. Listen to the recording and complete the sentences below.

1. The Front Office is the _____ and _____ of a hotel.

2. Hotels begin services to guests from _____.

3. One of the tasks of the Front Office is to handle _____.

4. The Front Office employees should have good _____ and strong _____.

5. One of the duties of the Front Office manager is to design and carry out _____ for the Front Office employees.

Section 2 Reading

Classification of Hotels

A hotel is a building or institution which provides lodgings, food and beverage, leisure facilities and other services for the public. It is served as a temporary home for people, ranging from the very basic to the ultra-deluxe. Though it is impossible to name categories exactly, some basic classifications have been developed by the industry. Generally hotels can be classified into five categories based on their facilities and functions: commercial hotels, resort hotels, residential hotels, convention hotels and motels. If classified according to their sizes, hotels can be divided into large, medium-sized and small ones. A large hotel possesses more than 600 guest rooms while a medium-sized hotel has rooms between 600 to 300 and a small hotel fewer than 300.

Hotels designed for business people are known as commercial or transient hotels, which are usually located in the business section of cities and towns. Commercial hotels are the most important types of hotels and they not only provides first-rate services for individuals and groups traveling for business purposes, but also manage to attract long staying guests and those traveling for pleasure and other reasons. Transient hotels are luxuriously and tastefully decorated and fully equipped with recreational facilities such as an indoor swimming pool, a bowling room, a massage salon, a gym, a billiard room, a spa and sauna room and so on. Among the best five-star commercial hotels in Beijing are Grand Hyatt Beijing, Beijing Jade Palace Hotel, Super House International.

Resort hotels are the second most important types of hotels which are established and fitted to meet every vacationer's need—relaxation, recreation, entertainment and so on. Most often resort hotels are built near historical interests and scenic spots—at beaches, near lakes and mountains or at a spa. Resort hotels make a strenuous effort to cater for every need of modern travelers. Comfort, recreation and delicacies, therefore, are always given first priority. Resort hotels are generally seasonal, but with the advent of indoor pools and attractive entertainment, some are operated well into the off season with lower hotel rates.

In addition to the two main types of hotels there is a third one called a residential hotel that is primarily designed for long-staying guests and usually found in America and Europe. Essentially a residential hotel is an apartment building, offering cozy single rooms for individuals such as single elderly people and full suites for families. It is also an ideal place for students who choose to live for lower room rates.

A convention hotel is intended for conference reception and usually provides modern facilities such as large convention rooms, multi-functional halls, recreational rooms for various kinds of conferences and entertainment. Convention hotels usually choose the most important political, economic and cultural center of a country or the most beautiful resort areas as their locations.

A motel or motor hotel first came into being in America in 1923. Motels are small one-story buildings usually found on smaller highways or roads. A motel provides a parking space for automobiles directly outside the door of a guest. This is different from a hotel, where travelers enter a lobby area and do not have as easy access to their automobiles. Motels can be more economical and convenient for people or families who go on a trip by car. Although motels are usually less expensive than hotels, they are not inferior in services. Many motels offer the same facilities as hotels, like air-conditioners, showers, cable TV and so on. Motels are usually individually owned, often with the owner's family providing all the services. A drawback of motels is that they do not have on-site restaurants, so guests have to eat away from their lodgings.

Vocabulary

access /ˈækses/ n. 通路,进入
advent /ˈædvənt/ n. (尤指不寻常的人或事)出现,到来
automobile /ˈɔːtəməbiːl/ n. 汽车
beverage /ˈbevəridʒ/ n. 饮料
billiards /ˈbiljədz/ n. 台球
commercial /kəˈməːʃəl/ adj. 商业的,贸易的
convention /kənˈvenʃən/ n. 大会,习俗,惯例
cozy /ˈkəuzi/ adj. 舒适的,安逸的
deluxe /dəˈlʌks/ adj. 豪华的,华丽的
drawback /ˈdrɔːbæk/ n. 缺点,障碍
essentially /iˈsenʃəli/ adv. 本质上,根本上
institution /ˌinstiˈtjuːʃən/ n. 机构,制度
massage /məˈsɑːʒ/ n. v. 按摩
recreational /ˌrekriˈeiʃənəl/ adj. 娱乐的,休养的
residential /ˌreziˈdenʃəl/ adj. 住宅区的
resort /riˈzɔːt/ n. 度假胜地

salon /sə'lɔn/ *n.* 沙龙
strenuous /'strenjuəs/ *adj.* 奋发的,努力的
transient /'trænziənt/ *adj.* 短暂的,瞬时的
ultra- /'ʌltrə/ *adj.* （前缀）极端的,过激的

Phrases & Expressions

be based on 以……为基础;以……为根据
be located in 位于……;坐落于……
provide sth. for sb. 为……提供……
in addition to 除……之外
come into being 出现;产生;形成
with the advent of 随着……的到来

Notes to the Text

1. If classified according to their sizes, hotels can be divided into large, medium-sized and small ones. 如果根据规模来分类,宾馆可以分为大型、中等和小型宾馆。在这个句子中 classified 是过去分词作状语,前面加上了连词 if。又如:
   If heated, water can be changed into vapor. 如果加热的话,水可以变成蒸汽。
   Although built in the 18th century, the church is still in good condition. 尽管建于 18 世纪,这座教堂仍然状况良好。
   Unless changed, the law will make it difficult for small businesses to make profits. 如果不改变的话,这项法令会使小企业很难赚取利润。
2. …but with the advent of indoor pools and attractive entertainment, some are operated well into the off season with lower hotel rates. 句中的 the advent of …的意思是:……的到来;……出现。又如: The advent of television makes people's life more interesting. 电视的出现使人们的生活变得更为有趣。

Exercise 1   Reading Comprehension

Answer the following Questions according to the text.

1. What is the definition of a hotel?

2. What recreational facilities may a commercial hotel provide for its guests?

3. Where is the resort hotel usually established and for whom does it often provide services?

4. For whom is the residential hotel mainly established?

5. What are the differences between a hotel and a motel?

Exercise 2   Word Training

Fill in the blanks with the words given below. Change the form where necessary.

deluxe	commercial	convention	resort	beverage
advent	cozy	access	inferior	drawback

1. By _____ the bride's father gives her away at her wedding.

2. People tend to get _____ souvenirs in shops of resort areas.

3. The big _____ to the plan is that it is very costly and time-consuming.

4. Many travelers enjoy living in a _____ cabin in the woods.

5. The top priorities of a company must be profit and _____ growth.

6. Every time he stays at a hotel, he asks for a suite with a _____ queen-sized bed.

7. The ski _____ are expanding to meet the growing number of skiers that come here.

8. Since the _____ of jet plane, travel has become faster and more comfortable.

9. Alcoholic _____ are served in the hotel lounge.

10. The hotel is in a central location with easy _____ to shops and restaurants.

Section 3   Translation

Ⅰ. *Translate the following sentences into Chinese.*

1. The rate is 250 U.S. dollars a night plus a 10 percent service charge.

2. The advertisement said the hotel could offer at least 15 percent seasonal discount.

3. I'm afraid I don't understand the charge. I didn't have any massage service.

4. I'd like a deluxe room with a queen.

5. Would you like to check the bill and see if the amount is correct?

II. *Translate the following sentences into English.*
1. 我想要一间能看到全城的房间。
2. 我们所有的房间都有浴室或淋浴。
3. 在我们宾馆居住,从第二晚后你便可以享受8折优惠。
4. 顺便问一下,使用那些设施需要额外付费吗?
5. 对不起,今晚的客房都已订满,我为您介绍一家别的宾馆好吗?

Section 4 Classified Word Bank

Read the following words and expressions aloud and then learn them by heart.

1.	单人间	single room
2.	双人间	double room
3.	大床间	king-sized room
4.	朝街房	front view room
5.	背街房	rear view room
6.	城景房	city view room
7.	园景房	garden view room
8.	海景房	sea view room
9.	湖景房	lake view room
10.	山景房	hill view room
11.	港景房	harbor view room
12.	经济间	economy room
13.	普通间	standard room
14.	高级间	superior room
15.	豪华间	deluxe room
16.	商务标间	business room
17.	行政标间	executive room
18.	普通套房	junior suite
19.	豪华套间	deluxe suite
20.	总统套房	presidential suite

Unit 4 At the Restaurant

Section 1 Listening and Speaking

I. Listen and Repeat

Dialogue 1 Helping Guests to Order

Alex wants to have dinner with his friend Cindy. They come to a Chinese restaurant in Beijing. The waiter is helping them to order.

Waiter: Good evening, sir. Here is the menu.

Alex: Thank you.

Cindy: What are your specialties?

Waiter: They are listed on the board, such as frogs' legs, the roast mutton, and stir-fried shrimp, etc. They are delicious and worth trying.

Alex: I know little about Chinese food, but I hear quick-fried tripe is very nice.

Waiter: Yes, it's well-known Peking snack.

Alex: I think I'll try it.

Waiter: What about you, madam?

Cindy: I'll have stir-fried shrimp. By the way, do you have Peking Roast Duck?

Waiter: Yes, we do.

Alex: Then we'll have a Peking Roast Duck.

Waiter: What would you like to drink? We have beer, fruit juice and wines.

Alex: I'd like to have some Chinese red wine.

Cindy: I prefer lemon juice.

Waiter: Why don't you try Maotai?

Alex: Maotai?

Waiter: Yes, it is world-famous Chinese liquor.

Alex: But I hear Chinese liquor is very strong.

Waiter: Yes, it's a little bit stronger than Whisky and Brandy. But it is really nice.

Cindy: I think we'll try it some other time.

Waiter: All right. I'll be back soon.

Part I
Arrival

Dialogue 2 Ordering Steak and Paying the Bill

Barbara is waiting at a table and a waiter is coming over to her.

Waiter: Sorry to keep you waiting. What would you like to have, madam?

Barbara: Could I see the menu, please?

Waiter: Ok, here it is.

Barbara: Thank you. (*After a few minutes*)

Waiter: Are you ready to order now?

Barbara: Yes, I'd like to have a steak.

Waiter: How would you like your steak? Rare, medium or well-done?

Barbara: I'd like it well-done, please.

Waiter: No problem. Does that come with salad?

Barbara: Okay.

Waiter: Is there anything else I can get for you?

Barbara: Yes, I'd like a glass of wine.

Waiter: OK.

(*After eating*)

Waiter: How's your steak?

Barbara: It's very nice. Could I have the bill, please?

Waiter: Just a moment, please. (*After a while*) Here is your bill.

Barbara: OK. May I have a receipt, please?

Waiter: Yes, of course.

II. Act Out

1. Listen to the dialogue. Then practice it with your partners using the words and expressions below to help you.

> **Manager**: madam, what, problem, sorry, new at the job, change, for you, sure, misunderstanding, from Brazil, English, not very good, perhaps, didn't understand, dish, change, immediately, French wine, always, good, don't think, wrong, brand, sour, for your taste, recommend, Chinese red wine, is that all.

Anne:	feel very unhappy, order, dish, fish, isn't fresh, vegetables, overcooked, mushy, complain, the waitress, seem, take any notice, what's more, when, spoke, didn't pay any attention, staring, little more like it, another, wine, strange, taste, yourself, perhaps, will.

2. Study the following sample dialogue. Then strike up a conversation with your partners using the sentences listed in the chart.

A: I don't think I ordered this.

B: Are you sure?

A: Yeah, I ordered braised abalone, not braised prawns. I'm afraid you've got it wrong.

1. I don't think I ordered this.
2. Do you have vegetarian dishes?
3. May I see the wine list?
4. Would you like salad or soup with that?
5. What is the special of the day?
6. I'd like my steak medium.
7. The meat isn't fresh. I want to have it changed.
8. Could we have a doggie bag?
9. Do I pay you or the cashier?
10. Can we order now?

III. Focus Listening

A. Listen to the recording and choose the correct answer for each question.

1. When a person can't arrive on time, he or she should _____.
   A. ask somebody else to go
   B. find excuses for the lateness
   C. keep silent and explain the next day
   D. call the host or hostess

2. All of the following are considered bad manners except _____.
   A. cleaning your teeth with toothpicks at table
   B. chewing with your mouth open

C. using the soup spoon to get the soup

D. slurping your soup

3. Which of the following is impolite in the United States?

    A. Eat something off your knife not off your fork

    B. Cut meat or vegetables into bite size pieces

    C. Eat one piece of meat or vegetable at a time

    D. Try not to drink too much or get drunk

4. What should you do when you want the dishes out of your reach?

    A. You just stand up and get the dishes

    B. You just eat the dishes you can reach

    C. You ask someone to do it for you

    D. You draw the dishes closer to you

5. To express that you have finished eating, you _____.

    A. say thank you and leave the table

    B. put your knife and fork side by side on the plate

    C. fold your napkin and put it beside your plate

    D. remain at a table and chat with others

B. Listen to the recording and complete the sentences below.

1. The well-known Chinese saying "Food is God for people" means food is the _____.

2. The Chinese cuisine is famous for its great variety and _____.

3. According to an old saying the characteristics of Chinese food are _____ in the south, _____ in the north, _____ in the east and _____ in the west.

4. Cooking can be viewed as an art that contains _____ and _____.

5. The Cantonese food is _____ and _____ and lays great emphasis on artistic presentation.

Section 2   Reading

Pubs in Britain

Britain is renowned for its amazing pubs and no trip to the country would be complete without a visit to one of them. Traditional pubs have long been thought to be the best place to sample the local culture by visitors. If you go to Britain and stay there for some time, you are sure to be impressed by the various kinds of pubs across the country.

British Pubs enjoy a long history. The idea for the first public house or pub was brought to Britain thousands of years ago by the Roman army who conquered Great Britain from 55 B. C. to 410 A. D. The first pub only served wine, but after the discovery of hops in the fourteenth century, British pubs began offering beer, as they do today. Nowadays pubs not only serve beer such as Lager, Bitter and Stout, but also offer wines, cider, soft drinks, and spirit like whisky, gin or vodka. Pubs also serve hearty meals of all kinds at a reasonable price.

British pubs differ from most pubs and bars throughout the world. They have their unique culture. Visitors who go there for the first may find it difficult to get a drink because there is no table service. In British pubs, you may have to go to the counter yourself to order food and drinks and pay for your purchase right there immediately. Many visitors feel puzzled about the arcane rituals of British pubs, but they do have some hidden purposes.

British men in general are well-mannered, refined and cultured, but they are reserved and shy. The pub culture, anthropologists revealed, is just designed to promote sociability for them. Standing in a pub for service allows you to chat with others waiting to be served. The bar counter is possibly the only site in the British Isles where friendly conversation with strangers is considered appropriate.

Today there are over 60 thousand pubs in the United Kingdom, some of which are very old and famous. For instance, The Eagle, one of the most popular pubs in Cambridge, can be traced back to the 15th century. It was in this pub that the Englishman Francis Crick and the American James Watson declared in February 1953 that they had discovered the secret of life—DNA double helix. At the Eagle you may come across a number of distinguished experts and scientists if you are fortunate.

In British pubs you are permitted to try to attract attention of the bartenders, but you should be careful of how to do it. Do not call out, tap coins on the counter, snap your finger, or wave like a drowning swimmer. Do not scowl, or sigh or roll your eyes. And whatever you do, do not ring the bell hanging behind the counter, which is used by the landlord to signal closing time. What you should do is to catch the bartender's eyes. You can also hold an empty glass or some money, but do not wave them about. Do adopt an expectant, hopeful, even slightly anxious facial expression. If you look too contented and complacent, the pub staff may assume that you are already served. If you are in a big group, it is best if only one or two people go to buy the drinks. Nothing irritates the regular customers and bartenders more than a gang of strangers blocking all access to the bar while they chat and dither about what to order.

In Britain no one under the age of 18 is allowed to drink in the pub. The fourteen-year-olds, however, may enter a pub unaccompanied if they order a meal. Children may enter a pub with their parents and stay there until 9 p.m., which provides families with the chance to enjoy decent meals together and allows pubs to continue in their traditional roles as community centers. As for business hours, most pubs operate between 11a.m. to 11p.m., but on Sundays they will have to close at 10:30 p.m..

Bartenders are called "landlords" and "barmaids" and they don't expect frequent tipping. To tip bartenders, it is customary to offer them a drink. You should never give them a cash gratuity. Pubs pride themselves on their egalitarian atmosphere. A tip in cash would be a reminder of their service role, whereas the offer of a drink is a friendly gesture.

Vocabulary

arcane /ɑːˈkein/ *adj.* 神秘的
bartender /ˈbɑːtendə/ *n.* 酒吧招待
bitter /ˈbitə/ *adj.* 苦酒
cider /ˈsaidə/ *n.* 苹果酒
complacent /kənˈpleisnt/ *adj.* 自满的,得意的
contented /kənˈtentid/ *adj.* 满足的,心安的
customary /ˈkʌstəməri/ *adj.* 习惯的,惯例的
distinguished /disˈtiŋwiʃt/ *adj.* 著名的,高贵的
dither /ˈdiðə/ *v.* 犹豫不决
egalitarian /igæliˈteəriən/ *adj.* 平等的
gratuity /grəˈtjuːəti/ *n.* 赏钱,赠物
hearty /ˈhɑːti/ *adj.* 大份的,丰盛的
helix /ˈhiːliks/ *n.* 螺旋
lager /ˈlɑːgə/ *n.* 熟啤酒
refined /riˈfaind/ *adj.* 精制的,优雅的
renowned /riˈnaund/ *adj.* 有名的,有声誉的
reserved /riˈzəːvd/ *adj.* 矜持的
scowl /skaul/ *vi.* 愁眉苦脸
sociability /ˌsəuʃəˈbiləti/ *n.* 社交性,善于交际
stout /staut/ *n.* 烈性啤酒

Phrases & Expressions

be renowned for 以……著名;以……闻名
be traced back to 可以追溯到……
come across 偶遇,不期而遇
call out 大声叫唤
pride oneself on 以某事自豪

Notes to the Text

1. Nowadays pubs not only serve beer such as Lager, Bitter and Stout, but also offer wines,

cider, soft drinks, and spirit like whisky, gin or vodka. 当今,酒吧不仅提供啤酒,如淡啤酒、苦啤酒、黑啤酒,还提供葡萄酒、苹果酒、软饮和烈酒如威士忌、杜松子酒或者伏特加酒。Lager, Bitter, Stout 是典型的英国酒吧啤酒。Bitter 较苦,Stout 又苦又浓,Lager 也叫 Shandy,它是由 lemonade(柠檬水)加啤酒,所以不太苦。如果叫烈酒也可以喝 whisky 或 vodka 等。

2. It was in this pub that the Englishman Francis Crick and the American James Watson declared in February 1953 that they had discovered the secret of life—DNA double helix. 就是在这间酒吧里,英国人佛朗西斯·克里克和美国人詹姆士·沃森在 1953 年宣布他们解开了生命的奥秘——脱氧核糖核酸双螺旋结构。文章中的 Eagle 酒吧也因此而出名。

Exercise 1   Reading Comprehension

Answer the following Questions according to the text.

1. What is the biggest difference between British pubs and most pubs and bars in the world?
2. What should you do to draw attention of the bartenders in British pubs?
3. What does the pub serve at present?
4. How do visitors get food and drinks in British pubs?
5. Why shouldn't a visitor to the pub tip bartenders in cash? What should you do when you want to tip them?

Exercise 2   Word Training

Fill in the blanks with the words given below. Change the form where necessary.

| atmosphere | gratuity | scowl | hearty | contented |
| dither | complacent | reserved | distinguished | customary |

1. He was unemotional, quiet and _____.
2. Stop _____ about it. Let's just go to the Chinese food restaurant nearby.
3. Some top-end restaurants in the metropolis will add a _____ of 10 to 15 percent.
4. My cousin provided me with a cozy room and _____ meals.
5. The hotel has made an elaborate preparation for their _____ foreign guests.

6. You simply can't afford to be _____ about the progress in your work.
7. It is _____ for the most important guest to sit at the end of the table.
8. His wife _____ at him and refused to say anything.
9. They cooperated for greater efficiency, fair pricing and _____ customers.
10. In a bar or a cafe, there is usually a very live and social _____.

Section 3　Translation

Ⅰ. *Translate the following sentences into Chinese.*
1. The Cantonese food is famous for its roast suckling pig while Beijing cuisine is known for its roast duck.
2. Would you like to try one of our desserts?
3. This round's on me.
4. Let's get down to some serious drinking.
5. What would you like with your steak? A salad?

Ⅱ. *Translate the following sentences into English.*
1. 你们这里有素食吗?
2. 特色菜在菜单的右边。
3. 您是不是想再看看菜单上的甜点?
4. 广东菜有点淡。
5. 这是我尝过的最好的酒。

Section 4　Classified Word Bank

Read the following words and expressions aloud and then learn them by heart.

1.	Baked Sesame Seed Cake	烧饼
2.	Deep-fried Dough Cake	油饼
3.	Deep-fried Dough Stick	油条
4.	Dumplings	饺子
5.	Fermented Bean Drink	豆汁儿
6.	Four-Joy Meatballs	四喜丸子
7.	Fried Cakes	炸糕

8. Fried Dough Twist	麻花
9. Fried Tofu, Home Style	家常豆腐
10. Glutinous Rice Ball	艾窝窝
11. Hand-Pulled Noodles with Beef	牛肉拉面
12. Hot & Sour Soup	酸辣汤
13. Jellied Tofu	豆腐脑儿
14. Kung Pao Chicken	宫保鸡丁
15. Mongolian Pot	火锅
16. Pork Lungs in Chili Sauce	夫妻肺片
17. Spring Rolls	春卷
18. Stewed Pork Ball in Brown Sauce	红绕狮子头
19. Stewed Tofu in Pottery Pot	砂锅豆腐
20. Sweet and Sour Mandarin Fish	松鼠桂鱼

Unit 5 Traffic

Section 1 Listening and Speaking

I. Listen and Repeat

Dialogue 1 Taking a Taxi

Charles has just got into a taxi. He is going to visit the Forbidden City in Beijing. The following is the dialogue between him and taxi driver.

Driver: Good morning. Where to, sir?

Charles: I'm going to the Forbidden City. I'd like to see the imperial palace. I hear it is magnificent.

Driver: Yes, it is. It has been listed by UNESCO as the largest collection of preserved ancient wooden structures in the world. It is said that the palace has 9,999 rooms and a half.

Charles: Wow! Is it far from here?

Driver: Yes, it is a good distance. It is about an hour drive from here.

Charles: Oh, watch out! A pedestrian is crossing the street.

Driver: (*Hit the brake*). My God! It was a close call.

Charles: It seems that people in Beijing cross the street anywhere they like!

Driver: Yeah, something should be done about it.

Charles: Could I roll up the window? It's too hot in here.

Driver: Of course you can. Just push the button on the door.

Charles: Mind if I smoke?

Driver: I'd prefer that you not smoke. Smoking is banned in the taxi in Beijing. Besides, I'm allergic to smoke.

Charles: Then I'd better not. Is it still far from here?

Driver: No, you can see it on the horizon. (*A few minutes later*) Oh, here we are! This is the entrance to the palace.

Charles: Thank you very much. What is the fare?

Driver: 58 yuan.

Charles: Here is a 100.

Driver: Thank you. Here is your change and ticket. Have a nice trip!

Dialogue 2　Inquiring About Transport to a Particular Place

Christina wants to go to Liulichang, a famous place in Beijing for Chinese calligraphy and paintings. At the moment she is asking for directions.

Christina: Excuse me. How can I get to Liulichang from here?

Policeman: It's quite a way. It's not within walking distance.

Christina: Can I take the subway?

Policeman: Yes, you can. There is a subway station right up there.

Christina: What is the name of the station?

Policeman: Sihui East. You can take the subway there.

Christina: Is it direct?

Policeman: No, it's Line 1. You have to change to Line 2 at the Jianguomen Station.

Christina: How many stops are there before I reach Jianguomen Station?

Policeman: Five stops, I think.

Christina: Where should I get off after I change to Line 2?

Policeman: At the Hepingmen Station. After you get out, just follow the signs.

Christina: I see. Thank you very much. By the way, can I get a good Chinese painting there?

Policeman: I think so. There are many famous artistic shops along the street. Some have a history of more than one hundred years. Rongbaozhai is one of them. It handles traditional Chinese calligraphy and paintings.

Christina: I see. Thank you very much. Bye.
Policeman: Bye.

II. Act Out

1. Listen to the dialogue. Then practice it with your partners using the words and expressions below to help you.

> **Jack**: excuse, Wangfujing, know, how, get, tell, which stop, get off, how many stop, conductor, announce, convenient, how much, fare, card, allow, 60 percent discount, cheap, public transport, where, purchase, thank.
> **Passerby**: many buses, take, Bus No. 52, Wangfujing bus stop, seven, automatic, bus-stop-reporting, name, each, reach, IC Card, 40 cents, passenger, without, convenient, authorized selling spots, right up there, up the road, welcome.

2. Study the following sample dialogue. Then strike up a conversation with your partners using the sentences listed in the chart.

A: **Could you move your stuff, please**?
B: No problem.
A: Thank you very much.
B: You are welcome.

1. Could you move your stuff, please?
2. Does this train go right through to Shanghai?
3. Can you tell me what stop to get off at?
4. Is this seat occupied?
5. Make a right at the light.
6. Is this the bus to the Bird's Nest?
7. How many stops are there to the Chinese Academy of Sciences?
8. I'm sorry, madam. You don't want me to run a red light, do you?
9. Go straight ahead through the intersection, then go north.
10. Can we take another road? I'm in a hurry?

Ⅲ. Focus Listening

A. Listen to the recording and choose the correct answer for each question.

1. If a driver doesn't wear a seat belt in the U. S. , he will be fined up to _____.
   A. 15 dollars   B. 50 dollars   C. 150 dollars   D. 500 dollars
2. Children under 12 should always _____.
   A. take the back seat   B. ride in the front
   C. wear a seat belt   D. sit in the middle
3. Which rule tells that you shall never drive when you are drunk?
   A. The first rule   B. The second rule   C. The third rule   D. The fourth rule
4. Which of the following is not the punishment for DUI?
   A. The payment of a large fine   B. A mandatory jail sentence
   C. The suspension of a driver's license.   D. Not driving for 2 years
5. Which of the following statements is true?
   A. When you see a stop sign but no one cross the street, just continue the drive.
   B. Drunken driving might lead to the revocation of a driver's license.
   C. You should always have your children sit beside you.
   D. You still have to wear your seat belt if you are reversing your vehicle

B. Listen to the recording and complete the sentences below.

1. The accident occurred in western _____.
2. In the road accident _____ people were killed and _____ others were injured.
3. The accident happened on _____.
4. The injured had been taken to _____ for treatment.
5. The traffic accident happened because of _____.

Section 2 Reading

Public Transport in Beijing

Buses

   Although there are various means of transport in the metropolitan city of Beijing, buses still play a fundamental role in it. The bus network in Beijing provides the primary mode of transport throughout the city as well as its environs. The Beijing Municipal Government gives a priority to the development of public transport, and the Beijing Public Transport Group operates thousands of buses on a wide array of routes serving the metropolis. With the advent of 2008 Beijing Olympic Games, Beijing has launched a massive program to improve its bus system. Thousands of old, dilapidated buses have recently given way to a new fleet of shiny, modern vehicles. The city has also introduced an electronic fare payment system, known as the IC Card, which is usable on both buses and subways. When one gets on the bus, he just needs to put his card close to the card reader, and after a beep the card-paying process is automatically completed. It is simple enough for a toddler to do it and it saves you the trouble of searching for coins or small notes in your pockets.

Another advantage is that the bus fare is surprisingly cheap. On January 1, 2007, Beijing began to implement a new pricing system for the city's transport, which has brought real benefits for the city dwellers. By issuing the traffic card, the local bus companies allow the passengers to enjoy attractive prices. With the fares for Beijing long-distance buses reduced on January 15, 2008, long-distance bus riders can also get 60 percent discount of the regular fares with the IC Cards. But those who do not own the cards will have to pay for the original price.

Subways

You can never imagine how rapidly the subway in Beijing has been developing in the past few decades! The first subway, Subway Line 1 can be traced back to the year 1965, when it began to be constructed. It was completed and put into operation on October 1, 1969 after more than four years of strenuous efforts. Nowadays although the subway network is not yet extensive to cover all districts of Beijing, there are subway lines distributed in most parts of city. Line 1 and Line 6 run across the city from the east to the west while Line 4 and Line 5 travel from the south to the north. Line 2 and Line 10 are loop lines which go around the second and third ring road. Line 13 traverses Haidian, Chaoyang and Changping District. These lines, together with Line 7, Line 8, Line 9, Line 14, etc., join Beijing together.

By subway you are accessible to many prominent places such as the Tian'anmen Square, the Forbidden City, the Temple of Heaven, the CCTV Station, the Beijing Railway Station, the Lama Temple, Wangfujing Street, etc.

Taxies

If you have never been to Beijing, taxis might be your best choice because they can provide newcomers with superb assistance and most convenience. Compared with the taxi fares in London, New York and other western metropolitan areas, fares in Beijing are extremely cheap. There is no extra charge for your luggage and you are not expected to tip the taxi driver. But taxis will charge you for the waiting time and late-night surcharge. For every accumulated five minutes of waiting time, you will be charged for an extra kilometer. And after 11 p.m., taxis will charge a 20 percent late-night surcharge. Taxies are available around the clock in the city streets, in front of big hotels, around the railway stations, airports and busy commercial centers. Taxi drivers are usually friendly, helpful and easygoing. When you get into a taxi you can chew the fat with them.

Bicycles

Although bicycles are not invented by the Chinese, China is best known as the "Bicycle Kingdom" because the number of bicycles in China is far greater than anywhere else. In the late 1980s China had more than 500 million bicycles. In the 1970s and 1980s bicycles were widely used not only in the affluent cities and townships but also in the less developed rural areas in China, especially for people who study or work in the vicinity of their homes. At that time a family might possess two or three bicycles. Just imagine how many bicycles there were for a country with the population of over one billion!

The situation, however, has changed in the past two decades with the development of China's economy and reform and open policy. People have become well-off and as a result can afford to buy their own cars. Nowadays some families even own two or three cars. Although the number of bicycles is declining dramatically, bicycles do not withdraw from the stage of history. The conventional bicycles, however, have been replaced by electric ones, which run faster and do not need any physical labor.

Vocabulary

accessible /ək'sesəbl/ *adj.* 易到达的,易得到的
affluent /'æfluənt/ *adj.* 富裕的
appraisal /ə'preizəl/ *n.* 评价,评估,鉴定
array /ə'rei/ *n.* 排列,陈列
dilapidated /di'læpi,deit/ *adj.* （建筑物,车辆）破烂不堪的
environs /in'vaiərənz/ *n.* 市郊,郊外
establishment /is'tæbliʃmənt/ *n.* 机构;单位（尤指企业、商店等）
fundamental /,fʌndə'mentl/ *adj.* 基础的,基本的
implement /'impliment/ *n.* 执行（计划、政策、建议）
massive /'mæsiv/ *adj.* 大而重的,巨大的,强大的
municipal /mju'nisipəl/ *adj.* 市的,市办的
parallel /'pærəlel/ *adj.* 平行的,并行的;相似的
primary /'praiməri/ *adj.* 第一位的,主要的
priority /prai'ɔriti/ *n.* 优先,优先权
prominent /'prɔminənt/ *adj.* 卓越的,显著的,突出的
strenuous /'strenjuəs/ *adj.* 艰苦的,需做出努力的
surcharge /sə:'tʃɑ:dʒ/ *n.* 额外费
toddler /'tɔdlə/ *n.* 初学走路的孩子
vicinity /vi'sinəti/ *n.* 附近,临近
withdraw /wið'drɔ:/ *v.* 撤回,撤退,退出

Phrases & Expressions

play a fundamental role in 在……起到重要作用

give a priority to 对……优先考虑
be put into operation 使……开始运作
the number of ……的数量
in the vicinity of 在……的附近

Notes to the Text

1. When you get into a taxi you can chew the fat with them. 上了出租车之后,你还可以与司机交谈。句中的 chew the fat 是非正式用语,意思是:促膝长谈,闲聊。英美人在日常生活中用了很多的非正式用语,又如:shoot the lights 闯红灯,hit the bottle 酗酒,hit the road 启程,上路,pull sb's leg 愚弄某人;开某人玩笑。
2. People have become well-off and as a result can afford to buy their own cars. 人们比以前富有了,因此一些有钱的人开始购买自己的汽车。well-off 是富有的、小康的意思。如:They are not extremely rich, but they are very well-off. 他们不是十分有钱,但还算富裕。

Exercise 1　Reading Comprehension

Answer the following Questions according to the text.

1. What does the Beijing Municipal Government give priority to according to the first paragraph?
2. What does Beijing do for the coming of the 2008 Olympic Games?
3. How many subway lines are mentioned in the article?
4. What is the recommended means of transport to people who have never been to Beijing?
5. Why do conventional bicycles give way to electric ones?

Exercise 2　Word Training

Fill in the blanks with the words given below. Change the form where necessary.

fundamental	priority	implement	parallel	vicinity
appraisal	accessible	prominent	primary	withdraw

1. He stated that all foreign forces would _____ as soon as the crisis ended.
2. Excellent service is _____ to the hospitality industry.
3. The municipal government said that _____ will be given to public transport.
4. The local authorities have decided to _____ new traffic regulations.
5. Ella put the portrait in a _____ position in her sitting-room.
6. A college education wasn't _____ to women until the 1920s.
7. Safety is a matter of _____ importance to travelers.
8. The car accident happened in the _____ of an intersection.
9. What's your _____ of the newly designed car?
10. Beijing Guang'an Avenue runs _____ to Chang'an Avenue.

Section 3 Translation

Ⅰ. *Translate the following sentences into Chinese.*
1. It will cost your double fare to leave the city.
2. I'm sorry you failed the test. You are a DUI case, so your license is suspended as of now.
3. He got a DUI conviction last night. He has to pay a fine of 1,800 yuan, and not allowed to drive for up to 5 months.
4. Go down this street, turn left at the third light and you'll see the freeway on-ramp sign.
5. Alex got two tickets back to back last week—one for speeding and the other for running a red light.

Ⅱ. *Translate the following sentences into English.*
1. 沿教堂街走两个街区,然后右转。
2. 不系安全带是违法的。
3. 你得在中山公园站换乘22路车。
4. 高速公路上的速度限制是每小时60英里。
5. 过了三道红绿灯后,到了第四道往右拐。

Section 4 Classified Word Bank

Read the following words and expressions aloud and then learn them by heart:

1. avenue		林荫道
2. breathalyzer		呼气式酒精浓度检测器

3. chain collision 连环撞车
4. crossroad 十字路口
5. double bend road 之字路
6. driver's license 驾驶执照
7. fork 岔路口
8. head-on collision 正面相撞
9. hit-run driver 肇事逃逸司机
10. intersection 交叉路口
11. on-ramp 高速公路入口处
12. overhead bridge 过街天桥
13. overpass 立交桥
14. rear-ending collision 后面冲撞
15. sidewalk 人行道
16. sobriety test 酒精检测
17. speed limit 限速
18. traffic light 红绿灯
19. traffic sign 交通标志
20. zebra crossing 斑马线

Part II

Tourism Consultation

Unit 1 Asking About Scenic Spots

Section 1 Listening and Speaking

I. Listen and Repeat

Dialogue 1 Asking about the Scenic Spots

Mary is an American tourist who stays at Beijing Great Wall Shelton Hotel. Now she is asking Mr. Zhang about the scenic spots in Beijing.

Zhang: Good morning, madam. May I help you?

Mary: Good morning. Is this the Tourist Travel Counter?

Zhang: Yes, what can I do for you?

Mary: This is my first time to Beijing. Could you please recommend me some scenic spots here?

Zhang: Certainly. Beijing is a beautiful city. There are a lot of tourist attractions here, such as Tian'anmen and Tian'anmen Square, the Forbidden City, the Summer Palace, the Temple of Heaven, the Great Wall, the Ming Tombs and so on. Apart from these, we also have Hutong Tour, Old City Tour, evening entertainment and…

Mary: Wait a minute, that's too much for me. I really don't know where I shall go for a visit.

Zhang: Beijing is an ancient city with a history of over 3,000 years. That's why there are so many historical sightseeing places for tourists.

Mary: Would you please tell me some main historical places?

Zhang: Of course. How long will you be staying here in Beijing?

Mary: For only three days.

Zhang: Then the Great Wall is a "must". It will take you a whole day to visit. The Forbidden City and Tian'anmen Square are for the second day tour, and you can spend the third day visiting the Summer Palace and the Temple of Heaven.

Mary: That's wonderful! Do you have a tour guide for me if I have the three-day tour?

Zhang: Yes, we offer this kind of service.

Mary: Thank you very much for your help.

Zhang: You are welcome. Here is our tour brochure. You can get everything in detail.

Mary: It's very nice of you. Bye!

Zhang: Bye!

Dialogue 2 Asking About a Tour

Mary wants to visit some places in Beijing. Now she is asking Mr. Zhang, a Travel Counter Clerk, about it.

Zhang: Good morning miss. Welcome to the Travel Counter. Can I help you?

Mary: Good morning. Do you have an optional tour?

Zhang: Yes, we do. Where do you want to visit?

Mary: I want to visit the highlights for tourists in Beijing. What kind of tour do you provide?

Zhang: We have three tours every day. The Great Wall and the Ming Tombs are a one-day tour. Tian'anmen Square and the Forbidden City, the Summer Palace and the Temple of Heaven are also one-day tours. They are the highlights for tourists in Beijing.

Mary: Can I book these tours at this hotel?

Zhang: Yes, of course.

Mary: How much is a one-day tour?

Zhang: Here is the price list. The Great Wall tour is more expensive than the other two, because it is 75 Kilometers away from the city.

Mary: What does the price include?

Zhang: It includes the admission tickets, English-speaking tour guide, coach, toll of superhighway, and the Chinese lunch.

Mary: I think I'll take the Great Wall tour first.

Zhang: How about the Forbidden City and the Summer Palace?

Mary: I'll decide whether to have it after I come back from the Great Wall.

Zhang: All right. Here is your receipt for the Great Wall tour tomorrow.
Mary: Thank you for your help.
Zhang: You are welcome.

II. Act Out

1. Listen to the dialogue. Then practice it with your partners using the words and expressions below to help you.

> **Feng**: morning, help, all right, Great Wall, Ming Tombs, good, a "must", Tian'anmen Square, Forbidden City, Summer Palace, Temple of Heaven, Fragrant Hill, western, Hutong Tour, enjoy, style, old, Beijingers, brochure, welcome.
> **Jane**: arrange, one-day tour, been to, recommend, other, sightseeing places, Yes, want, see, scenic spots, suburb, special tours, any place else, recommend, wonderful, in detail, thank.

2. Study the following sample dialogue. Then strike up a conversation with your partners using the sentences listed in the chart.

A: May I help you?
B: Yes. **Could you please recommend some scenic spots in Beijing?**
A: Certainly. Beijing is a metropolitan city. There are many beautiful parks, ancient temples, and historical structures in Beijing.

1. Could you please recommend some scenic spots in Beijing?
2. Could you tell me how I can get to the Summer Palace?
3. What's the price for the City Tour?
4. Where can I have the Hutong Tour?
5. Do you have any French-speaking tour guides?
6. How many people are there in the coach tour?
7. Do you have non-smoking coaches?
8. What time do you think we will get to the Great Wall?
9. Could you show me the Palace Museum on the map?
10. Any place else that you can recommend for me?

Ⅲ. Focus Listening

A. Listen to the recording and choose the correct answer for each question.

1. Beijing has a history of over _____ years.
   A. 2,000　　　　B. 3,000　　　　C. 4,000　　　　D. 5,000
2. Which of the following is not a major sightseeing place in Beijing?
   A. The Great Wall　　　　　　　B. the Summer Palace
   C. The Forbidden City　　　　　D. Wangfujing Street
3. Mary will stay in Beijing for only _____ days.
   A. two　　　　B. three　　　　C. four　　　　D. five
4. _____ is not one of the three one-day tours advised for Mary.
   A. Zhongshan Park and the Tian'anmen Square
   B. The Great Wall and the Ming Tombs
   C. The Summer Palace and the Temple of Heaven
   D. Tian'anmen, the Tian'anmen Square and the Forbidden City
5. To make Mary's tour more convenient and enjoyable, the Travel Counter _____.
   A. gives her a brochure
   B. advises her to take a one-day tour
   C. takes on an English-speaking guide for her
   D. introduces all the scenic spots to her

B. Listen to the recording and complete the sentences below.

1. Most of the tourists like to visit the _____ of the famous scenic spots in Beijing.
2. The travel counter of the hotel arranges the optional tour or _____ every day.
3. Other tours in Beijing are slightly _____ than visiting the Great Wall.
4. The Great Wall is about _____ kilometers away from Beijing.
5. People like taking this kind of tour because the price is _____.

Section 2　Reading

Scenic Spots in Beijing

　　Nowadays, many people travel in search of a better life or in order to satisfy the needs and curiosity of themselves, or just for fun. When traveling in Beijing, tourists will choose the major sightseeing places for a visit. For foreign tourists, they can get travel information from the travel agencies or places that provide such a kind of service. So Travel Counter at the hotel is really necessary. The clerks working at the hotel Travel Counter should not only provide a good service for the foreign tourists but also familiarize themselves with the famous scenic spots in Beijing.

Scenic Spots in Beijing

There are mainly six scenic spots in Beijing. They are Tian'anmen and Tian'anmen Square, the Forbidden City, the Summer Palace, the Temple of Heaven, the Great Wall and the Ming Tombs.

Tian'anmen and Tian'anmen Square are located in the center of Beijing. Tian'anmen was first built in 1420 of the Ming Dynasty. At that time it was the main entrance to the former Imperial City. Since the founding of the People's Republic of China, Tian'anmen has been a symbol of new China. Tian'anmen Square was a "T" shaped square during the Ming and Qing Dynasties. It has been greatly changed since 1950s. Now Tian'anmen Square is 44 hectares in area, and it is the largest city center square in the world. Tian'anmen Square attracts millions of people from all over the world every year. It is a place for celebrations during the important festive occasions.

The Forbidden City has a history of over 500 years. It was first built in 1420 during the Ming Dynasty, and used to be the former Imperial Palace for the Ming and Qing emperors. The Forbidden City was the place where the emperors lived and handled state affairs. There were altogether 24 emperors who lived and conducted state affairs in the Forbidden City for a total of 491 years. On October 10th, 1925, the whole complex was converted into a museum and opened to the public. The Forbidden City is not only the best-preserved imperial palace in China but also the largest ancient palatial structure in the world.

The Summer Palace is located on the northwest outskirts of Beijing, about 20 kilometers away from the center of the city. It has a history of over 250 years and mainly comprises Longevity Hill and Kunming Lake. This beautiful garden served as an imperial garden in the old days, but it was turned into a public park in 1928. Today the Summer Palace is very famous in the world and it attracts millions of people every year.

The Temple of Heaven is situated in the southern part of Beijing. It was built in 1420 in the Ming Dynasty. It was the place where the emperors of the Ming and Qing Dynasties worshiped the God of Heaven and prayed for a good harvest. The Temple of Heaven is not only the largest group of temple buildings in China, but also the largest heaven-worshipping architecture in the world.

The Ming Tombs are located in Changping District, about 50 kilometers to the northwest of Beijing. There were 13 Ming emperors, 23 empresses, many imperial concubines, princes and princesses that were buried in this imperial cemetery. These 13 tombs are the best preserved of all Chinese imperial tombs. Because there were 13 Ming Emperors buried in the area, it is called the "Thirteen Ming Tombs" in Chinese.

The Great Wall is one of the most famous ancient construction wonders in the world. For many centuries, the Great Wall kept out the invading troops of the northern nomadic tribes. The Great Wall witnessed the rise and fall of many dynasties and changes on the earth. Now, the Great Wall is a famous historical scenic spot for tourists, and it plays a very important role in the friendship between the Chinese people and people of the world.

Vocabulary

agency /ˈeidʒənsi/ n. 代理处，代理，旅行社
ancient /ˈeinʃənt/ adj. 远古的，旧的
concubine /ˈkɔŋkjubain/ n. 妃子，妾
dynasty /ˈdainəsti/ n. 朝代，王朝
emperor /ˈempərə/ n. 皇帝，君主
empress /ˈempris/ n. 皇后
hectare /ˈhektɑː/ n. 公顷（等于1万平方米）
imperial /imˈpiəriəl/ adj. 皇帝的
palace /ˈpælis/ n. 宫，宫殿
pray /prei/ v. 祈祷，恳求
prince /prins/ n. 王子
princess /ˈprinses/ n. 公主
scenic /ˈsiːnik/ adj. 风景的
sightseeing /ˈsaitsiːiŋ/ n. 观光
spot /spɔt/ n. 斑点，污点，地点，场所，现场
symbol /ˈsimbəl/ n. 象征
tomb /tuːm/ n. 坟墓 v. 埋葬
wonder /ˈwʌndə/ v. 想知道，怀疑 n. 奇观，奇迹
worship /ˈwəːʃip/ v. 崇拜，尊敬

Phrases & Expressions

Travel Counter 旅游柜台
Imperial Palace 皇宫
imperial garden 御花园
the Thirteen Ming Tombs 十三陵
Longevity Hill 万寿山

Notes to the Text

1. It was the place where the emperors of the Ming and Qing Dynasties worshiped the God of

Heaven and prayed for a good harvest. 这是明清两代帝王祭天、祈谷的地方。祭天（worship the God of Heaven）是指古代中国皇帝冬至到天坛举行祭祀天神的活动。祈谷（pray for a good harvest）是指古代中国皇帝孟春到天坛举行祈求五谷丰登的活动。

2. For many centuries, the Great Wall kept out the invading troops of the northern nomadic tribes. 在几个世纪，长城抵御了北方游牧民族军队的侵略。北方游牧民部落（the northern nomadic tribes）是指古代中国北方过着不定居生活的牧民部落。

Exercise 1　　Reading Comprehension

Answer the following questions according to the text.

1. What does a foreign tourist need when he or she is traveling in Beijing?
2. What should a Travel Counter clerk know when he or she talks with a foreign tourist?
3. What are the main sightseeing places in Beijing?
4. Do you know the different functions of Tian'anmen Square, the Forbidden City, the Summer Palace, the Temple of Heaven, the Great Wall and the Ming Tombs?
5. Where did the emperors live in the Ming and Qing Dynasties?

Exercise 2　　Word Training

Fill in the blanks with the words given below. Change the form where necessary.

| famous | symbol | dynasty | pray | garden |
| worship | travel | agency | center | imperial |

1. Many people believe that _____ is a part of people's life.
2. Carvings can date back to the Ming _____.
3. People can get the travel information from the travel _____.
4. Tian'anmen Square is located in the _____ of Beijing.
5. When he was young, Tony absolutely _____ his grandpa who worked for FBI.
6. As everybody knows, the dove is a _____ of peace.
7. Beihai Park is the oldest imperial _____ in the world.
8. In the old days the emperor went to the Temple of Heaven to _____ for a good harvest.

9. The tomb for the emperor is called _____ tomb.
10. There are many _____ ancient scenic spots in Beijing.

Section 3 Translation

Ⅰ. *Translate the following sentences into Chinese.*
1. The most common reason for travel is associated with our needs.
2. Why do you call the Imperial Palace the Purple Forbidden City?
3. What dose "power behind the throne" mean?
4. Do you know the layout of Tian'anmen Square in the Ming and Qing Dynasties?
5. The Summer Palace was called the Garden of Clear Ripples in the Qing Dynasty.

Ⅱ. *Translate the following sentences into English.*
1. 她说日出时的海岸很美丽。
2. 北京不但是一个古老的城市,而且也是一个旅游观光的好地方。
3. 我想去司马台长城,你们有宣传小册子吗?
4. 饭店的旅游柜台对来北京的散客旅游者非常重要。
5. 皇帝为什么要在颐和园建一个石舫呢?

Section 4 Classified Word Bank

Read the following words and expressions aloud and then learn them by heart:

1.	tour brochure	旅游小册子
2.	package tour	跟团旅游
3.	optional tour	选择性旅游
4.	one-day sightseeing	一日游
5.	business trip	商务旅行
6.	honeymoon tour	蜜月旅行
7.	group tour	团体旅游
8.	outbound travel	出境游
9.	tour guide	导游
10.	local guide	地陪
11.	national guide	全陪

12. tour escort   领队
13. return ticket   往返票
14. single ticket   单程票
15. tourist attractions   旅游景点
16. summer resort   避暑胜地
17. holiday resort   度假胜地
18. national park   国家公园
19. natural scenery   自然景观
20. places of cultural and historical interest   人文景观

Unit 2 At the Travel Agency

Section 1 Listening and Speaking

I. Listen and Repeat

Dialogue 1 Asking About a Tour at the Travel Agency

David is an American student. Now he is at Beijing International Travel Service asking about the tour for his parents. Miss. Wang is receiving him.

David: Excuse me, is this Beijing International Travel Service?

Wang: Yes, what can I do for you?

David: My parents will come to China this summer vocation. I'd like to take them to travel in the country, but I have no idea where to go. Could you give me some recommendations?

Wang: Certainly. How long is your tour?

David: It's about 10 to 15 days.

Wang: Do you prefer to go to the south or the north?

David: What's the difference?

Wang: The tour to the south includes more scenic spots. For example, Hang Zhou and Su Zhou have beautiful exquisite gardens; Lijiang is well-known for its well-preserved townscape. Shanghai is a modern consumer city and Kunming is a city with a nice temperature all year round.

David: I hear Sanya is a well-known scenic spot in the south.

Wang: Exactly. Sanya is superior in geography, climate and natural resources. It is known as "the Oriental Hawaii" and "Sunshine City" because of its special tropical scene as well as its attractive nature.

David: I see. What is the tour to the north?

Wang: It is also very interesting. Xi'an is renowned for its terra-cotta warriors and horses, and the Mausoleum of Emperor Qin Shi Huang. Shenyang has many historical sites such as Shenyang Palace Museum, the Eastern Imperial Tombs, the Northern Imperial Tombs, etc. Harbin is famous for its Ice-lantern Show.

David: Oh, I have never been there before. I love this tour too.

Wang: Here is our tour brochure with a price list and tour information in detail.

David: It's wonderful! I'll come back after I make the decision. Thank you very much.

Wang: You are welcome.

Dialogue 2 Arranging a Tour

Bruce wants to visit some places in Beijing. Now he is at CYTS. Miss Zhang is helping him arrange the tour.

Zhang: Good Morning, sir. Welcome to China Youth Travel Service. Can I help you?

Bruce: Yes, I'd like to see some places in Beijing. Could you please help me arrange the tour?

Zhang: Yes, of course. Please tell me what kind of tour you are interested in?

Bruce: I have already been to the Forbidden City, the Summer Palace, the Temple of Heaven and the Great Wall. I'd like to see some new scenic spots around Beijing. Would you please give me some recommendations?

Zhang: Certainly. I think the Tanzhe Temple is good for you. It is 45 kilometers southwest of Beijing. It is very famous. As the saying goes, "First there was the Tanzhe Temple, then came Beijing."

Bruce: Is it a whole day tour?

Zhang: Well, on your way back, you can go to the White Cloud Taoist Temple, the largest Taoist temple in Beijing.

Bruce: Okay, do you have any other recommendations?

Zhang: Yes, have you heard about Peking Man?

Bruce: Yes, I have.

Zhang: Why not go to the Cave of Peking Man. It is about 50 kilometers southwest of Beijing. These Peking men lived there about 200,000 to 700,000 years ago. It's really worth going.

Bruce: Fantastic! I really want to go there.

Zhang: Confucius Temple and the Former Imperial College are also nice places to go, because…

Bruce: I just went there last week. They are near the Lama Temple, is it right?

Zhang: Oh, yes. How about the Folk Tour in the countryside?

Bruce: I think I'll take the tour to the Cave of Peking Man.

Zhang: All right, please fill out this form first, then I'll arrange a tour guide and a car for you.

Bruce: Thank you very much.

Zhang: My pleasure.

Ⅱ. Act Out

1. Listen to the dialogue. Then practice it with your partners using the words and expressions below to help you.

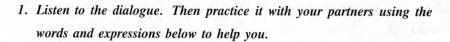

Wang: morning, welcome, travel agency, of course, where, go, Xi'an, terra cotta figure, Su Zhou, garden, Gulin, landscape, temple, south, we can, Fragrant Hill Park, located, western suburbs, 20 to 30 kilometres, serve as, imperial garden, Qing Dynasty, all right, here is, in detail, after, reading.

David: arrange, week-tour, first, China, recommend, interesting, scenic spot, worth seeing, can, for a week, places, in the suburbs, countryside, how far, characteristics, week-tour first, arrange, come back, brochure, thank, help.

2. Study the following sample dialogue. Then strike up a conversation with your partners using the sentences listed in the chart.

A: What can I do for you?

B: I'd like to visit some scenic spots in Beijing. Could you arrange it for me?

A: Yes, of course.

1. What can I do for you?
2. Could you please arrange some interesting scenic spots for me?

3. How much is the full-day tour?
4. How far is it from here?
5. Do you have any brochures in English?
6. What kind of tours do you have?
7. Why not go to the Liulichang Cultural Street? It is very ancient.
8. What is the characteristic of that place?
9. Do you have any other recommendation?
10. Do you have any French-speaking guide?

III. Focus Listening

A. Listen to the recording and choose the correct answer for each question.

1. From the recording we know that Johnson is _____.
   A. an American student studying at Beijing University
   B. a tourist spending summer vacation in Beijing
   C. an employee at Beijing International Travel Service
   D. a tour guide for international travel

2. Johnson went to Beijing International Travel Service to _____.
   A. ask for a job   B. arrange a tour
   C. serve as an intern   D. work as a volunteer

3. How long was the tour for Johnson?
   A. 8 days   B. 9 days   C. 12 days   D. 15 days

4. The south tour includes all of the following except _____.
   A. Hangzhou   B. Lijiang   C. Sanya   D. Xi'an

5. What is the price of north tour?
   A. 4,000 yuan B. 5,000 yuan C. 6,000 yuan   D. 7,000 yuan

B. Listen to the recording and complete the sentences below.

1. The Tanzhe Temple is _____ kilometers in the southwest suburbs of Beijing.
2. As the saying goes, "First there was _____, then came Beijing"
3. The White Cloud Taoist Temple is the _____ Taoist temple in Beijing.
4. Peking Man lived about _____ years ago.
5. Confucius Temple is near the _____.

Section 2 Reading

At the Travel Agency

Many people prefer to travel on their holidays; many people spend their leisure time by traveling, and many people say that their dream after retirement is to travel around the world.

To meet the different needs of tourists, different types of travel agencies offer a variety of travel products and services for them. When people decide to travel, they usually choose a travel agency to help them. It is at the travel agency that tourists get travel information, obtain tour brochures, make enquires about itineraries, decide which tour to take, book train or airline tickets and so on.

There are various kinds of tours for people to choose, such as the optional tour, the package tour, coach tour, Hutong tour, folk tour, etc.

Tour Brochure

  4-day tour: Tian'anmen and Tian'anmen Square, the Forbidden City, the Summer Palace, the Temple of Heaven, the Great Wall, the Ming Tombs, Hutong tour and Lama Temple.

  3-day tour: Tian'anmen and Tian'anmen Square, the Forbidden City, the Summer Palace, the Temple of Heaven, the Great Wall and the Ming Tombs.

  2-day tour: Tian'anmen and Tian'anmen Square, the Forbidden City, the Summer Palace, the Great Wall and the Ming Tombs.

  1-day tour: Tian'anmen and Tian'anmen Square, the Forbidden City, the Summer Palace or the Great Wall and the Ming Tombs.

  Half-day Tour: Forbidden City or the Great Wall.

Coach Tour: RMB 500 for 4-day tour

      RMB 400 for 3-day tour

      RMB 300 for 2-day tour

      RMB 200 for 1-day tour

      RMB 100 for Half-day tour

Departure time: 8:30 a.m. Every day.

The coach tour includes the admission tickets, tour guide, coach and the toll of superhighway, as well as the Chinese lunch.

Vocabulary

admission /əd'miʃən/ n. 允许进入,承认某事之陈述,供认
agency /'eidʒənsi/ n. 代理处,行销处,代理
coach /kəutʃ/ n. 车
departure /di'pɑ:tʃə/ n. 启程,出发,离开
dream /dri:m/ v. 做梦,梦见,梦想,想到 n. 梦想
express /iks'pres/ n. 快车,快递,专使
fee /fi:/ n. 费(会费、学费等),酬金
holiday /'hɔlədi/ n. 假日,节日,假期
information /,infə'meiʃən/ n. 通知,信息
itinerary /ai'tinərəri/ n. 路线
leisure /'li:ʒə/ n. 空闲,闲暇,悠闲
optional /'ɔpʃənəl/ adj. 可选择的,随意的
package /'pækidʒ/ n. 包裹,包
prefer /pri'fə:/ v. 更喜欢,宁愿
product /'prɔdəkt/ n. 产品,产物
retirement /ri'taiəmənt/ n. 退休,引退,退却
service /'sə:vis/ n. 服务,服务性工作
ticket /'tikit/ n. 票,入场券
travel /'trævl/ v. 旅行,传播 n. 旅行
variety /və'raiəti/ n. 变化,多样性,品种,种类

Phrases & Expressions

Meet the needs of 满足……的需求
a variety of 多种多样的
travel agency 旅行社
in detail 详细地
admission tickets 门票

Notes to the Text

1. There are various kinds of tours for people to choose, such as the optional tour, the package tour, coach tour, Hutong tour, folk tour, etc. 有很多的旅游供人们选择，比如有选择性旅行、包价旅游、乘游览车旅游、胡同游、民俗游等。

   选择性旅游（optional tour）：由旅游者任意选择某一项旅游或多项旅游。包价旅游（package tour）：一揽子旅游服务，旅游者没有选择的余地，一切旅游活动都是安排好了的。

Exercise 1   Reading Comprehension

Answer the following questions according to the text：

1. What kind of business does a travel agency have?
2. What kind of information should the tourists get from the travel agency?
3. Can you arrange a 3-day tour?
4. Does the coach tour include the admission tickets?
5. What is the departure time for the tour?

Exercise 2   Word Training

Fill in the blanks with the words given below. Change the form where necessary.

| admission | itinerary | temple | departure | prefer |
| leisure | package | special | variety | optional |

1. I'd like to a _____ tour to Egypt. I want to see the pyramids.
2. English, math and computer science are compulsory for all freshmen, but psychology and art are _____.
3. He's willing to talk about issues which most people _____ to avoid.
4. Many white-collar workers are concerned with their opportunities for _____.
5. We need to use _____ tyres on our car when we are driving in snowy conditions.
6. Oh, my God! How many _____ do you have in Beijing then?
7. When preparing meals, you need to think about _____ and taste as well as nutritional

value.
8. The next place on our _____ was the Tower of London.
9. The _____ time has been changed to 9 a.m. next Monday.
10. The _____ price is $20 for adults and $10 for children.

Section 3   Translation

Ⅰ. *Translate the following sentences into Chinese.*
1. Mr. Zhang wants to travel abroad on his vacation.
2. Johnson has been to most scenic spots in Beijing.
3. The sells manager at the travel agency is very busy during the high season.
4. Students can enjoy half price of the admission tickets.
5. I have never been to Tibet. Could you arrange that for me?

Ⅱ. *Translate the following sentences into English.*
1. 我已经去故宫了,所以我很想去一些其他有意思的地方。
2. 我们有各种旅游线路,不知你想到什么地方去玩?
3. 儿童能减免门票吗?
4. 我对喇嘛教很感兴趣,除雍和宫外北京还有其他喇嘛寺庙吗?
5. 让我们谈谈行程的具体事宜吧。

Section 4   Classified Word Bank

Read the following words and expressions aloud and then learn them by heart.

1.	group ticket	团体票
2.	day return	当日往返票
3.	electronic ticket	电子机票
4.	discount ticket	打折票
5.	special fare ticket	特价票
6.	student fare ticket	学生票
7.	off/low season	淡季
8.	high/peak season	旺季
9.	admission ticket	门票

10. express train	特快车
11. through train	直达快车
12. passport	护照
13. visa	签证
14. registration form	登记表
15. travel agency	旅行社
16. identity card	身份证
17. youth hostel	青年招待所
18. luxury hotel	豪华饭店
19. residential hotel	公寓旅馆
20. boardinghouse	寄宿公寓

Unit 3 At the Bank

Section 1 Listening and Speaking

I. Listen and Repeat

Dialogue 1 Cashing checks

Alan is at Bank of China. He wants to cash some checks and change the money into RMB. Miss Zhao, a bank clerk, is serving him.

Zhao: Good morning, sir. May I help you?

Alan: Yes, can you cash these traveler's checks for me?

Zhao: Certainly. How much do you want to cash?

Alan: 200 U.S. dollars. Would you please tell me the exchange rate today?

Zhao: It's 6.25 Yuan to the dollar.

Alan: Thank you. Here is my traveler's check.

Zhao: All right. Could you show me your passport, please?

Alan: Yes, here you are.

Zhao: Thank you. Please fill out the form and have your signature on each check.
Alan: Okay.
Zhao: Here is your money and receipt. 200 U. S. dollars will be 1,250 Yuan.
Alan: Thank you. Could you change these hundred bills into some smaller ones?
Zhao: Sure, how would you like them?
Alan: Two in fifty-yuan notes, five in twenty and ten-yuan notes.
Zhao: All right, here you are.
Alan: Thank you very much.
Zhao: It's my pleasure.

Dialogue 2   Exchanging money

Alan is going to exchange his RMB for U. S. dollars at the Hotel Foreign Exchange. He also wants to get some coils. Miss Zhao is receiving him.

Zhao: Good morning. Can I help you?
Alan: Yes, I'm going home tomorrow, but I still have some RMB here. Could you please help me change them back into U. S. dollars?
Zhao: I'm sorry I can't exchange your RMB for U. S. dollars. You can only do it at Bank of China or the Foreign Exchange Bank at the airport.
Alan: Then I'll do it at the airport.
Zhao: Is there anything else I can do for you?
Alan: Well, could you change some Chinese coins for me please? I'm a coin collector.
Zhao: Certainly. How many coins do you want?
Alan: Can I have 40 yuan coins?
Zhao: All right, 10 Yuan for 1-yuan coins, 10 Yuan for 50-cent coins and 20 Yuan for 10-cent, 5-cent, 2-cent and 1-cent coins. Will that be all right?
Alan: No problem. Thank you very much.
Zhao: You are welcome.

II. Act Out

1. Listen to the dialogue. Then practice it with your partners using the words and expressions below to help you.

> **Zhao**: Welcome, Bank of China, help you, of course, how much, do you, cash, show, passport, one U. S. dollar, 6.25 Yuan, have, signature, each check, here is, money and receipt, certainly, how many coins, here you are. You are welcome.

> **Alan**: cash, traveler's check, dollars, do it, hotel foreign exchange, three hundred dollars, exchange rate, sign here, give me some coins, 20 Yuan, thank.

2. Study the following sample dialogue. Then strike up a conversation with your partners using the sentences listed in the chart.

A: Good morning, madam. **Can I change some money here**?

B: Certainly. How much do you want to change?

A: I want to change five hundred U.S. dollars into RMB.

1. Can I change some money here?
2. Where can I cash my traveler's checks?
3. Can I change the local money back into U.S. dollars?
4. What is the current exchange rate?
5. I need some change, please.
6. Could you please sign your name on each check?
7. Could I change these big bills for some smaller ones?
8. The ATM ate my card.
9. How would you like that? Large or small bills?
10. May I see some ID?

Ⅲ. Focus Listening

A. Listen to the recording and choose the correct answer for each question.

1. Alan is staying at _____.
   A. Beijing Hotel   B. Jianguo Hotel
   C. Tiantan Hotel   D. Beijing International Hotel
2. Alan has come to the hotel Foreign Exchange Counter to _____.
   A. cash his traveler's check   B. exchange money
   C. enquire about the exchange rate   D. get some change.
3. The current exchange rate is _____ to the dollar.
   A. 6.25 yuan   B. 6.35 yuan
   C. 6.45 yuan   D. 6.55 yuan
4. How much money does Alan want to exchange?

A. 300 U. S. dollars　　　　　　B. 400 U. S. dollars
　　C. 500 U. S. dollars　　　　　　D. 600 U. S dollars
5. How many fifty-Yuan bills does Alan ask for?
　　A. 10　　　　B. 20　　　　　C. 30　　　　　D. 50

B. Listen to the recording and complete the sentences below.
1. Frank will _____ home tomorrow.
2. He has only _____ Chinese yuan.
3. The mask of Peking Opera shows the _____ of Beijing.
4. The vase is made of Cloisonné, the traditional _____ of China.
5. The local money might be used for the _____ expenses.

Section 2　Reading

Bank and Credit Card

Bank

　　When traveling, people have to take money with them. But different countries usually use different currencies. A tourist has to have the currency of the country he is going to visit, so that he can pay taxi or bus fares, to tip porters, or to buy souvenirs for his friends and relatives. It's for this reason that he will have to go to the bank to change money.

　　Generally speaking, a tourist has to visit the bank during his travel, because the bank is the place where the tourist can exchange money. But since different currencies have different exchange rates, it will be quite helpful for the tourist to get the information from the bank about them.

　　What is the exchange rate? It is the value of the money of one country compared to the money of another country. People know the value of their own money through the exchange rate, but since the floating exchange rate system is adopted, the rate does not fix but changes according to the world banking, market or financial conditions.

　　Many tourists change their money at the bank or hotel foreign exchange. But before they do it, they usually check the rate of exchange on that day. Every bank provides such information for the tourists. After they get the basic knowledge of the currency of the country, they can decide how much money should be exchanged, and then spend money in

that country.

Sometimes when tourists finish their travel in a country, they still have some local money left. Very often they want to change them back at the bank, but actually they should keep it until they get to the airport, because the local money can be used for the last-minute expenses, such as the airport departure tax, souvenirs and so on.

Credit Card

Since more and more people like to travel and cash is not that convenient for them to carry, they prefer credit cards. Credit card is a small, rectangular plastic card, which is not only easy to carry but also offer many advantages. For instance, when people travel, they can buy something at a store, have meals at a restaurant, enjoy favorable price and service etc. They can also draw money from the bank. With credit cards people can get something they cannot afford at one time, because the bank allows people to pay for the charges in several payments over a period of time.

Today, more and more people use credit cards instead of cash to buy what they need. They no longer need to carry a lot of money with them whenever they go for a trip. This is very convenient for tourists when they travel, therefore, they don't have to worry about the cash in their purses and wallets.

Vocabulary

according /əˈkɔːdiŋ/ *adv.* 依照
afford /əˈfɔːd/ *vt.* 买得起,花费得起
carelessness /ˈkɛəlisnis/ *n.* 粗心,疏忽
check /tʃek/ *vt.* 检查,核对
compare /kəmˈpɛə/ *n.* 比较
condition /kənˈdiʃən/ *n.* 条件,情形,环境
convenient /kənˈviːnjənt/ *adj.* 便利的,方便的
currency /ˈkʌrənsi/ *n.* 货币,流通
exchange /iksˈtʃeindʒ/ *n.* 交换,调换,兑换
expenses /ikˈspens/ *n.* 费用,开支
financial /faiˈnænʃəl/ *adj.* 财政的,金融的
market /ˈmaːkit/ *n.* 市场,销路,行情

perhaps /pə'hæps/ adv. 或许，多半
porter /'pɔːtə/ n. 行李搬运工，守门人，门房
rate /reit/ n. 比率，速度，等级
souvenirs /'suːvəniə/ n. 纪念品
thief /θiːf/ n. 小偷，贼
through /θruː/ prep. 穿过，通过
tip /tip/ n. 顶，梢，小费，vt. 给小费
value /'væljuː/ n. 价值，估价，评价

Phrases & Expressions

generally speaking 一般来讲
exchange rate 兑换率
flouting exchange rate 浮动汇率制
credit card 信用卡
for instance 例如

Notes to the Text

1. …because the local money can be used for the last-minute expenses, such as the airport departure tax, souvenirs and so on. ……因为当地货币可以用来支付最后的开支,比如机场离境税,纪念品等。紧急关头的消费(the last-minute expenses)是指预料之外的花费、支出。机场离境税(the airport departure tax)是指离开某个国家时,在机场需交付的离境税。

2. Credit card is a small, rectangular plastic card, which is not only easy to carry but also has many advantages. 信用卡是一张很小的、长方形的塑料卡片,它不仅易于携带而且拥有很多好处。信用卡(credit card)是指由银行发行、代替货币进行交易的一种卡。使用信用卡交易可以允许一定量的透支,但如不能按时偿还,需要支付给银行很高的利息。用信用卡也可以进行一定量的提款。

Exercise 1　Reading Comprehension

Answer the following questions according to the text.

1. Where do the tourists go if they want to change money?

2. What is the definition of exchange rate?
3. What exchange rate system is used now?
4. What can tourists do with the local money they have before leaving?
5. Why do people prefer credit card than cash?

Exercise 2 Word Training

Fill in the blanks with the words given below. Change the form where necessary.

| financial | convenient | afford | widely | cash |
| condition | change | souvenir | local | prefer |

1. Johnson still had some _____ money before he left China.
2. There are a couple of American tourists at the _____ stand.
3. Some factories closed down owing to the _____ crisis in Asia.
4. The church was built in the 1890s but still in good _____.
5. People should know the exchange rate when they _____ their money.
6. The traveler's check is _____ used by tourists.
7. Young people _____ credit card to cash.
8. Excuse me. Where can I _____ my traveler's checks?
9. We can't _____ to go on vacation this summer.
10. It is very _____ for people to use credit cards especially for the tourists.

Section 3 Translation

Ⅰ. *Translate the following sentences into Chinese.*

1. Being a tourist, he should have the local money of that country he is visiting.
2. Do you know why people should have their signatures on each traveler's check when exchanging money?
3. More and more people prefer credit card when they consume.
4. Foreign tourists can change their RMB back into U.S. dollars at Bank of China.
5. People are interested in the exchange rate when they change money, because the exchange rate shows the value of his country's currency.

Ⅱ. *Translate the following sentences into English.*
1. 饭店的外币兑换处给旅游者提供了换钱的方便服务。
2. 旅游者换钱时对汇率都有知情权,银行工作人员有提供此信息的义务。
3. 一般来说,换钱时都要根据当天的汇率换钱。
4. 旅行支票可以在中国银行兑换现金,信用卡也能在中国银行兑换现金。
5. 在中国,不仅年轻人使用信用卡,中老年人也使用。

Section 4　Classified Word Bank

Read the following words and expressions aloud and then learn them by heart:

1.	account number	账号
2.	open an account	开户
3.	deposit book	存折
4.	credit card	信用卡
5.	blank check	空白支票
6.	traveler's check	旅行支票
7.	cash check	现金支票
8.	check for transfer	转账支票
9.	overdraw	透支
10.	check	支票
11.	to cash	兑现
12.	to deposit	存款
13.	deposit form	存款单
14.	currency exchange	货币兑换
15.	exchange rate	兑换率
16.	signature	签字
17.	receipt	发票
18.	travel agent	旅行代理商
19.	travel fair	旅游展销会
20.	tour coupon	旅游优惠券

Unit 4　Emergency Cases When Traveling

Section 1　Listening and Speaking

I. Listen and Repeat

Dialogue 1　Falling Ill

In a scenic spot Jenny is not feeling well. Miss Yang, the tour guide, comes up to her. Jenny's husband John is worrying about her.

Yang: You look pale and are dripping with sweat. Do you need my help?

Jenny: Yes, please. I feel terrible; I think I'm sick.

Yang: Calm down, please. I'll call the ambulance right now.

Jenny: Thank you.

Yang: Does she have any serious illness, John?

John: Yes. She has heart disease. Since today is very hot, she might suffer from a heart attack.

Yang: In this case, please don't move her. Let her lie down and keep calm. The doctor and the ambulance will be here right away.

John: I'll take good care of her. Please call the doctor again. She is growing faint.

Yang: All right. I'll call again. In order to save time, I'll go and ask the employees of the scenic spot for help, and let them show the way for the ambulance.

John: Thank you very much.

Yang: You are welcome. I'll be back in a minute.

John: Okay. (*After a while, Miss Yang comes back with a doctor*)

Doctor: What's wrong with her?

John: She is short of breath.

Doctor: She needs to go to hospital right away. Let's put her on the stretcher first.

John: Okay. (*To Miss Yang*) Thank you very much for your help.

Yang: Don't mention it. Let's go and accompany her to the hospital.

Dialogue 2   Losing Passport

Peter is a foreign tourist and Miss Zhou is his tour guide. Now he is telling her that he lost his passport in the hotel lobby.

Zhou: Peter, what's the matter with you? You look worried.

Peter: I've got a problem. I can't find my passport now. I think it's missing.

Zhou: Oh, I'm sorry to hear that. But have you searched for it in your hotel room?

Peter: Yes, but I can't find it anywhere in it. I can't find it in my suitcase or my clothes pockets.

Zhou: Don't worry. Try to think where you used your passport for the last time.

Peter: I used it yesterday when I signed my traveler's checks in the souvenir shop. I went there to find it but they didn't have it, either. What shall I do then?

Zhou: If your passport doesn't turn up, you will have to get a new one.

Peter: Could you tell me how to get a new one?

Zhou: Certainly. First, let's report it to the local public security office and go there to get a certificate of loss.

Peter: Okay, What else should we do next?

Zhou: Next I need to report it to my travel agency and get the document indicating the loss of your passport from my travel agency. After that you should go to the Entry and Exit Office of the Beijing Municipal Public Security Bureau with the supporting document from my travel service and your photos to apply for a "lost passport certificate."

Peter: Can I have my photos taken at the Beijing Municipal Public Security Bureau?

Zhou: Of course you can. Then you should go to your embassy in Beijing to apply for a new passport with the documents from the Beijing Municipal Public Security Bureau.

Peter: Where can I get the visa then?

Zhou: With the newly issued passport, you will go back to the Beijing Municipal Public Security Bureau again to apply for the visa.

Peter: Thank you very much for your help.

Zhou: You are welcome.

II. Act Out

1. Listen to the dialogue. Then practice it with your partners using the words and expressions below to help you.

> **Yang**: watch, step, serious, need, help, worry, call, ambulance, right away, before, came, move, make yourself, comfortable, here, minute, save time, meet, at the gate, look, doctor, take, hospital, accompany, hospital.
>
> **Peter**: God, hurt, ankle, terribly pain, thank, how soon, doctor, arrive, afraid, stand, pain, thank.
>
> **Doctor**: Let, put, stretcher, that, fine.

2. Study the following sample dialogue. Then strike up a conversation with your partners using the sentences listed in the chart.

A: I feel terrible. **I think I've got a heart attack.**

B: I'll call in a doctor for you right away.

A: Thank you very much for your help.

A: You are welcome.

1. I think I've got a heart attack.
2. I think I am going to vomit.
3. I think I've got a heatstroke.
4. I fell off a tree. I think my leg is broken.
5. I've got a splitting headache.
6. I am so dizzy. I can't stand up.
7. My ankle is swollen.
8. I'm growing faint and I'm short of breath.
9. I'm having terrible chest pains.
10. I cut myself on broken glass, and I am bleeding very badly.

Ⅲ. Focus Listening

A. Listen to the recording and choose the correct answer for each question.

1. The temperature reached _____ degrees centigrade on the day when Xiao Wang took a group to the Forbidden City.

    A. 36   B. 37   C. 38   D. 39

2. What happened to Angela during the trip to the Forbidden City?

    A. She was lost.   B. She was injured.

C. She lost her passport.   D. She had a stroke
3. What was the first thing Xiao Wang did after giving Angela some cold water?
   A. He called the ambulance.   B. He moved her to the shade.
   C. He fanned her with a newspaper.   D. He tried to let her sit down.
4. Which of following statements is not true?
   A. Xiao Wang helped to put Angela on the stretcher.
   B. Xiao Wang did not accompany Angela to the hospital.
   C. Angela thanked Xiao Wang for his help.
   D. Angela asked Xiao Wang to dinner.
5. All of the following statements are true except _____.
   A. Xiao Wang is a qualified tour guide
   B. Xiao Wang is often praised by his boss
   C. Angela is an American tourist
   D. Angela recovered very soon

B. Listen to the recording and complete the sentences below.
1. The passport can certify one's _____ and citizenship.
2. The passport can also _____ a citizen to travel abroad.
3. If a tourist has really lost his passport, you will have to help him to _____.
4. The tourist who has lost his passport has to go to the _____ of his country in China to apply for a new passport.
5. With the newly issued passport, the tourist will have to go back to the _____ to apply for the visa.

Section 2   Reading

Traffic Accident

When traveling, it is quite common for people to experience something unpleasant. They may fall ill or get lost; they may lose their wallets or passports; they may even meet with danger, accident or death. In such cases, it is very important for tour guides to know what they should do or whom they should turn to for help. Now let's learn what a tour guide must do in case a traffic accident happens during a trip.

If you are a tour guide or the person who is in charge of a group, when a traffic accident happens on a trip, you should handle it in the following way:

Firstly, make the injured as comfortable as possible and call for an ambulance or have someone else do it immediately. You can ask the people who are not injured to help you with the rescue work. Move the injured tourists out of the coach as quickly as possible. The injured, especially those who are seriously injured should be sent to the nearby hospital immediately.

Secondly, keep the scene of the accident intact before the police arrive; then go and stop any cars or buses on the spot in order to send the injured to the nearby hospital.

Thirdly, report the accident promptly to the transportation and public security departments and the office of the travel service for instructions as how to handle the accident. You should ask the travel service to dispatch another coach to the spot, so that you can take them back to the hotel or continue the tour.

Fourthly, try to keep the tourists calm and try to reduce the adverse effect of the accident to the minimum before the relevant personnel arrive.

Fifthly, the wounded should get the "Certificate of Medical Treatment" and the "Certificate of Traffic Accident" signed by the Public Security Bureau, so that the wounded can register a claim for compensation from the insurance company.

Lastly, no matter what kind of accident happens, you should file a written report right after the accident. The report should include the cause of the accident, how it was handled and the result of it. It should be truthfully accurate and in details.

Vocabulary

accurate /'ækjurit/ *adj.* 正确的,精确的
adverse /'ædvə:s/ *adj.* 不利的,敌对的,相反的
ambulance /'æmbjuləns/ *n.* 救护车
case /keis/ *n.* 事情,病例,案例,情形,场合
claim /kleim/ *n.* (根据权利提出)要求,主张;认领
compensation /ˌkɔmpen'seiʃən/ *n.* 补偿,赔偿
dispatch /dis'pætʃ/ *v.* 派遣;发送
immediately /i'mi:djətli/ *adv.* 立即,马上,直接地
injured /'indʒəd/ *adj.* 受伤的,受损害的
insurance /in'ʃuərəns/ *n.* 保险,保险费
intact /in'tækt/ *adj.* 完整无缺的
minimum /'miniməm/ *n.* 最小值,最小化

reduce /ri'djuːs/ vt. 减少,缩小
register /'redʒistə/ n. 记录,登记
relevant /'relivənt/ adj. 有关的,相应的
rescue /'reskjuː/ n. 援救,营救
security /si'kjuərəti/ n. 安全
wallet /'wɔlit/ n. 皮夹,钱夹
wounded /'wuːndid/ adj. 受伤的

Phrases & Expressions

get lost 迷路
meet with… 遭遇……
in such cases 在这种情况下
turn to 求助……
in charge of 负责……
call (for) an ambulance 叫救护车
no matter what 无论……

Notes to the Text

1. Secondly, keep the scene of the accident intact before the police arrive 你还应该在警察到达之前保护现场完整。保护现场完整(Keep the scene of the accident intact)也是导游要做的事情,这对于以后处理事故非常有益。
2. Anyway, the wounded should get the "Certificate of Medical Treatment" and the "Certificate of Traffic Accident" signed by the Public Security Bureau... 句中的"Certificate of Medical Treatment"(医疗证明)是指由医疗部门开出的治疗过程证明书;而"Certificate of Traffic Accident"(交通事故证明)是指由公安局签发的处理交通事故过程的证明书。

Exercise 1　Reading Comprehension

Answer the following questions according to the text.
1. What unpleasant things might happen to tourists during their trips?
2. When a traffic accident happens on the trip, what should a tour guide do first?

3. What should a tour guide do secondly according to the text?
4. Why do the wounded need to get the "Certificate of Medical Treatment" and the "Certificate of Traffic Accident"?
5. What should the report include?

Exercise 2　Word Training

Fill in the blanks with the words given below. Change the form where necessary.

| register | drink | common | dispatch | insurance |
| claim | rescue | security | medicine | injure |

1. Alison and her husband _____ six people from the fire last night.
2. Traffic accidents are quite _____ for people when they travel.
3. The news agency _____ a reporter to the city to cover the riot.
4. Mary went to the front office to _____ the necklace she lost the other day.
5. The car is _____ in my wife's name.
6. Travelers should have emergency _____ when they start to travel.
7. For _____ reasons, passengers are requested not to leave any luggage unattended.
8. When traveling, travelers should take some _____ with them in case of emergency.
9. Ten people were seriously _____ in a road accident.
10. In order to prevent the traffic accident from happening, the driver ought not to _____ alcohol.

Section 3　Translation

Ⅰ. *Translate the following sentences into Chinese.*

1. Travelers often suffer from heatstroke in summer.
2. When someone faints during a traffic accident, what should you do first?
3. You must carry your passport and ID card when you travel.
4. When a tourist does lose his passport, the tour guide should help him to get a new one.
5. Being a tourist, you should always carry your mobile phone in case of emergency.

Ⅱ. *Translate the following sentences into English.*
1. 作为一名旅游者,当交通事故发生时,你应该做什么并向谁求助呢?
2. 旅游时身体不适,应及时休息或就医。
3. 发生交通事故的处理方法包括:找人寻求帮助、叫救护车、寻求警察帮助、就地拦截车辆送伤者就医等。
4. 我们应帮助受伤者,把事故的影响降到最低限度。
5. 旅游发生意外时,首先不能慌张,然后寻求救助。

Section 4　Classified Word Bank

Read the following words and expressions aloud and then learn them by heart:

1.	look pale	面色苍白
2.	feel dizzy	感到晕眩
3.	be dripping with sweat	汗水直淌
4.	have a heart attack	心脏病发作
5.	suffer from heatstroke	中暑
6.	have a fever	发烧
7.	have a cold	感冒
8.	have a headache	头疼
9.	have a stomachache	胃疼
10.	have a sore throat	嗓子疼
11.	have a stuffy nose	鼻子不通
12.	feel like vomiting	想吐
13.	be short of breath	呼吸急促
14.	be allergic to dogs	对狗过敏
15.	My eyes are swollen	我眼睛肿了
16.	badly injured	受重伤的
17.	dangerous driving	危险驾驶
18.	drive without license	无证驾驶
19.	drive onto the pavement	冲上人行道
20.	call for an ambulance	打电话叫救护车

Beauty Spots

Unit 1 Natural Scenery

Section 1 Listening and Speaking

I. Listen and Repeat

Dialogue 1 Talking About Jiuzhaigou Valley

Brant is talking with Annie about Jiuzhaigou Valley in their tourism English class.

Brant: Have you heard of Jiuzhaigou Valley, the famous scenic spot in Sichuan Province?

Annie: Yes, of course. But I have never been there.

Brant: What a pity!

Annie: I hear that Jiuzhaigou is called "Fairyland" for its natural and primitive scenery.

Brant: Yeah, there is a beautiful fairy tale about it.

Annie: Really? What is it?

Brant: It's said that once upon a time, a god named Dage made a magic mirror from wind and cloud, and sent it to his beloved goddess Semo. However, Semo dropped the mirror onto the ground because of her carelessness, and it turned into 108 colorful lakes. Therefore, there are about 108 lakes of various sizes and shapes in Jiuzhaigou Valley.

Annie: Wow! That's a beautiful fairy tale. Is Nuorilang Waterfall famous in Jiuzhaigou Valley?

Brant: Yeah, it is one of the largest falls in China.

Annie: Is there any special meaning for Nuorilang Waterfall?

Brant: Well, Nuorilang, in Tibetan language, means "splendid and magnificent".

Annie: It really deserves the name!

Brant: I agree. Shall we pay a visit to Jiuzhaigou together on our summer vacation?

Annie: That's a good idea.

Dialogue 2 A Trip to Huanglong

Miss Li, the tour guide, is now introducing Huanglong to the tourists.

Tourist: Where are we going today?

Guide: We are going to the Huanglong Scenic and Historic Interest Area.

Tourist: What does Huanglong mean in Chinese?

Guide: It means yellow dragon.

Tourist: I learned on the Internet that Huanglong is the World Wonder and Fairy Land on Earth. It was listed on the World Nature Heritage Site List in 1992.

Guide: Yeah, it is famous for its magical landscape of calcium carbonate deposits, as well as its rich forest and rare animals.

Tourist: Amazing! Where is it?

Guide: It is located in Songpan County, Sichuan Province.

Tourist: How did Honglong get its name?

Guide: It is said that there are numerous colorful ponds in different sizes and shapes, which have a shining golden color due to the gold-colored calcium carbonate deposits at the bottom of the water, so during sunlight, it's just like a golden dragon out of the water. That's the origin of the name.

Tourist: What is the most famous attraction in Huanglong?

Guide: *Shitazhenhai* (the Stone Pagoda Pool) is the most famous in Huanglong. The calcium carbonate deposits give different colors to the water, which is really amazing.

Tourist: I hear that the local people value Feicui Spring so much.

Guide: Yeah. The water in Feicui Spring has medical value. After drinking or bathing in its water, people will recover from diseases.

Tourist: Sounds great. I am looking forward to enjoying it.

Guide: OK, let's go.

II. Act Out

1. *Listen to the dialogue. Then practice it with your partners using the words and expressions below to help you.*

Guide:	head for, Mt. Huang, name after, ancient, emperor, try to, elixirs, became, God, therefore, Stranger pines, rock crevices, various, shapes, grotesque rocks, different, angles, animals, people, lotus, peak, 1,860 metres, seas of clouds, swirling, third wonder, hot springs, treat diseases, dermatosis, arthritis, take a bath.
Tourist:	call, mountain, fantastic story, known, wonders, amazing, second, Lotus Flower Stone, beautiful, take, photos, fantastic, charming landscape, sound great, good idea.

2. Study the following sample dialogue. Then strike up a conversation with your partners using the sentences listed in the chart.

A: Have you ever been to the Great Wall?

B: Yes, of course.

A: Then you must have heard the famous saying "He who has never been to Great Wall is not a true man".

B: Sure.

1. Have you ever been to the Great Wall?
2. Are you interested in Fragrant Hills Park?
3. How long are we going to stay in Jiuzhaigou Valley?
4. Do you have any brochures in English?
5. Excuse me. Is there a gift shop nearby?
6. I think Mogao Caves really live up to their reputation.
7. Our ancestors thought that Mt. Huang was so high that it scraped the sky.
8. Is the Summer Palace impressed you so much?
9. Have you noticed anything special in Tianchi Lake?
10. How did Huaqing Hot Spring get its name?

III. Focus Listening

A. Listen to the recording and choose the correct answer for each question.

1. Niagara Falls is located _____.

   A. in the state of New York

B. in the province of Ontario

C. in South America

D. in North America

2. Which of the following falls does not belong to the three world-famous falls?

   A. Niagara Falls

   B. Victoria Falls

   C. Cataratas Falls

   D. Yosemite Falls

3. In native American Indian language the word "Niagara" means _____?

   A. the strait   B. the Iroquois

   C. the rock   D. the wonder

4. Niagara Falls consists of all of the following except _____.

   A. American Falls   B. Khone Falls

   C. Bridal Veil Falls   D. Horseshoe Falls

5. Which fall is the largest in the world?

   A. Cataratas Falls   B. Niagara Falls

   C. Victoria Falls   D. American Falls

B. Listen to the recording and complete the sentences below.

1. _____ was in charge of the construction of the Leshan Giant Buddha.

2. The height of the Leshan Giant Buddha is _____ metres.

3. The Leshan Giant Buddha took _____ years to complete.

4. _____ people can sit on each instep of the Leshan Giant Buddha.

5. The purpose of constructing the Leshan Giant Buddha is to _____ and to protect the people traveling on the river.

Section 2   Reading

Kanas Lake in Xingjiang

   Xinjiang Uygur Autonomous Region, also called Xinjiang for short, covers an area of 1.66 million square kilometers, accounting for one-sixth of the total area of the Chinese territory. Xinjiang is rich in tourism resources and its unique scenery attracts tourists from both home and abroad. In Xinjiang you can see high mountains, glaciers, lakes, grasslands, vast Gobi and deserts, various natural reserves, historical sites and so on. Over 1,000 kinds of wild animals and plants live and grow there, including some endangered species.

Located on the middle part of the Altai Mountain of Xinjiang, Kanas Lake covers an area of 44.78 square kilometers. It is 1,374 meters above sea level and the deepest place reaches 188 meters. If you look at the map you can find that China is shaped like a rooster and Kana Lake is just that most beautiful tail plume  of the rooster. Nowadays, Kanas Lake in Xinjiang, Qinghai Lake in Qinghai Province, Namtso Lake in Tibet, Lake Tianchi in Jilin Province, and West Lake in Zhejiang Province are known as the country's five great lakes.

Kanas Lake is also reputed to be one of the most famous color-changing lakes in the world. The color of the water in the lake is different and changes with the season and climate. It becomes caesious grey in May, light green or dark blue in June, milky in July, blackish green in August and emerald in September and October.

Kanas, in Mongolian, means "beautiful, rich and mysterious". Legend has it that the lake used to be a mirror for a fairy to dress and make up. One day, the fairy dropped some flower seeds on the Lakeside due to her carelessness. Immediately there were flowers and

trees growing everywhere around the lake and the fairyland of Kanas thus came into being.

Besides the breathtaking scenery of the lake, the nearby Crouching Dragon Bay, the Moon Bay, the Wild Duck Bay and the Fish Observing Pavilion are all worth seeing.

It's said that that there are monsters in the lake. They are 10 to 15 meters long and their heads are 4 meters wide. The first person who claimed to have seen the lake monster was an associate professor in the biology department of Xinjiang Normal University. That was in the late 1970s. Since then, the report about the mysterious creature has never stopped. Many scientists and researchers went there to conduct investigation. But it was not until 1987 that a well-equipped scientific research team formed by domestic and foreign experts discovered a sizeable red fish, which was about three or four meters long. The team thus announced that the mysterious creature had been discovered. The so-called "lake monster" was actually giant Hucho Taimen, called Giant Red Fish by the local people. Later the investigation team published a book about the lake monster. But until now people still don't know any detailed information about this kind of giant red fish.

Vocabulary

autonomous /ɔː'tɒnəməs/ adj. 自治的
claim /kleim/ v. 声称；要求；认领
crouch /'krautʃ/ v. 蜷缩，蹲伏
detail /'diːteil/ n. 详细
domestic /də'mestik/ adj. 国内的
endangered /in'deindʒəd/ adj. 濒临灭绝的；有危险的
fairy /'fɛəri/ n. 仙女，精灵
fairyland /'fɛərilænd/ n. 仙境
investigation /inˌvesti'geiʃən/ n. 调查
monster /'mɒnstə/ n. 怪物，妖怪
mysterious /mis'tiəriəs/ adj. 神秘的，不可思议的
pavilion /pə'viljən/ n. 亭，阁
plume /pluːm/ n. 羽毛
province /'prɒvins/ n. 省
recognize /'rekəgnaiz/ v. 认可，公认，认出
reserve /ri'zəːv/ n. 保护区
rooster /'ruːstə/ n. 公鸡
scenery /'siːnəri/ n. 风景，景色
sizeable /'saizəbl/ adj. 相当大的
territory /'teritəri/ n. 领土，版图
unique /juː'niːk/ adj. 独特的，唯一的

Phrases & Expressions

account for 占……百分比；说明，解释
be rich in 在……富有
be recognized as 被认为是……
come into being 形成，产生

conduct investigation 进行调查

Notes to the Text

1. Kanas Lake：喀纳斯湖位于新疆，距乌鲁木齐市 1 000 公里之遥，蒙古语意为"峡谷中的湖"。
2. Kanas Lake in Xinjiang, The Qinghai Lake in Qinghai Province. The Namtso Lake in Tibet, Tianchi in Jilin Province, West Lake in Zhejiang：青海的青海湖、新疆的喀纳斯湖、西藏的天湖、吉林省的天池和浙江省的西湖被誉为中国五大湖。
3. Crouching Dragon Bay，卧龙湾，the Moon Bay，月亮湾，the Wild Duck Bay，鸭泽湾，the Fish Observing Pavilion 观鱼亭。
4. Hucho Taimen：哲罗鱼，为凶猛的冷水性纯淡水鱼类，当地人把它称作大红鱼，专家认为它也就是所谓的湖怪。

Exercise 1　Reading Comprehension

Answer the following Questions according to the text.

1. What are the five great lakes in China?
2. What is the meaning of Kanas in Mongolian?
3. How did Kanas Lake become a fairyland?
4. Where is the location of the Kanas Lake?
5. What is the lake monster?

Exercise 2　Word Training

Fill in the blanks with the words given below. Change the form where necessary.

| resort | recognize | scenery | mysterious | mineral |
| reflect | pavilion | fairyland | investigation | unique |

1. Africa is a _____ land to him.
2. This place has become a famous summer _____.
3. Some countries in Africa are rich in _____ deposits.

4. Mary could see her face _____ in the water of the lake.

5. He had made a thorough _____. No wonder he knew so much about it.

6. Sometimes they just drive slowly down the lane enjoying the _____.

7. The _____ on the hill looks down on the river.

8. The interesting and charming creature is _____ to Australia.

9. The garden was a _____ of beautiful flowers and sweet odors.

10. The receptionist _____ her at once.

Section 3   Translation

Ⅰ. *Translate the following sentences into Chinese.*

1. As the Chinese saying goes, "East or west, Guilin's landscape is the best".
2. The snow scene of West Lake earns very high praise from people, especially the view of "Melting Snow at Broken Bridge".
3. The roaring tide of the Qiantang River is a magnificent spectacle under heaven.
4. The Silvery Beach in Beihai City is renowned for its "long beach, white sand", hence it is called "No.1 Beach in China".
5. Both banks of the Hukou are flanked by green mountains. As the water-channel looks very much like the mouth of a pot, it gets its name "Hukou".

Ⅱ. *Translate the following sentences into English.*

1. 断桥位于白堤的东面。
2. 泰山是这里最有名的景点。
3. 不知道你有没有注意到云南省的风景很特别。
4. 一起去参观乐山大佛怎么样？
5. 好一个"阳朔山水甲天下"，看来真是一点也不夸张！

Section 4   Classified Word Bank

Read the following words and expressions aloud and then learn them by heart.

1. Aegean Sea	爱琴海
2. Ayers Rock	艾尔斯巨石
3. Bali, Indonesia	巴厘岛

4.	Boulder Bank	天然长堤
5.	Cake of Good Hope	好望角
6.	Crocodile Farm	泰国北览鳄鱼湖
7.	Easter Island	复活岛
8.	fairyland	人间仙境
9.	Fiji Island	斐济岛
10.	Grand Canyon	大峡谷
11.	Great Barrier Reef	大堡礁
12.	Great Lakes	五大湖
13.	Iguassu Falls	伊瓜苏瀑布
14.	Niagara Falls	尼加拉瓜瀑布
15.	Sahara Desert	撒哈拉大沙漠
16.	The Himalayas	喜马拉雅山
17.	West Lake	西湖
18.	Yellowstone National Park	黄石国家公园
19.	Yosemite National Park	美国约塞米蒂国家公园
20.	Yungang Caves	云冈石窟

Unit 2 Historical Sites

Section 1 Listening and Speaking

Ⅰ. Listen and Repeat

Dialogue 1 Talking About the Great Wall

Brant is talking with Miss Zhang, the tour guide, about the Great Wall.

Brant: Have you ever been to the Great Wall, the famous world heritage listed by UNESCO?

Zhang: Yes. I have.

Brant: Why is it called the Great Wall?

Zhang: In fact, it was built by different states as independent walls until Qin Shihuang, emperor of the Qin Dynasty, united the states and had them joined up.
Brant: What was the purpose of building the Great Wall?
Zhang: It was built as a defensive fortification.
Brant: How long is the Great Wall?
Zhang: The total length of the Great Wall is about 6,000 kilometers.
Brant: Have you heard the legend about the Great Wall?
Zhang: Do you mean the story of "Meng Jiangnu's Bitter Sweeping?
Brant: Yeah.
Zhang: Of course I have. Meng Jiangnu was a woman whose husband was forced to leave home to build the Great Wall. She went thousands of miles to the Shanhai Pass to see him but only found that he had died of exhaustion and been buried under the wall. On hearing the tragic news, Meng Jiangnu could not stop crying. She cried and cried and finally with a tremendous noise, a 400-kilometer-long section of the Great Wall collapsed over her bitter wail.
Brant: What a tragedy!
Zhang: In memory of Meng Jiangnu, people later built a temple, called the Jiangnu Temple, near the Great Wall. And Meng Jiangnu's story has been passed down from generation to generation.
Brant: It's a moving story. I must go there and pay a visit to the temple.

Dialogue 2 A Trip to the Leaning Tower of Pisa
The tour guide is now introducing the Leaning Tower of Pisa to the visitors.
Tourist: Where are we going today?
Guide: We are going to the Leaning Tower of Pisa.
Tourist: I hear it took a long time for people to build it.
Guide: You said it. Actually it took 176 years, from 1174 to 1350.
Tourist: Unbelievable! Why did it take such a long time?
Guide: Well, the Tower of Pisa started as early as 1174 but when the third floor was completed, it was found that the tower was leaning to the southeast, so the construction had to stop. Over one hundred years later, a famous engineer Pisa took precise measurement of the tower and concluded that it would not collapse with such a little inclination. So the construction resumed but it was delayed considerably.
Tourist: Why did people construct this tower?
Guide: It was said that the kingdom of Pisa won a big war and plundered a lot of treasures.

In order to commemorate that moment, the kingdom of Pisa decided to construct a freestanding bell tower behind the Cathedral of Pisa.

Tourist: I see. But can you tell me why the tower leans?

Guide: That's because of the poorly laid foundation and loose substrate that has allowed the foundation to shift direction.

Tourist: Oh, I understand. Thank you very much.

Guide: You are welcome.

Ⅱ. Act Out

1. Listen to the dialogue. Then practice it with your partners using the words and expressions below to help you.

Sha:	head for, Lijiang Ancient Town, Lijiang Autonomous County, Naxi Ethnic Minority, province, 2400 metres, sea level, list as, cultural heritage, UNESCO, reign, Mu（木）family, 500 years, character Mu, frame, another, Kun（困）, mean, siege, descendant, trap, rat, hole, main, water source, wall pictures, distribute, temples, picture words, record, lection, religion, unique, popular, pleasant, spring, last, 241 days, hot summer, pleasure.
Tourist:	hear, known as, the Oriental Venice, true, city wall, hear, Hei Longtan, famous, wonderful, say something, Dongba Characters, weather, pleasant, sound great, take, photos.

2. Study the following sample dialogue. Then strike up a conversation with your partners using the sentences listed in the chart.

A: Have you ever been to the Confucius Temple?

B: Yes, **it is the largest mansion in the Chinese history.**

A: Did you take any photos?

B: Yes, of course.

1. **It is the largest mansion in the Chinese history.**
2. People said that Confucius had 3,000 students, 72 of whom were prominent.
3. The Confucius Temple is one of the largest architectural complexes in China.
4. The Confucius Temple is the place where people offer sacrificial services.
5. The Confucius Forest is a good place for people to get some relief.

6. Confucius delivered lectures in his later years in Apricot Terrace.
7. In 1997, Lijiang was inscribed on the list of the World Cultural Heritage Sites.
8. In the 1920s, archaeologists discovered the complete skull of Peking Man.
9. Confucius makes a great contribution to the Chinese culture.
10. The Ancient Lijiang Town is praised as the "Oriental Venice".

III. Focus Listening

A. Listen to the recording and choose the correct answer for each question.

1. Which of the following statements about London Tower Bridge is not true?
   A. It is situated in the River Thames.
   B. It is a well-known sightseeing place in London.
   C. It was officially opened in 1910.
   D. It has the upper walkway and lower roadway.

2. London Tower Bridge is _____ meters in length.
   A. 270   B. 217   C. 65   D. 1,000

3. The upper walkway of London Tower Bridge closed in 1910 because _____.
   A. people could enjoy London's new skyline from there.
   B. it became a haunt for prostitutes and pickpockets.
   C. visitors took pictures from the specially designed windows.
   D. there was a historical exhibition there.

4. We know from the article that the word "bascule" means _____ in French.
   A. raise   B. derive   C. open   D. seesaw

5. Why is the lifting system of the bridge not used as often as before?
   A. Because the lifting mechanism becomes too complex.
   B. Because it was used 1,000 times a year before.
   C. Because there are too many ships on the River Thames.
   D. Because the Thames is no longer used much as a trade or shipping route.

B. Listen to the recording and complete the sentences below.

1. There are _____ pieces of steles from various dynasties in the temple.
2. The temple is divided into _____ courtyards.
3. The temple was built in _____, the second year after the death of Confucius.
4. The Confucius Temple is famous for its _____, calligraphy and ancient trees.
5. Even the ancient emperors would _____ to show their respect for Confucius.

Section 2　Reading

The Terra-cotta Warriors and Horses

　　The Terra-cotta Warriors and Horses are the most significant archeological excavations of the twentieth century. It is praised as the eighth wonder of the world. In 1987, Qin Shihuang's Mausoleum, together with the Museum of the Terra-cotta Warriors and Horses was listed as a world cultural heritage site by UNESCO. The site of Terra-cotta Warriors and Horses is around 1.5 kilometers east of Qin Shihuang's Mausoleum, which lies in the Lintong County, Shaanxi Province. The figures of warriors and horses displayed are only part of the burial objects of Qin Shihuang's Mausoleum.

　　After becoming the ruler of the Qin State, Qin Shihuang began to have his tomb constructed. It took about 700,000 laborers 11 years to build it. It is said that the workmen were buried along with the emperor in order to seal their mouths. The mausoleum is 76 meters high. It has a square earthen base and consists of an interior city and exterior city.

　　In 1974, while digging a well to fight drought, some farmers from Lintong County, about thirty kilometers east of Xi'an, unearthed some brown pottery fragments, which led to the great discovery of the terra-cotta warriors and horses. As everybody knows, three large pits were discovered near the mausoleum, and altogether more than 7,000 life-size terra-cotta warriors, horses, chariots and weapons have been unearthed from these pits. Most of them have been restored to their former grandeur. It presents us with an epic of an ancient war battlefield in the large pits. The Terra-cotta Warriors and Horses are arranged according to the battle formations of Qin Dynasty.

No.1 Pit, found in 1974, is the largest with an area of 14,269 square meters. It was first opened to the public on National Day, 1988. It comprises 11 passage trenches and long corridors. There are 38 columns of terra-cotta warriors and horses at the front. Some warrior figures are holding catapults, arrows and bows in their hands; some are carrying bronze swords in their belts. They look bright and sharp just as new ones. The height of terra-cotta warriors varies from 1.78 meters to 1.97 meters. The terra-cotta horses are 1.72 meters high and 2 meters long. They are made vividly with big bright eyes, large nostrils, stout legs and plump waists and hips.

No. 2 Pit was discovered in 1976, which is located 20 meters in the northeast of No.1 Pit. No. 2 Pit was officially opened to the public in 1983. There are over a thousand warriors and 90 wood chariots.

No. 3 Pit, with 68 warriors, war chariots and horses, began to receive visitors in 1989. The warriors, armed with weapons in a battle formation, have different features and facial expressions just like real ones.

The terra-cotta warriors and horses and bronze chariots are treasures rarely seen in the world. With exquisite workmanship and strong artistic appeal, they fully demonstrate the extraordinary wisdom and superb creative power of the ancient Chinese people. Moreover, they also provide valuable materials for the study of arts, sculpture, pottery making, military affairs and so on. It is just for this reason that the discovery of the terra-cotta warriors and horses will make great contribution to the world. Ever since the Terra-cotta Warriors and Horses Museum was built, people all over the world came here for a visit. It has become a must for both domestic and foreign visitors. Every year the museum attracts millions of people throughout the world.

Vocabulary

archeologist /ˌɑːkiˈɔlədʒist/ n. 考古学家
arrange /əˈreindʒ/ v. 安排
battlefield /ˈbætlfiːld/ n. 战场
craftsmanship /ˈkrɑːftsmən/ n. 工匠,技工
domestic /dəˈmestik/ adj. 家庭的,国内的
excavation /ˌekskəˈveiʃən/ n. 挖掘,发掘
expression /iksˈpreʃən/ n. 表达

exquisite /'ekskwizit/ *adj.* 优美的，精致的
feature /'fi:tʃə/ *n.* 特征
heritage /'heritidʒ/ *n.* 遗产
landmark /'lændmɑ:k/ *n.* 明显的目标，里程碑
mausoleum /,mɔ:sə'liəm/ *n.* 陵墓
nostril /'nɔstril/ *n.* 鼻孔
pyramid /'pirəmid/ *n.* 角锥，金字塔
respect /ris'pekt/ *n.* 尊敬，敬重
sculpture /'sklptʃə/ *v.* 雕刻
spectacular /spek'tækjulə/ *adj.* 引人入胜的
terra-cotta /,terə'kɔtə/ *n.* 陶瓦，赤土陶器
trench /trentʃ/ *n.* 战壕
vivid /'vivid/ *adj.* 生动的，鲜明的

Phrases & Expressions

be listed as 被列为……
lie in 位于……
be opened to the public 对公众开放
provide...for... 为……提供……
military affairs 军事事务

Notes to the Text

1. The Terra Cotta Warriors and Horses：秦始皇兵马俑，它是秦始皇陵的陪葬坑，位于秦始皇陵园东侧1,500米处，是世界最大的地下军事博物馆。
2. UNESCO：全称United Nations Educational, Scientific and Cultural Organization。UNESCO属联合国专门机构，简称联合国教科文组织。1964年11月正式成立，同年12月成为联合国的一个专门机构。总部设在法国巴黎。其宗旨是通过教育、科学和文化促进各国间合作，对和平和安全做出贡献。
3. the eight wonders of the world：世界八大奇迹。世界八大奇迹指的是埃及的金字塔、亚历山大港灯塔、爱琴海太阳神像、奥林匹亚宙斯神像、阿尔特米斯月神庙、摩索拉斯陵墓、巴比伦空中花园和秦始皇兵马俑地下军阵。

Part III
Beauty Spots

Exercise 1 Reading Comprehension

Answer the following Questions according to the text.

1. What is the height of Qin Shihuang's Mausoleum?
2. Which pit of the Terra-cotta Warriors and Horses is the largest?
3. Where is the site of the Terra-cotta Warriors and Horses?
4. How many terra-cotta warriors, horses, chariots and horses have been unearthed?
5. What was listed as a world cultural heritage site by UNESCO in 1987?

Exercise 2 Word Training

Fill in the blanks with the words given below. Change the form where necessary.

landmark	contribute	chariot	sculpture	mausoleum
exquisite	heritage	spectacular	feature	excavate

1. The Song Dynasty _____ three great inventions to the world civilization.
2. Among the most _____ sights are the great sea-bird colonies.
3. The expert found the bronze _____ in the pits.
4. Beautiful gardens are a characteristic _____ of Suzhou and Hangzhou.
5. I am studying painting and _____ at an art school.
6. Qin Shihuang's _____ lies in the Lintong County, Shaanxi Province.
7. The archaeologists _____ an ancient city.
8. China has an exceptionally rich cultural _____.
9. He has _____ tastes and manners.
10. The Empire State Building is a New York _____.

Section 3 Translation

Ⅰ. *Translate the following sentences into Chinese.*

1. The life-size terracotta warriors and horses are just like real ones. They are truly magnificent.

2. The Temple of Heaven used to be a place where emperors of the Ming and Qing dynasties worshiped and offered sacrifices to Heaven.
3. Being a summer resort of the Qing royal family, the Summer Palace is the most intact, the best preserved and the largest of its kind of the classical gardens in China.
4. The sculptures of Yungang Grottoes absorbed the Indian Buddhist art and developed traditional Chinese sculpture art.
5. The Qiao Family Compound covers an area of some 8,724 square meters, and consists of 6 main courtyards, in which there are 20 minor ones.

Ⅱ. *Translate the following sentences into English.*
1. 兵马俑给我们展示了生动的古代战场的情景。
2. 曲阜位于泰山之南,是儒学的始祖孔子的故乡。
3. 故宫也称紫禁城,是明清两朝的皇宫。
4. 十三陵是非常重要的考古发现。
5. 三星堆博物馆为政治、军事、经济提供了宝贵的财富。

Section 4   Classified Word Bank

Read the following words and expressions aloud and then learn them by heart.

1.	Forbidden City	故宫
2.	Notre Dame de Paris	巴黎圣母院
3.	Eiffel Tower	埃菲尔铁塔
4.	Arch of Triumph	凯旋门
5.	Louvre	罗浮宫
6.	Pantheon	万神殿
7.	Leaning Tower of Pisa	比萨斜塔
8.	Parthenon	帕提侬神庙
9.	Big Ben	大本钟
10.	British Museum	大英博物馆
11.	Buckingham Palace	白金汉宫
12.	St. Paul's Cathedral	圣保罗大教堂
13.	Stratford-on-Avon	斯特拉特福镇(莎士比亚诞生地)
14.	London Tower Bridge	伦敦塔桥

15.	Westminster Abbey	威斯敏斯特教堂
16.	Statue of Liberty	自由女神像
17.	Panama Canal	巴拿马运河
18.	Pyramid	金字塔
19.	Sydney Opera House	悉尼歌剧院
20.	Suez Canal	苏伊士运河

Unit 3   Religious Shrines

Section 1   Listening and Speaking

Ⅰ. Listen and Repeat

Dialogue 1   Talking About the White Horse Temple

Charles is talking with Miss Jiang, the tour guide, about the White Horse Temple.

Charles: I hear the White Horse Temple is the first Buddhist temple in China, is that right?

Jiang: Yes, it is.

Charles: Can you tell me something about it?

Jiang: Yeah, it was built in 68 AD in the Eastern Han Dynasty. It was a place to preach Buddhist scriptures.

Charles: Where is it located?

Jiang: It is located in Luoyang City, Henan Province.

Charles: How did the temple get its name?

Jiang: Well, it's said that all the scriptures were carried to the temple by a white horse.

Charles: Oh, I see.

Jiang: Have you ever watched the TV series, Journey to the West or Xiyouji?

Charles: Yes, it tells how four monks went to the Western Heaven to acquire Buddhist scriptures.

Jiang: Yes, Tang Xuanzang, the master, together with his three disciples went on a pilgrimage for Buddhist scriptures from Luoyang to the Western Heaven. It took them 17 years to get the scriptures. They suffered from various kinds of difficulties and troubles.

Charles: But it is only a Chinese myth.

Jiang: You can say that. But according to some historians and Buddhist masters, Tang Xuanzang really existed although his disciples were fictitious characters. It's said that after returning to his homeland with scriptures, he became the Buddhist abbot of the White Horse Temple, teaching scriptures there.

Charles: Marvelous! If I have an opportunity, I'll pay a visit to it.

Jiang: It's really worth seeing.

Dialogue 2　A Trip to Shaolin Temple

The tour guide is now introducing the Shaolin Temple to the tourists.

Guide: Look! Here is the Hall of Heavenly Kings.

Tourist: Oh, it looks solemn and a bit scary.

Guide: It is said that it is responsible for checking behaviors of people, helping people who are in trouble, and blessing people who are kind.

Guide: Now, we are heading for the Mahavira Hall, which is an important celebration place. People will pray for something here.

Tourist: Look, there are a lot of statues along the wall. They have different facial expressions.

Guide: These are the famous 18 Buddhist Arhats. Each of them is a Kung Fu master. Look at the floor! Can you find something unusual?

Tourist: The pits! There are a lot of pits on the floor.

Guide: Yeah. The Monks left a lot of footprints when they practiced Shaolin Kung Fu, which is believed to be one of the most famous martial arts.

Tourist: Oh, my goodness! They must have practiced very hard.

Guide: Yeah. If they wanted to master Shaolin Kung Fu, they must have several years' hard training.

Tourist: Can we go inside and have a look?

Guide: Yeah. Let's go. (After a while) Well, the next spot is Dharma Cave.

Tourist: What is it?

Guide: Dharma used to sit in this cave facing the walls and meditated patiently for five years. Finally, he reached the immortal spiritual state and created the Buddhist Zen.

Tourist: Amazing! A great person! Can I take some photos here?
Guide: Sure! Go ahead!

II. Act Out

1. Listen to the dialogue. Then practice it with your partners using the words and expressions below to help you.

Miao: head for, Yuantong Temple, built, foot, Luofeng Hill, originally, Butuoluo Temple, know, Bodhisattva Guan-yin, 32 Dharma names, restored, in 1301, architecture, design, four Chinese characters, archway, mean, best view, passing, see, wide path, huge pool, octagonal, pavilion, middle, my pleasure.
Tourist: hear, biggest, Kunming City, call, now, I see, famous for, wonderful, beautiful scenery, surroundings, look more like, garden, take photos.

2. Study the following sample dialogue. Then strike up a conversation with your partners using the sentences listed in the chart.

A: Have you ever heard of the White Horse Temple?
B: Yes, **it is the first Buddhist temple in China**. I am looking forward to visiting it.
A: Me, too.

1. The White Horse Temple is the first Buddhist temple in China.
2. I hear that two-thirds of the emperors in the Eastern Han Dynasty used the White Horse Temple.
3. It's said that Xuan Zang became the Buddhist abbot of the White Horse Temple.
4. The Lingyin Temple was built in 326 AD, and it is one of the ten oldest temples in China.
5. The Famen Temple is located in Fufeng County, Baoji City, Shaanxi Province.
6. The three pagodas of the Chongsheng Temple are located at the foot of Zhonghe Peak, a kilometer northwest of Dali Ancient City.
7. The Big Wild Goose Pagoda is a masterpiece of the Chinese Buddhist architecture.
8. The Leshan Giant Buddha is one of the hand-made stone sculptures in the world.
9. The sculpture of the Longmen Grottoes has the myths of religion.
10. The Yuantong Temple is the biggest temple in Kunming City.

Ⅲ. Focus Listening

A. Listen to the recording and choose the correct answer for each question.

1. A monk named Hui Gen Left _____ jade Buddha states in the Jade Buddha Temple of Shanghai.
   A. 2 B. 3 C. 4 D. 5
2. Mount Putuo is located _____ according to the article.
   A. in Shanghai B. in Burma
   C. in Zhejiang Province D. in Henan Province
3. When was the Jade Buddha Temple completed?
   A. In 1918 B. In 1882 C. In 1834 D. In 1896
4. The sitting Jade Buddha is _____ meters in height.
   A. 1.92 B. 1.34 C. 0.96 D. 1.18
5. Which of the following statements about the sitting Buddha statue is not true?
   A. It was carved with exquisite workmanship.
   B. It was carved out of pure flawless white jade.
   C. The jewels on its head, arms and feet are all genuine.
   D. It is on the first floor of the Jade Buddha Chamber.

B. Listen to the recording and complete the sentences below.

1. The A-Ma Temple was built on a _____.
2. It is said that A-Ma was a _____ from Putian, Fujian Province.
3. To worship A-Ma originated from the _____.
4. _____ arrived at the Macao and landed opposite the A-Ma Temple.
5. People thought A-Ma could cope with _____ for the fishermen.

Section 2   Reading

Church of Hagia Sophia

  The Church of Hagia Sophia is one of the most extraordinary buildings in the history of architecture from the period of Byzantium. It played a significant role in the Byzantine Empire as well as the Ottoman Empire.

  The word "Hagia" in Greek means "Divine", and "Sophia" means "Wisdom". "Divine Wisdom" is one of the attributes of Jesus Christ. The church was completed in 360

AD during the reign of Constantinus. Because of war and revolt, the church was burnt in 404 AD. In 532 AD Emperor Justinian decided to have this church reconstructed, and it was completed 6 years later. It took more than ten thousand labors 6 years to build it. Emperor Justinian was a devout believer of Christianity. He not only used the church as a means for enlarging the scope of Christianity, but all coronation and major baptism ceremonies took place here. This church served as the heart of the empire.

When the Turks conquered Istanbul in 1453, the first thing Mehmed, the conqueror, did was to turn the church into a mosque. From then on, the church served as a great mosque, with four mosque minarets built around the church. The mosaics and frescoes on the walls in Byzantine period were covered with clays, because they were forbidden in Islam. Actually this helped the preservation of the mosaics and frescoes. It was in 1932 that Mustafa Kemal Ataturk, the emperor of Turk, ordered to turn the mosque into a museum. He believed that it was a world heritage and people could come and see it. Therefore, in 1932, the clay was removed, and it was reopened to the public as a museum. The Church of Hagia Sophia is famous for two kinds of religion, Christianity and Islam.

While approaching the church, you will be impressed by the red big building with a splendid dome. The building is huge and vast. When going through the main gate, you will find two different entrances. In the second entry hall, there's a big bronze gate, which was built during the reign of Justinian. That is the main imperial gate to the church, which was reserved for the emperor's passage. Right above the gate on the right, there's a mosaic picture. Jesus Christ is in the middle, on the right hand side is Angel Gabriel and on the left is Blessed Virgin. This mosaic is spectacular because the pieces for the mosaic are quite little, which makes the mosaic very clear. Even the cheek color or the wrinkles of Jesus Christ can be easily recognized.

The interior of the Hagia Sophia is vast. It is covered with a big central dome, which is 56 m wide, 150 feet high. The dome of the Hagia Sophia church was decorated with Arabic calligraphy and writings during the Ottoman Era. The Hagia Sophia church is strengthened with columns in green and purple color. Purple is the sacred color of Byzantium. The emperors were born to purple color fabrics. They used this color in their costumes and were buried in purple color fabrics.

Vocabulary

baptism /'bæptizəm/ n. 浸洗, 严峻考验
ceremony /'serimoni/ n. 典礼
christianity /ˌkristi'æniti/ n. 基督教
church /tʃəːtʃ/ n. 教堂
conquer /'kɔŋkə/ vt. 征服, 战胜
coronation /ˌkɔrə'neiʃən/ n. 加冕礼
divine /di'vain/ adj. 神的, 上帝的
dome /dəum/ n. 圆屋顶
empire /'empaiə/ n. 帝国
extraordinary /ik'strɔːdənəri/ adj. 非凡的, 出色的, 令人惊奇的
fabric /'fæbrik/ n. 织物, 衣料; (社会)结构
fresco /'freskəu/ n. (用水彩颜料在湿灰浆墙面上画的)壁画
Jesus /'dʒiːzəs/ n. 耶稣
minaret /'minəret/ n. 尖塔
mosaic /məu'zeiik/ n. 镶嵌, 镶嵌图案
mosque /mɔsk/ n. 清真寺
revolt /ri'vəult/ v. & n. 反抗, 起义, 反叛
spectacular /spek'tækjulə/ adj. 壮观的
splendid /'splendid/ adj. 壮丽的, 辉煌的

Phrases & Expressions

be impressed by 对……留下深刻印象
be covered with 被……所覆盖
play an significant role... 在……起到重要作用; 在……扮演重要角色
be decorated with... 用……装饰……
serve as 用作……; 充当……

Notes to the Text

1. Hagia Sophia Church：圣索菲亚大教堂。圣索菲亚大教堂修建于拜占庭（Byzantium）帝国也就是东罗马帝国（Eastern Roman Empire）。圣索菲亚教堂最初是由东罗马帝国帝王君士坦丁（Constantine）大帝建造，由于地震和叛乱，圣索菲亚大教堂经历过数次重修，尤以东罗马帝国帝王查士丁尼大帝（Justinian）的重修著称。拜占庭帝国衰落后，土耳其奥斯曼国王穆罕默德攻入拜占庭（Byzantine），大教堂从此成了伊斯兰教徒的清真寺。现为博物馆。

2. Byzantine Empire：拜占庭帝国。又被称作东罗马帝国（Eastern Roman Empire），是在西罗马帝国崩溃后依然存在的罗马帝国东半部。拜占庭帝国通常被认为开始自公元395年直至1453年（实际始于8世纪）。在其上千年的存在期内它一般被人简单地称为"罗马帝国"。拜占庭之名源于一座靠海的古希腊移民城市，公元330年罗马皇帝君士坦丁在此建城，作为罗马帝国的陪都，并改名为君士坦丁堡（Constantinople）。东罗马帝国衰败后，土耳其奥斯曼（Ottoman）国王穆罕默德攻入拜占庭（Byzantine），改名伊斯坦布尔（Istanbul）。

3. Ottoman Empire：奥斯曼帝国是中古后期兴起的。它的建立者是游牧于里海东南部的一支突厥人。13世纪时，蒙古人开始向西扩张，迫使这支突厥人不断迁移。最初他们依附于塞尔柱突厥人建立的罗姆苏丹国。1242年，罗姆苏丹国在蒙古人的打击下瓦解，于是这支突厥人获得了充分发展的机会。部落酋长埃尔托格鲁尔死后，他的儿子奥斯曼继位。1300年，奥斯曼宣布他的部落为独立的伊斯兰国家。1326年，奥斯曼夺取拜占庭帝国的重镇布鲁萨，控制了马尔马拉海峡，并把首都迁到布鲁萨。这一新的国家称为奥斯曼帝国。

4. Mustafa Kemal Ataturk：穆斯塔法·基马尔，土耳其国父。

5. Blessed Virgin：圣母马利亚，基督耶稣的母亲。

Exercise 1   Reading Comprehension

Answer the following Questions according to the text.

1. What does the word Hagia mean in Greek?
2. Who conquered the Istanbul?
3. When was the church rebuilt?
4. What is the height of the central dome?

5. What is the width of the central dome?

Exercise 2　Word Training

Fill in the blanks with the words given below. Change the form where necessary.

| revolt | impress | era | ceremony | enlarge |
| extraordinary | decorate | empire | conquer | splendid |

1. Perhaps the most _____ building of the nineteenth century was the Crystal Palace.
2. The tribesmen will _____ if you ask them to pay taxes.
3. We're _____ the production scale to produce more and better computers.
4. The wedding _____ took place in the local church.
5. Modern medical science has _____ many kinds of diseases.
6. Our house commanded a _____ view of the Potala Palace.
7. I am very _____ with the Temple of Heaven.
8. The Roman _____ was divided in the fourth century AD.
9. As the _____ wore on, she switched her attention to films.
10. He _____ his room with pictures of all his favorite movie stars.

Section 3　Translation

Ⅰ. *Translate the following sentences into Chinese.*

1. The Church of Hagia Sophia was built with a dome-on-dome technique.
2. Hagia Sophia is thought of as one of the supreme achievements in the history of architecture.
3. In the center of the Byzantine Empire is Byzantine, or Constantinople, which is Turkey's Istanbul today.
4. The uniqueness of the Hagia Sophia Church is that it adopts the Greek style of Cross in the design of plane and employs a giant dome for the roof.
5. The internal decoration of the Church of Hagia Sophia uses the mosaic inlaid with colored marbles.

II. *Translate the following sentences into English.*
1. 基督教时代从耶稣诞生时算起。
2. 圣约翰神明座堂(the Cathedral of St. John the Divine)位于美国纽约市。
3. 在17世纪圣彼得大教堂完成前,圣索菲亚大教堂是世界上最大的教堂。
4. 圣索菲亚大教堂也因为伊斯兰教和基督教的同时存在而闻名。
5. 公元1453年,奥斯曼土耳其帝国将君士坦丁堡改名为伊斯坦布尔。

Section 4   Classified Word Bank

Read the following words and expressions aloud and then learn them by heart.

1.	Christianity	基督教
2.	Catholicism	天主教
3.	Protestantism	耶稣教
4.	Judaism	犹太教
5.	Islamism	伊斯兰教
6.	Brahmanism	婆罗门教
7.	Buddhism	佛教
8.	Daoism	道教
9.	Lamaism	喇嘛教
10.	Buddhist scriptures	佛经
11.	The Holy Bible	圣经
12.	the Old Testament	旧约
13.	the New Testament	新约
14.	Religious rites	宗教仪式
15.	Prayer	祈祷
16.	God	神
17.	Goddess	女神
18.	The Holy City	圣城
19.	The holy land	圣地
20.	Worship	朝拜

Unit 4 Holiday Resorts

Section 1 Listening and Speaking

I. Listen and Repeat

Dialogue 1 Talking About Xilamuren Grassland

Frank is talking with Ms Wei, the tour guide, about Xilamuren Grassland.

Wei: Hello, Frank. Have you heard of the Xilamuren Grassland?

Frank: Yes, but I have never been there.

Wei: What a pity!

Frank: Where is it located?

Wei: It is located 100 kilometers north of Hohhot.

Frank: What does Xilamuren mean in Mongolian?

Wei: It means yellow river.

Frank: I hear that the tourist can stay in the traditional Mongolian yurt for camping.

Wei: Yeah, the yurts are made of wool and furnished with blankets, quilts, and pillows. So they are very good for camping.

Frank: What kind of entertainment does the Xilamuren Grassland have?

Wei: You can enjoy wrestling, horse riding, camel riding, archery and so on.

Frank: It sounds amazing.

Wei: Yeah. In the evening you can also enjoy music from the horse head fiddle as well as traditional singing and dancing.

Frank: Wow! I cannot wait. I am looking forward to it.

Dialogue 2 A Trip to Changbai Mountain

The tour guide is now introducing Changbai Mountain to the tourists.

Tourist: Where are we going today?

Guide: We are going to Changbai Mountain

Tourist: Oh, where is it?

Guide: It is located in the northeast part of China

Tourist: What is it famous for?

Guide: It is famous for Tianchi, rare animals, marvelous lakes, hot springs and lush forests.

Tourist: I hear that Tianchi is like a piece of jade in the sky. It is a fairyland on earth!

Guide: Yes, you said it. It is really amazing! By the way, would you like to try the hot spring?

Tourist: I hear that there are various kinds of minerals in the hot spring.

Guide: Yeah. Taking a bath in the hot spring can treat many kinds of diseases, such as arthritis, dermatitis, diabetes, etc.

Tourist: Sounds great! I am looking forward to enjoying it.

Guide: Me, too.

Tourist: OK, let's go.

II. Act Out

1. Listen to the dialogue. Then practice it with your partners using the words and expressions below to help you.

> **Mei**: ladies and gentlemen, Mt. Song, Dengfeng, Henan Province, exactly, beautiful, given, name, International Geological Park, UNESCO, rich cultural history, natural scenery, distinctive features, monks, scholars, deliver, Buddhism, Taoism, Confucianism, link, you are right.
>
> **Tourist**: tell, where, located, also, call, Zhongyue, five, landscape, difference, Mount Song, other mountains, hear, Mount Song, history museum, mean, learn, history, development, besides, wonderful.

2. Study the following sample dialogue. Then strike up a conversation with your partners using the sentences listed in the chart.

A: Have you ever been to Hainan?

B: No, but I hear **Hainan itinerary is more flexible and the cost is low.**

A: Yeah, would you like to go with me?

B: No problem.

1. Hainan itinerary is more flexible and the cost is low.
2. Kunming is called "Spring City" because it is always as warm as spring.
3. The Aegean Sea is well-known for its clear blue waters and dramatic scenery.

107

4. Shanghai's Nanjing Road is known as "China's No.1 Business Street".
5. There are a lot of magnificent European style buildings at the Bund in Shanghai.
6. Mount Lu is well-known for its magnificent peaks, unique waterfalls and historical sites.
7. Yu Garden is the paragon of classical gardens of Shanghai.
8. Mount Tai is most famous for its spectacular sunrise and sunset.
9. How beautiful West Lake is! It seems that we were traveling on a fairyland.
10. Mount Huang is renowned for its legendary pines, picturesque rocks, the sea of clouds, and hot springs.

III. Focus Listening

A. Listen to the recording and choose the correct answer for each question.

1. How many main islands are there in Hawaii?
   A. 7　　　　B. 8　　　　C. 9　　　　D. 10
2. Hawaii is famous for all of the following except _____.
   A. lush valleys　　　　　　B. towering volcanoes
   C. sandy beaches　　　　　D. customs and traditions
3. Who colonized Hawaii 1,700 years ago?
   A. Polynesians　　　　　　B. Caucasians
   C. Japanese　　　　　　　 D. Native Americans
4. Hawaii became the 50th state of the United States in _____.
   A. 1850　　　B. 1859　　　C. 1950　　　D. 1959
5. The climate of Hawaii is _____ during the whole year.
   A. hot　　　B. damp　　　C. mild　　　D. rainy

B. Listen to the recording and complete the sentences below.

1. Gulangyu lies in the _____ of Xiamen City.
2. The population of Gulangyu is about _____.
3. Only _____ are allowed to use on the island.
4. With the spread of the Christianity _____ comes into Gulandyu Island.
5. Many pianists have come to the island, so the island is also called _____.

Part III
Beauty Spots

Section 2 Reading

Shangri-la

Shangri-la derives from the Tibetan word, which means a beautiful and peaceful place. In the year 1933, James Hilton, a British writer, published a novel named *Lost Horizon*. This book tells about three American pilots who were flying over the Sino-Indian plateau during World War II, when their plane crashed into a remote valley surrounded by high mountains. It was in this book that the word Shangri-la appeared for the first time. The book depicts the beautiful scenery of Shangri-la: the snow-capped mountains, the lush grasslands, the red soil plateaus, the magnificent waterfalls, and the harmonious relationship between the nature and the human race. It is just like a paradise on earth. After rescued by the local Tibetans, the three American pilots finally returned home.

According to the historical record, in 1933, there was an American transport plane which crashed in the town of Zhongdian in Yunnan Province when flying on the Sino-Indian route. After a careful investigation, it was concluded that the beautiful "Shangri-la" described in the *Lost Horizon* was the city of Zhongdian located in the Tibetan Autonomous Prefecture of Yunnan Province. When Frank Capra turned the novel into a Hollywood movie, it was an instant success. Today, Shangri-la has become a word of the English language and used everywhere from Chinese hotel chains to holiday cottages

In Shangri-la there are three snow-capped mountains, Meili, Baimang and Haba. Meili is the most beautiful and famous mountain in the world. The highest peak of Meili is 6,740 meters above sea level. Not only can you see different kinds of trees from the top to the foot of the mountain, but you can also see spectacular waterfalls cascade down the mountainside. Cattle graze leisurely on the meadows with exotic flowers and luxuriant grass. In the innermost depths of the forests is an exotic world of rare birds and animals. In addition, Meili Snow Mountain is also regarded as a holy mountain by the Tibetan Buddhists. Every year, thousands of Buddhists come here to worship.

There are 16 ethnic groups in Shangri-la and each of them has their own unique culture, traditional customs, life styles and religions. They lead a peaceful and quiet life. Because of the influence of the natural environment and conditions, their personalities are kind, honest, and hospitable. The largest lamasery of Shangri-la is Songzanlin Lamsery, where there are 800 lamas.

The distance from Zhongdian to Kunming is 700 kilometers, and in 1999, an airline route was established between the two places. You can travel between them at any time. Now, it is easy to book plane tickets from any ticket agencies in Kunming, therefore it is very convenient for travelers to fly to Shangri-la.

Vocabulary

autonomous /ɔːˈtɔnəməs/ *adj.* 自治的

cottage /ˈkɔtidʒ/ *n.* 小屋

crash /ˈcræʃ/ *n.* 撞击

describe /disˈkraib/ *v.* 描述

exotic /igˈzɔtik/ *adj.* 外来的, 外国来的

grassy /ˈgrɑːsi/ *adj.* 绿色的, 像草的

harmonious /hɑːˈməunjəs/ *adj.* 和谐的, 协调的

instant /ˈinstənt/ *adj.* 立即的

investigation /inˌvestiˈgeiʃən/ *n.* 调查

luxuriant /lʌgˈzjuəriənt/ *adj.* 丰产的, 奢华的

mountain /ˈmautin/ *n.* 山脉

novel /ˈnɔvəl/ *n.* 小说

pilot /'pailət/ n. 飞行员
plateau /'plætəu, plæ'təu/ n. 高原
province /'prɔvins/ n. 省（一个国家的行政区）
religion /ri'lidʒən/ n. 宗教，信仰
scattered /'skætəd/ adj. 离散的，分散的
scenery /'si:nəri/ n. 景色
surround /sə'raund/ v. 围绕
transport /træs'pɔ:t/ n. 交通工具

Phrases & Expressions

derive from 源自……，源于……
fly over 在……上空飞行
above sea level 海拔
in the innermost depths of 在……的最深处
in addition 另外
lead a...life 过着……的生活

Notes to the Text

1. Shangri-La（香格里拉）：位于云南省西北部的滇、川、藏大三角区域，地处迪庆香格里拉腹心地带。
2. James Hilton：英国作家詹姆斯·希尔顿。
3. Lost Horizon：小说《失去的地平线》。"香格里拉"一词，是1933英国小说家詹姆斯·希尔顿在小说《失去的地平线》中所描绘的一块永恒和平宁静的土地。

Exercise 1 Reading Comprehension

Answer the following Questions according to the text.
1. What is the meaning of Shangri-La?
2. What are the three snow-capped mountains in Shangri-La?
3. How many ethnic groups are there in Shangri-la?
4. How many lamas are there in Songzanlin Lamsery?
5. How far is it from Zhongdian to Kunming?

Exercise 2　Word Training

Fill in the blanks with the words given below. Change the form where necessary.

snowcapped	crash	harmony	investigation	derive
religion	scatter	exotic	autonomous	convenient

1. His elder son was killed in an air _____ last month.
2. We see pictures of _____ birds from the jungle of Brazil.
3. Tourists find the 24-hour service very _____.
4. Almost every country has some form of _____.
5. Many English words _____ from Latin and French.
6. The Inner Mongolian _____ Region is in the north of China.
7. Let freedom ring from the _____ Rockies of Colorado!
8. My cat and dog live in perfect _____.
9. The murder case is still under _____.
10. The police came and the crowd _____.

Section 3　Translation

Ⅰ. *Translate the following sentences into Chinese.*

1. As the Chinese saying goes, "the landscape of the Five Famous Mountains tops those elsewhere, and the landscape of Mount Huang belittles that of the Five Famous Mountains."
2. The scenery here is like a three-dimensional picture. I feel I've walked into a beautiful painting.
3. Lijiang Ancient Town is surrounded by green mountains with crystal clear water running through it; hence the name Dayan Zhen.
4. Mount Huang is located in the south of Anhui Province. It is a world-famous holiday resort.
5. Come on. Don't leave him hanging. You'd better tell him about the legend of Peak Flying from Afar.

II. *Translate the following sentences into English.*
1. 云南民族村是云南多民族省份的缩影。
2. 苏州由20多个湖环抱而成,有"东方威尼斯"之称。
3. 西藏有你说的那么好吗？我已经等不及要去看看了。
4. 不管刮风下雨,我们明天都要去游览庐山。
5. 九寨沟是世界自然奇观之一。

Section 4　Classified Word Bank

Read the following words and expressions aloud and then learn them by heart.

1.	Beidaihe Beach	北戴河海滨(中国)
2.	Cannes	戛纳(法国)
3.	Copenhagen	哥本哈根(丹麦)
4.	Doha	多哈(西亚)
5.	Dubai	迪拜(西亚)
6.	Goteborg	哥德堡(瑞典)
7.	Hong Kong	香港(中国)
8.	Istanbul	伊斯坦布尔(土耳其)
9.	Macau	澳门(中国)
10.	Maldives	马尔代夫
11.	Manila	马尼拉
12.	Marseilles	马赛(法国)
13.	Penglai	蓬莱(烟台)
14.	Rhodes	罗德(希腊)
15.	Sanya	三亚(中国)
16.	Sendai	仙台(日本)
17.	Sentosa	圣淘沙(新加坡)
18.	The Hague	海牙(荷兰)
19.	The Mediterranean	地中海
20.	Venice	威尼斯(意大利)

Part IV

Festivals and City Tours

Unit 1 Festivals

Section 1 Listening and Speaking

I. Listen and Repeat

Dialogue 1 Talking About the Chongyang Festival
The tour guide is now introducing the Chongyang Festival to the tourists.
Tourist: Do you know the Chongyang Festival?
Guide: Yeah, it is on the ninth day of the ninth month of the Chinese lunar calendar. So it's also called the Double Ninth Festival.
Tourist: Is there any special meaning for the Chongyang Festival?
Guide: The festival is based on the theory of Yin and Yang. Yin is feminine and negative while Yang is masculine and positive. Odd number belongs to Yang. The Double Ninth Festival is the day when the two largest odd numbers meet, so it is called Chongyang. Chong means double.
Tourist: What do people do on that day?
Guide: The festival is in autumn, so it is perfect for outdoor activities, like hiking and climbing mountains.
Tourist: Why do people carry dogwood?
Guide: It is said that dogwood is a plant with a strong fragrance. People think it can drive away the evil spirits and keep you safe from harm.
Tourist: You mean dogwood can bless people, is that right?

Guide: Yeah.
Tourist: Then why do people drink chrysanthemum wine?
Guide: It's believed that chrysanthemum wine can make old people keep fit and live longer.
Tourist: So Double Ninth Day is especially for the elderly.
Guide: Yes, you are right.
Tourist: Then I'll send some chrysanthemum wine as a gift to my parents. I hope they live longer.
Guide: That's a good idea.

Dialogue 2   Talking about Thanksgiving Day

Miss Zhang, the tour guide, is talking about Thanksgiving Day with Edwin.

Zhang: Hi, Edwin, can you tell me something about Thanksgiving Day?
Edwin: OK. What would you like to know?
Zhang: Why do people call it Thanksgiving Day?
Edwin: Well, Thanksgiving Day came from the pilgrims, or the first settlers in America, who shared the first harvest with the Indians and gave thanks to God for the bounty of the autumn harvest. They also thanked the Indians for their help. That's why it's called Thanksgiving Day.
Zhang: What day is Thanksgiving Day?
Edwin: It is on the fourth Thursday of each November.
Zhang: What do people eat on that day?
Edwin: People usually have some traditional foods, like turkey, sweet corn, pumpkin pies, etc.
Zhang: What do people do on Thanksgiving Day?
Edwin: They often go to church, watch football games and so on. Parades are also a big part on that day.
Zhang: It is amazing! I really want to join it.

II. Act Out

1. *Listen to the dialogue. Then practice it with your partners using the words and expressions below to help you.*

Tourist: when, celebrate, Lantern Festival, what day, mean, celebration, Spring Festival, good, hear, guess, lantern riddles, interesting, special food, what is it, sounds great, where, try, good.

> **Liang:** began, Han Dynasty, 15th day, first lunar month, middle, end, February, lion dance, dragon dance, daytime, enjoy, lantern show, park, street, riddles, on lanterns, solve a riddle, prize, Yuanxiao, also, Tangyuan, traditional food, rice flour dumplings, sweet fillings, restaurant, buy, home, boil.

2. Study the following sample dialogue. Then strike up a conversation with your partners using the sentences listed in the chart.

A: Have you ever heard of the Spring Festival?
B: Yes, **it is the most important festival in China.**
A: Do you take any photos on that day?
B: Sometimes.

1. The Spring Festival is the most important festival in China.
2. Christmas Day is one of the most important festivals in the West.
3. National Day is sometimes celebrated by setting off firecrackers.
4. The Dragon Boat Festival started in the Period of Warring States and has a history of more than 2,000 years.
5. Sweet dumplings or Yuanxiao is special food for the Lantern Festival.
6. Tasting the mooncake and watching the moon are wonderful things in the Mid-Autumn Festival.
7. On April Fools' Day many people play tricks on those they are familiar with.
8. But Tomb-Sweeping Day is by no means the only time when sacrifices are made to ancestors.
9. On Halloween, children usually knock at people's doors and say to them, "treat or trick?".
10. Valentine's Day is celebrated on February 14 of each year.

Ⅲ. Focus Listening

A. Listen to the recording and choose the correct answer for each question.

1. The Mid-Autumn Festival is on the _____ day of the eighth lunar month.
   A. 5th B. 8th C. 15th C. 25th
2. The round-shaped mooncake symbolizes not only the moon but also _____.
   A. family reunion   B. good luck
   C. good health   D. happiness
3. It's said that the tradition of eating mooncakes started in the _____ Dynasty.

A. Yuan   B. Han   C. Ming   D. Qing
4. Which of the following statements is not true?
   A. People could no longer bear the cruel ruling of the Mongols.
   B. The peasant armies secretly planned a revolt.
   C. The peasant armies used the mooncakes to pass the message.
   D. The peasant armies failed to overthrow the Mongolian government.
5. People began to eat mooncakes in the Mid-Autumn Festival in honor of _____.
   A. the Yuan Dynasty   B. the revol
   C. Zhu Yuanzhang   D. the imperial army

B. Listen to the recording and complete the sentences below.
1. People, especially the young will set off _____ on New Year's Eve.
2. People decorate their house with pictures, _____, and _____.
3. People will eat Jiaozi and drink some _____ on the first day of the Spring Festival.
4. Youngsters can get _____ from their parents or grandparents.
5. At the temple fair people can eat local snacks or enjoy _____.

Section 2   Reading

The Duanwu Festival

    The Duanwu Festival, also called the Dragon Boat Festival, is on the fifth day of the fifth lunar month. It is said that the festival started in the Period of Warring States and has a history of more than 2000 years.

    Originally, the festival was used to offer sacrifices to the river god to pray for favorable weather and bumper harvests because the god was believed to have the power to control the river and distribute rainfalls.

    Later, the Duanwu Festival became a special occasion to commemorate Quyuan, the great patriotic poet and a minister of the State of Chu in the Warring States. At that time, Chu was threatened by the State of Qin, which was stronger than any of the other six states: Qi, Chu, Yan, Han, Zhao and Wei. Qin wanted to annex the other states. Quyuan proposed that Chu should unite the other states to resist Qin, but his proposal was denied by other crafty officials who used contemptible means to persuade the King to drive him out of the capital. Finally Quyuan was exiled.

    Quyuan wrote many outstanding poems to express his patriotic feelings. Many times he

warned the king of the danger of the increasingly corrupt imperial court and suggested ways to strengthen the military forces to fight against Qin. However, all of his suggestions were brushed aside or rejected.

During his exile, he learnt the news that his motherland had been conquered by the state of Qin. He was so grieved that he drowned himself in the Miluo River. It was the 5th day of the 5th lunar month in 278 B. C.. On hearing the news, people rowed their boats and tried to find his corpse but in vain. To prevent the fish and other sea animals from attacking his corpse, people threw a lot of food into the river. An old doctor even poured a jug of realgar wine into the river, hoping to make all aquatic beasts drunk. They wished him to rest in peace. This suggested how people loved and respected him. Later people used reed leaves to wrap zongzi for this purpose. Thus the custom of eating zongzi, staging the dragon boat race and drinking realgar wine came into being.

Zongzi is the traditional Chinese food for the Duanwu Festival. It is a pyramid-shaped dumpling made of glutinous rice wrapped in bamboo or reed leaves. Although thousands of years have gone by, people still maintain the age-old custom of eating zongzi.

Different parts of the country have different kinds of zongzi. In North China since dates are abundant in the area, zongzi is often made of rice mixed with dates. But in East China's Jiaxing County, zongzi is stuffed with pork. In Guangdong Province, people put pork, ham, chestnuts and other ingredients into zongzi, making them very rich in flavor. In Sichuan Province, Zongzi is usually served with a sugar dressing. In the past zongzi was only a kind of family food, but now it has gone into the market. So do not forget to taste some delicious zongzi in the Duanwu Festival.

The dragon boat race is very popular during the Duanwu Festival, especially in South China. The length of the dragon boat is from 20 to 40 meters. It needs several people to row it together. As the captain stands on the boat head waving a small flag to help coordinate the rowing, boatmen row the boat in cadence and with drumbeats, and the cheering from the huge crowds on both sides of the river makes the dragon boat race very exciting.

For thousands of years, in addition to zongzi and dragon boat race, drinking realgar wine is also very popular in the Duanwu Festival. It was believed that realgar was an antidote for various poisons, and it could drive away the evil spirit and kill insects. Therefore, it is advisable to drink some realgar wine during the Duanwu Festival.

Vocabulary

antidote /ˈæntidəut/ n. 解毒剂
boatman /ˈbəutmən/ n. 船夫
conquer /ˈkɔŋkə/ v. 征服, 占领, 攻取
coordinate /kəuˈɔːdinit/ v. 协调, 调整
distribute /disˈtribjuːt/ v. 分配, 分发, 分销
drumbeat /ˈdrʌmbiːt/ n. 鼓声, 打鼓
festival /ˈfestəvəl/ n. 节日, 喜庆日 adj. 节日的, 快乐的
fillings /ˈfiliŋ/ n. 馅, 填充物
glutinous /ˈgluːtinəs/ adj. 很黏的, 黏性很大的
increasing /inˈkriːsiŋ/ adj. 日益增加的, 增大的
lunar /ˈlunə/ adj. 阴历的, 月亮的
official /əˈfiʃəl/ n. 官员 adj. 官方的, 正式的
patriotic /ˌpætriɔtik, ˌpei-/ adj. 爱国的, 有爱国心的
poison /ˈpɔizn/ n. 毒药 vi. 放毒
political /pəˈlitikəl/ adj. 政治的, 行政上的
refuse /riˈfjuːz/ v. 拒绝
strengthen /ˈstreŋθən/ v. 加强, 巩固
suggestion /səˈdʒestʃən/ n. 建议, 提议

Phrases & Expressions

pray for 祈祷……
fight against 与……战斗; 对抗……
brush aside 不理, 漠视

in vain 徒劳,白费力
rest in peace 安息

Notes to the Text

1. The Duanwu Festival：端午节,农历五月初五,端是"开端""初"的意思。初五可以称为端五。
2. Quyuan：屈原。屈原是中国最伟大的浪漫主义诗人之一,也是我国已知最早的著名诗人和伟大的政治家。
3. Zongzi：粽子。粽子是端午节的节日食品,传说是为祭投江的屈原而发明的,是中国历史上迄今为止文化积淀最深厚的传统食品。

Exercise 1　Reading Comprehension

Answer the following Questions according to the text.

1. What day is the Dragon Boat Festival?
2. Who did the Dragon Boat Festival commemorate according to the text?
3. What do the people eat on that day?
4. What do the people usually do on that day?
5. Why do people drink realgar wine in the Duanwu Festival?

Exercise 2　Word Training

Fill in the blanks with the words given below. Change the form where necessary.

| refuse | political | evil | originally | distribute |
| festival | increasingly | poison | conquer | cheer |

1. Christmas is one of the Christian _____.
2. A long period of _____ stability is very important to the development of economy.
3. It becomes _____ difficult to find employment in big cities around the world.
4. The Normans _____ England in 1066.
5. Gases from cars _____ the air of our cities

6. Please _____ the examination papers round the class.

7. They led the crowd in _____ for their school team.

8. The United States has _____ him a visa

9. The novel _____ came from a true love affair.

10. Being greedy for money is the root of all _____.

Section 3   Translation

Ⅰ. *Translate the following sentences into Chinese.*
1. Mother's Day was first suggested in the United States in 1872 by Julia Ward Howe.
2. Tomb-Sweeping Day is a traditional ancient Chinese festival.
3. In the Mid-Autumn Festival, the Chinese have the custom of enjoying the full moon and eating mooncakes.
4. The Lantern Festival is on the 15th day of the first lunar month.
5. Firecrackers and Jiaozi are the two most important things during the Spring Festival.

Ⅱ. *Translate the following sentences into English.*
1. "圣诞节"这个名称是"基督弥撒"的缩写。
2. 复活节是庆祝耶稣基督的复活。
3. 清明节祭祖是中国人的传统习惯。
4. 吃饺子可以给新的一年带来好运。
5. 美国每年十一月的第四个星期四庆祝感恩节。

Section 4   Classified Word Bank

Read the following words and expressions aloud and then learn them by heart.

1. New Year's Day	元旦
2. The Spring Festival	春节
3. The Lantern Festival	元宵节
4. Tomb-sweeping Day	清明节
5. The Dragon Boat Festival	端午节
6. The Mid-Autumn Festival	中秋节
7. The Double Ninth Festival	重阳节

8.	May Day	五一国际劳动节
9.	Teachers' Day	教师节
10.	National Day	国庆节
11.	Valentine's Day	情人节
12.	Easter	复活节
13.	April Fool's Day	愚人节
14.	Mother's Day	母亲节
15.	Father's Day	父亲节
16.	Independence Day	美国独立日
17.	Halloween Day	万圣节
18.	Thanksgiving Day	感恩节
19.	Christmas Eve	平安夜
20.	Christmas Day	圣诞节

Unit 2 Famous Cities

Section 1 Listening and Speaking

Ⅰ. Listen and Repeat

Dialogue 1　Visiting Shanghai

Mr. Black is a tourist from the USA. Miss Wang is a tour guide from a travel agency in Shanghai.

Wang: Let's get into the taxi, Mr. Black.

Black: OK. Today we're going to have a sightseeing tour around Shanghai. Miss Wang. I'm at your disposal.

Wang: (*After entering the taxi*) First of all, we'd better go to Shanghai Friendship Store to buy some souvenirs. And then, we'll drive to "Yu Yuan Garden" bazaar. If it's time for lunch, you'd better have a snack there.

Black: All right. I'll do as you've suggested. (*After lunch, they reenter the taxi*) Where are we going now, Miss Wang?

Wang: We are going to the ancient Long Hua Temple.

Black: OK.

Wang: (*Nearly half an hour later*) Look! From the windscreen, we can see clearly the ancient pagoda standing high over there.

Black: Oh, it's wonderful!

Wang: This ancient Long Hua Temple was built 1,700 years ago.

Black: Wow! It's really very ancient.

Wang: (*After looking around the temple*) Oh, Mr. Black. It's time for us to go back to the Hilton Hotel now.

Black: OK.

Dialogue 2 Visiting London City

Mr. Song is a tourist from China. Helen is a tour guide from a travel agency in London.

Song: I'd like to visit London. Could you recommend me some tourist attractions?

Helen: Well, the British Museum, Buckingham Palace, the Houses of Parliament, Big Ben, Tower Bridge, Hyde Park, Oxford Street are all good places in the city.

Song: But I can stay here for only one day. Do you think I can visit all of them?

Helen: No, you can't if you want to have a good look at them instead of just having a quick glance.

Song: That's too bad.

Helen: I suggest you call a taxi. It would save you a lot of time.

Song: Then where should I go first?

Helen: I think Buckingham Palace is really worth going because it's quite unique. After seeing Buckingham Palace, you can go on to visit the British Museum, Oxford Street, Hyde Park, etc.

Song: OK. Thank you very much.

Helen: It's my pleasure.

II. Act Out

1. Listen to the dialogue. Then practice it with your partners using the words and expressions below to help you.

> **Sun**: good city, no idea, so much, picture, taken, Statue of Liberty, thank, not yet, tell, something, better, elevator, other, places, thank.

Joe: yes, take, see, New York City, of course, glad, help, welcome, visit, Empire State Building, build, in 1931, 381 meters high, hard, believe, climb, how, top, Brooklyn Bridge, UN Building, magnificent, pleasure.

2. Study the following sample dialogue. Then strike up a conversation with your partners using the sentences listed in the chart.

A: **I'm going on a trip to Cairo next week.**

B: How long will you be staying there?

A: For a couple of days.

1. I'm going on a trip to Cairo next week.
2. From up here we can get a bird's-eye view of the city.
3. We can take you to most tourist attractions of the city in a couple of days.
4. The Stone Forest is a famous scenic spot in Yunnan Province.
5. If we take a boat trip, we can enjoy the magnificent sights along the Seine.
6. Can you tell me what the main public transport in London is?
7. I'm afraid that two days' time isn't enough for us to see all the places of interest in Paris.
8. Suppose you haven't been abroad yet, which country would you like to visit first?
9. The Statue of Liberty is a colossal neoclassical sculpture on Liberty Island in New York Harbor.
10. Venice is one of a few cities in the world where the noises of cars are never heard because cars are not allowed.

III. Focus Listening

A. **Listen to the recording and choose the correct answer for each question.**

1. Shanghai is the most important _____ and commercial city in China.
   A. industrial   B. political   C. cultural   D. economic

2. _____ will make visitors taste the changes in China over the past 20 years.
   A. Western-style architectures   B. Overseas businessmen
   C. More and more new highrises   D. More scenic spots

3. All of the following are major scenic spots in Shanghai except _____.
   A. the Jade Buddha Temple   B. the Baima Temple
   C. the Yuyuan Garden   D. the Oriental Pearl Tower

4. Shanghai has the _____ largest airport of China.
   A. first   B. second   C. third   D. fourth
5. Which of the following statements is true?
   A. Tourists can see the past in Shanghai.
   B. Tourists can present the future of Shanghai.
   C. People can buy lots of souvenirs in Shanghai.
   D. Shanghai owns the second largest seaport in China.

B. Listen to the recording and complete the sentences below.

1. Hong Kong is a largely _____ of the People's Republic of China.
2. Hong Kong faces the Guangdong Province in the north and _____ to the east, west and south.
3. Hong Kong enjoys considerable autonomy under the "_____" policy.
4. _____ in Hong Kong are the responsibility of the PRC Government.
5. Hong Kong has a population of 7 million people, but only _____ of land.

Section 2　Reading

London

What is the population of London? That is not easy to decide, because as with all very large towns, it depends on what you regard as its boundary. Towards the edge there are the areas called suburbs, some of them almost like separate towns, but still more or less a continuous part of the central populated area. In "Greater London", which includes all the suburbs and some of the surrounding countryside, the population is eight million. Although, according to the latest reports, these figures have now been surpassed by Tokyo, London remains one of the three or four largest cities in the world. In extent it is vast. Charing Cross, near Trafalgar Square, is usually taken as the central point, and from here the populated area extends unbroken for about eight miles in all directions, forming a huge circle about sixteen miles in diameter.

London has been called "the Great Wen". A

wen is an ulcer; like an ulcer London has just grown and grown, until skilled surgery has been needed to stop it.

Within that great wen there are thirty-two Boroughs, each with a separate council like that of any large independent town. The oldest part is called simply "The City". It is the original London, and was surrounded many centuries ago by a wall with gates in it whose names still survive (Bishopsgate, etc.) Today it is the home of the great banks and insurance offices, and of the great Stock Exchange where the nation's business is conducted. The City is administered by the Lord Mayor of London, elected yearly from among the most prominent businessmen.

To the East is the large area called the East End. This is London's poorest quarter. Despite a considerable amount of new building, it gives a general impression of dinginess, and does not easily outlive its reputation for roughness and squalor, though the people are often generous and hospitable to a degree rarely found in richer homes. The East End contains a large Jewish community, closely connected with the clothing and tailoring trades, and includes the very large riverside docks which make London one of the three largest ports in the world. People of all colors and nationalities may be seen living there.

To the West are the fine shops and theatres of the area vaguely known as the West End, the part best known to the tourist. Oxford Street with its huge department stores is the favorite street for shopping, and if you go westwards along it you will pass first Regent Street, with more big department stores, then Bond Street, with its smaller luxury shops, until you come eventually to Park Lane, containing one of the most famous and most expensive hotels in London, the Dorchester. Park Lane stands between one of London's most fashionable districts, Mayfair, and the largest of all London's parks, Hyde Park, which with the neighboring Kensington Gardens forms a grassy area of a whole square mile, scattered with trees and crossed by a long narrow lake called the Serpentine.

London is too big, too crowded, often ugly and dirty. But no one can deny that it is vastly impressive, exciting, and to a sensitive person, moving. There are many attractions. There is the famous zoo in Regents Park, there is Madame Tussaud's fascinating exhibition of life-like wax figures of famous men and women, there are the many wonderful museums, especially the British Museum in Bloomsbury with its colossal library, and the group of museums in South Kensington which can give you a whole education for a small charge. There is the new Post Office Tower, 630 feet high, housing equipment for television broadcasting and telephone communication. There is the Royal Observatory at Greenwich, which provides the whole world with a standard longitude and a standard time for the purposes of geography and navigation.

Vocabulary

administer /əd'ministə/ v. 管理,给予,执行
attraction /ə'trækʃən/ n. 吸引力,吸引人的事物
charge /tʃɑːdʒ/ n. 费用
colossal /kə'lɔsl/ adj. 巨大的,庞大的
communication /kə,mjuːni'keiʃən/ n. 通信,信息
extend /iks'tend/ v. 扩充,延伸
generous /'dʒenərəs/ adj. 慷慨的,大方的
impressive /im'presiv/ adj. 给人印象深刻的,感人的
longitude /'lɔndʒitjuːd/ n. 经度,经线
navigation /,nævi'geiʃən/ n. 航海,导航
prominent /'prɔminənt/ adj. 卓越的,突出的
reputation /,repju(ː)'teiʃən/ n. 名誉,名声
scatter /'skætə/ v. 分散,散开
separate /'sepəreit/ adj. 分开的,单独的
surpass /sə'pɑːs/ v. 超越,胜过
ulcer /'ʌlsə/ n. 溃疡,腐烂物

Phrases & Expressions

depends on 依靠
regard …as… 认为
according to 根据,依照
connect…with… 连接,联系
in all directions 四面八方

Notes to the Text

1. wen：肿瘤。用来比喻人口不断增长的大城市。
2. London Stock Exchange：伦敦证券交易所。它是世界第三大股票交易所,欧洲第一大股票交易所,现有三千多家公司在交易所上市。伦敦证券交易所是一间提供企业融资、股票及债券交易的国际性证券交易所。
3. Oxford Street：牛津街,位于伦敦市中心。牛津街不足两公里,却云集了超过300家的大型商场。在这里,人们除了看名牌,享受高级服务之外,店铺的建筑特色也是一道令人赏心悦目的风景线。
4. Regent Street：摄政街。位于伦敦市中心,摄政街上坐落的那些伦敦城历史最悠久的商店一定会给您留下深刻的印象。
5. Trafalgar Street：特拉法尔加广场(在英国伦敦的威斯敏斯特)。
6. Hyde Park：海德公园。在泰晤士河东部的中心,海德公园西接肯辛顿公园(Kensington Park),东连绿色公园(Green Park)。

Exercise 1   Reading Comprehension

Answer the following Questions according to the text.

1. Why isn't the population of London easy to decide?
2. What is the population in Greater London?
3. Where are the great banks and insurance offices located?
4. Where do people of all colors and nationalities live in London?
5. Which street is the favorite one for shopping?

Exercise 2   Word Training

Fill in the blanks with the words given below. Change the form where necessary.

depend	surpass	original	connect	include
cross	equipment	charge	scatter	provide

1. They _____ the sufferers with food and clothes as well as money.
2. The gang of thieves _____ at the sight of the police patrol car.

3. Most restaurants add a 10 per cent service _____.
4. We bought several new pieces of _____ for our new lab.
5. I had job interview this morning. Keep your fingers _____!
6. Sorry, my job doesn't _____ dancing with the boss!
7. They did not at first _____ his uncle with the murder.
8. I must change the _____ plan for lack of money.
9. His idea _____ mine in originality.
10. He _____ on his uncle for his school fees after his father's death.

Section 3 Translation

Ⅰ. *Translate the following sentences into Chinese.*
1. Oxford Street with its huge department stores is the favorite street for shopping.
2. New York is called the "paradise for adventurers". It is the financial and trade center of the United States.
3. Los Angeles is the world's largest metropolitan area, where we can find the largest China town in America.
4. As the old Chinese saying goes, "In heaven there is a paradise, and on earth Suzhou and Hangzhou".
5. Shenzhen boomed to fame overnight. It rose in a number of years from a tiny boarder town to a giant city.

Ⅱ. *Translate the following sentences into English.*
1. 悉尼与堪培拉哪一个是澳大利亚首都？
2. 我打算带你参观这个城市的所有名胜。
3. 我下个星期将到旧金山作一次旅行。
4. 我想游览日内瓦的所有名胜。
5. 我要强调的是迟到恕不等候。

Section 4 Classified Word Bank

Read the following words and expressions aloud and then learn them by heart.

1. Wellington		惠灵顿
2. Brasilia		巴西利亚

3.	Ottawa	渥太华
4.	Guatemala	危地马拉
5.	Lima	利马
6.	Washington DC	华盛顿特区
7.	Vienna	维也纳
8.	Brussels	布鲁塞尔
9.	Copenhagen	哥本哈根
10.	Paris	巴黎
11.	Berlin	柏林
12.	Athens	雅典
13.	Rome	罗马
14.	Amsterdam	阿姆斯特丹
15.	Stockholm	斯德哥尔摩
16.	Helsinki	赫尔辛基
17.	St. Petersburg	圣彼得堡
18.	Kiev	基辅
19.	Geneva	日内瓦
20.	Warsaw	华沙

Unit 3　Museums and Palaces

Section 1　Listening and Speaking

Ⅰ. Listen and Repeat

Dialogue 1　At the Museum

Ann is visiting the National Museum of China. Mr. Yang is an attendant in it.

Yang: Good morning, miss. Welcome to the museum.

Ann: Thank you. Wow! The museum is so large.

Yang: Yes, it covers an area of nearly 200,000 square meters and has a permanent collection of 1,050,000 items. Many of them are precious and rare artifacts not to be found in museums anywhere else in China or the rest of the world.

Ann: It's marvelous! Can you give me some examples?

Yang: Yes, of course. Among the most important items are the "Simuwu Ding" from the Shang Dynasty, a large and rare inscribed Western Zhou Dynasty bronze water pan, the Han Dynasty jade burial suits, etc.

Ann: When was museum established?

Yang: It was established in 2003 by the merging of two separate museums, the Museum of the Chinese Revolution, and the National Museum of Chinese History.

Ann: Do you have any brochures for the museum?

Yang: Yes, they are available at the information desk.

Ann: Can I take some pictures of the exhibits?

Yang: No, photography in the museum is strictly prohibited.

Ann: I see. By the way, do I need to buy another ticket if I come again tomorrow?

Yang: Yes. The ticket you have bought is for one day only.

Ann: Thank you very much.

Yang: You're welcome.

Dialogue 2 Visiting the Palace Museum

Helen is a tourist from Canada. Mr. Li, the tour guide, is showing her around the Palace Museum.

Li: Here is the Palace Museum. How do you like it?

Helen: It is large and magnificent.

Li: Yes, it covers an area of 72 hectares. And it has 9,999 rooms.

Helen: When was it built?

Li: It was built from 1406 to 1420.

Helen: It's really ancient. It was 70 years before Columbus discovered America.

Li: That's right.

Helen: How many emperors used to live here?

Li: Twenty-four.

Helen: When did the last emperor move out of the imperial palace?

Li: In 1924. Actually the last emperor Pu Yi was forced to leave the palace.

Helen: I hear the Palace Museum is also called the Forbidden City, isn't it?

Li: Yes, it is. According to a Chinese myth, the Heavenly King lived in the Purple Palace. And the ancient Chinese emperors claimed that they were the sons of Heaven and they should also live in the purple palace, hence the name.

Helen: Then why did people call it the Forbidden City?

Li: That's because the palace was surrounded by a moat and high walls as a defense. It was so sacred that common people could not even dream of ever going in. Even some of the high officials could not go there if they were not invited. Therefore the imperial palace was called the Forbidden City.

Helen: Oh, I see. Thank you very much.

Li: You are welcome.

Ⅱ. Act Out

1. Listen to the dialogue. Then practice it with your partners using the words and expressions below to help you.

Mary: where, National Museum of China, when, built, how many, exhibits, foreigners, museum, souvenir shops, English-speaking docents, wonderful.
Zhou: located, east side, Tian'anmen Square, completed, in 1959, 690,000 square metres, 610,000 items, display, primitive, modern, visit, mysterious, splendid culture, 5000 years, selling souvenirs, publications, speak, different languages.

2. Study the following sample dialogue. Then strike up a conversation with your partners using the sentences listed in the chart.

A: The British Museum is one of the greatest museums in the world.

B: Yes, it is. It has a permanent collection of some 8 million works.

A: When was it established?

B: In 1753.

1. The British Museum is one of the greatest museums in the world.
2. The Metropolitan Museum of Art contains more than two million works.
3. The Louvre Museum is the world's most visited museum, and received more than 9.7 million visitors in 2012.

4.	The Powerhouse Museum is Sydney's largest public museum and is home to some 400,000 artifacts.
5.	The Palace Museum, also called the Forbidden City, is one of the country's most important sights.
6.	The Asian Art Museum of San Francisco has approximately 18,000 works of art and artifacts from all major Asian countries and traditions.
7.	The Palace of Westminster is the meeting place of the House of Commons and the House of Lords.
8.	The American Museum of Natural History is one of the largest and most celebrated museums in the world.
9.	The National Museum of American History preserves and displays the heritage of the United States in the areas of social, political, cultural, scientific and military history.
10.	The Museum of London documents the history of London from prehistoric to modern times.

Ⅲ. Focus Listening

A. Listen to the recording and choose the correct answer for each question.

1. How many suggested itineraries can you choose from in Vatican Museum?
   A. 2   B. 3   C. 4   D. 5
2. The Vatican Museums cover _____ square meters.
   A. 5,000   B. 5,500   C. 15,000   D. 55,000
3. The museums provide _____ for the disabled.
   A. lifts   B. wheelchairs   C. pushchairs   D. special toilets
4. The museums are housed in _____ palaces.
   A. 2   B. 3   C. 4   D. 5
5. Which of the following statements is not true?
   A. There are three courtyards inside the palaces.
   B. Parents with young children can use pushchairs.
   C. The Vatican Museums are not as famous as the British Museum.
   D. The itineraries can take anything from 45 minutes to 5 hours.

B. Listen to the recording and complete the sentences below.

1. The British Museum started in _____.
2. The collection now comprises about _____ items.
3. The British Museum draws _____ visitors each year.
4. The back entrance is usually _____ than the main one.
5. The Great Court is the largest covered public square in _____.

Section 2 Reading

The Louvre Museum

The vast Louvre Museum was constructed as a fortress by Philippe Auguste in the early 13th century and rebuilt in the mid-16th century for use as a royal residence. In 1793 the Revolutionary Convention turned it into the Louvre Museum, the nation's first national museum.

The paintings, sculptures and art works on display in the Louvre Museum have been assembled by French governments over the past five centuries. Among them are works of art and artisanship from all over Europe and important collections of Assyrian, Etruscan, Greek, Coptic and Islamic art and antiquities. Traditionally the Louvre's raison d'etre is to present Western art from the Middle Ages to about the year 1848 as well as the works of ancient civilizations that formed the starting point for Western art. However, in recent years it has acquired or begun to exhibit other important collections as well.

When the museum opened in the late 18th century it contained 2,500 paintings and objects of art; today some 35,000 are on display. The 'Grand Louvre' project inaugurated by the late President Mitterrand in 1989 doubled the museum's exhibition space, and new and renovated galleries have opened in recent years devoted to objects of art such as the crown jewels of Louis XV, as well as ancient art collected from Africa, Asia, Australia and the Americas.

The Louvre is located in a good place. The side facing the Seine is some 700m long and it is said that it would take nine months just to glance at every piece of art here. Most people do their duty and come, but many leave overwhelmed, unfulfilled, exhausted and frustrated at having got lost on their way to da Vinci's La Joconde, better known as Mona Lisa. Since it takes several serious visits to get anything more than a brief glimpse of the works, your best bet-after checking out a few you really want to see—is to choose a particular period or section of the Louvre and pretend that the rest is in another museum somewhere across town.

The most famous works from antiquity include the Seated Scribe, the Code of Hammurabi and that armless duo, the Venus de Milo and the Winged Victory of Samothrace. From the Renaissance, don't miss Michelangelo's The Dying Slave and works by Raphael. Botticelli and Titian.

The main entrance and ticket windows in the Cour Napoleon are covered by the 21m-high Grande Pyramide, a glass pyramid designed by the Chinese-born American architect Pei. You can avoid the queues outside the pyramid or at the Porte Des lions entrance by entering the Louvre complex via the Carrousel du Louvre entrance.

The Louvre is divided into four sections: the Sully, Denon and Richelieu Wings and Hall Napoleon. Sully creates the Cour Carree (literally square courtyard) at the eastern end of the complex. Denon stretches along the Seine to the south; Richelieu is the northern wing along rue de Rivoli.

The split-level public area under the Grande Pyramide is known as the Hall Napoleon. The hall has an exhibit on the history of the Louvre, a bookshop, a restaurant, a café, auditoriums for concerts, lectures and films, and Cyberlouvre, an internet research center with online access to some 20,000 works of art. The centerpiece of the Carrousel du Louvre, the shopping center that runs underground from the pyramid to the Arc de Triomphe du Carrousel, is an inverted glass pyramid, also created by Pei.

Vocabulary

access /'ækses/ n. 通路, 入口, 进入权

antiquity /æn'tikwiti/ n. 古代,古老,古迹
architect /'a:kitekt/ n. 建筑师
artisanship /'a:tizənʃip/ n. 手艺,工艺,手艺活
Assyrian /ə'siriən/ adj. 亚述的,亚述人的,亚述语的 n. 亚述人
construct /kən'strʌkt/ vt. 建造,创立
convention /kən'venʃən/ n. 惯例,常规,习俗;大会
Coptic /'kɔptik/ adj. 科普特人的,埃及基督徒的
Etruscan /i'trʌskən/ adj. 伊特鲁里亚的,伊特鲁里亚人的 n. 伊特鲁里亚人
fortress /'fɔ:tris/ n. 堡垒,要塞
frustrate /frʌs'treit/ v. 使生气,使烦恼,使沮丧;使挫败,阻挠
inaugurate /i'nɔ:gjureit/ vt. 创新,开辟
Islamic /iz'læmik/ adj. 伊斯兰的,伊斯兰教的
overwhelm /'əuvə'welm/ vt. 受打击,制服,压倒
raisondêtre /'reizɔn'detrə/ n. （法）存在的目的或理由
renaissance /rə'neisəns/ n. 复兴,复活,文艺复兴
renovate /'renəuveit/ vt. 修复
sculpture /'skʌlptʃə/ n. 雕刻,雕塑,雕塑品

Phrases & Expressions

on display 展示,陈列
devote...to... 把……献给……;献身于……
get lost 迷路
be known as 被认为是……
access to 使用某物的能力(机会,权利)

Notes to the Text

Philippe Auguste （法国人）菲力普·奥古斯都
da Vinci 达·芬奇
rue de Rivoli. （法国地名）里沃利路
Cour Carree （法语）宫殿广场
Cour Napoleon 罗浮宫中的拿破仑中庭
Arc de Triomphe du Carrousel 小凯旋门

Exercise 1 Reading Comprehension

Answer the following Questions according to the text.
1. When was the Louvre turned into the Louvre Museum?
2. When did the Museum open to the public?
3. Who inaugurated the 'Grand Louvre' project?
4. How many sections is the Louvre Museum divided into? What are they?
5. What does the Hall Napoleon have?

Exercise 2 Word Training

Fill in the blanks with the words given below. Change the form where necessary.

| renovate | assemble | acquire | glance | glimpse |
| devote | frustrate | overwhelm | pretend | access |

1. He _____ at the menu, and then started to order.
2. Doesn't it _____ you that audiences in the theatre are so restricted?
3. The couple spent thousands of dollars _____ the house.
4. I _____ that things are really okay when they are not.
5. The vote was _____ —283 in favor, and only 29 against.
6. Some of the fans had waited 24 hours outside the hotel to catch a _____ of their heroine.
7. He _____ his life to promoting world peace.
8. My home is located within easy _____ of shops and other facilities.
9. There was not even a convenient place for students to _____ between classes.
10. He _____ a bad reputation because of his bad manners.

Section 3 Translation

Ⅰ. *Translate the following sentences into Chinese.*
1. The Crystal Palace is one of the most famous buildings in the world.

2. Rectangular in shape, the Forbidden City is the world's largest palace.
3. In the Summer Palace, the Long Corridor and the bridges are both very famous.
4. Tourists from all over the world have been flooding into this famous Palace.
5. The Louvre is divided into four sections: the Sully, Denon and Richelieu Wings and Hall Napoleon.

Ⅱ. *Translate the following sentences into English.*
1. 罗浮宫是世界三大博物馆之一。
2. 伦敦科技博物馆每年吸引330万到访者。
3. 大英博物馆是世界上最古老、最威严的博物馆。
4. 布达拉宫已被列为世界遗产。
5. 伦敦维多利亚与阿尔伯特博物馆是世界上最大的装饰艺术和设计博物馆。

Section 4 Classified Word Bank

Read the following words and expressions aloud and then learn them by heart:

1.	Damascus Museum	大马士革博物馆
2.	Guggenheim Museum	古根海姆博物馆
3.	Victoria Museum	维多利亚博物馆
4.	Doha National Museum	多哈国家博物馆
5.	Deutsches Museum	德意志博物馆
6.	Museum Island	博物馆岛
7.	Egyptian Museum	埃及博物馆
8.	Picasso Museum	毕加索博物馆
9.	Museum of Bardo	巴尔多博物馆
10.	H. C. Anderson's House	安徒生博物馆
11.	War Museum	战争博物馆
12.	Doftana Museum	多夫塔纳博物馆
13.	British Museum	大英博物馆
14.	Palace Museum	故宫博物院
15.	Louvre Museum	罗浮宫
16.	Van Gogh Museum	凡·高博物馆

17. National Museum of China	中国国家博物馆
18. Discover World Museum	发现世界博物馆
19. American Museum of Natural History	美国自然史博物馆
20. National Archaeological Museum	国家文物博物馆

Unit 4 Parks

Section 1 Listening and Speaking

I. Listen and Repeat

Dialogue 1 Hong Kong Disneyland

Jackie has just been to Hong Kong Disneyland. Now she is telling Leo about her experience in the park.

Leo: Hi, Jackie! Have you ever been to Hong Kong Disneyland? I hear it is fantastic.

Jackie: Yes, I was there last week. The weather was hot. But the heat did not prevent thousands of people from visiting it.

Leo: When did the park open to visitors?

Jackie: It opened to visitors on September 12, 2005.

Leo: Can people enjoy themselves there?

Jackie: Yes, of course. The park consists of four themed lands similar to other Disneyland parks: Main Street, U.S.A., Fantasyland, Adventureland and Tomorrowland. Visitors can try the rides, the shows and all the other things at the theme park.

Leo: I hear the Walt Disney Company opened its first amusement park in Los Angeles in 1955. This park is the eleventh, right?

Jackie: Yes. But Hong Kong Disneyland is the second Disney theme park in Asia. Tokyo got the first one in 1983.

Leo: Can we enjoy delicious food at Hong Kong Disneyland?

Jackie: Yeah. If you are a guest of Disney, you can taste various kinds of foods there.

Leo: By the way, how long will it take to get there from the center of Hong Kong?

Jackie: Well, it takes about half an hour by underground train.
Leo: Oh, it is very convenient.

Dialogue 2 Hong Kong Ocean Park

Frank is planning his tomorrow's trip to Hong Kong Ocean Park. Now he is talking about it with Amanda.

Amanda: Have you decided where to go for tomorrow's trip?
Frank: I plan to visit Hong Kong Ocean Park.
Amanda: Splendid! It is a famous tourist attraction in Hong Kong. It brings to life the wonderful ocean world.
Frank: Yes, it is a marine-based adventure park. Visitors to the ocean park can not only enjoy the rides and attractions that can be found in most parks, but they can also learn about life in the ocean.
Amanda: Yes, there is a four-story aquarium called Atoll Reef displaying more than 2,000 fishes in 250 different species.
Frank: It is the largest aquarium in Hong Kong.
Amanda: Yes, and if you're more adventurous, the Dragon, a steel roller coaster will take you for a hurricane speed super ride, and give you the ride of a lifetime.
Frank: That's wonderful! I hear Hong Kong Ocean Park also features a Giant panda exhibit.
Amanda: Yes, 2 more pandas named Le Le and Ying Ying were added to the ocean park on May 1, 2007. After quarantine, they made their first public appearance in the ocean park on July 1, 2007.
Frank: By the way, do you know its opening hours?
Amanda: Yeah, from 10:00 a.m. to 10:00 p.m..
Frank: How about the price?
Amanda: HK $345 for adults and HK $173 for children aged 3 to 11.
Frank: I see.

Ⅱ. Act Out

1. Listen to the dialogue. Then practice it with your partners using the words and expressions below to help you.

> **Jim**: suggestions, tomorrow's trip, how far, tell, what, expect, political activities, long history, which part, attractive, buy, souvenirs, how long, have a good view.

Part IV
Festivals and City Tours

> **Qian**: suggest, Summer Palace, an hour's bus ride, three parts, political activities, living quarters, scenic spot area, administration, place, Cixi, state affairs, officials, principal, Halls of Benevolence and Longevity, 800 years, witness, prosperity, decline, honor, disgrace, Long Corridor, Seventeen Arch Bridge, frame, Kunming Lake, Buddha Fragrance Chamber, a lively whole, stretch, 300 metres, whatever, wish.

2. Study the following sample dialogue. Then strike up a conversation with your partners using the sentences listed in the chart.

A: Could you recommend me some scenic spots in Beijing?
B: I suggest you visit the Summer Palace. **It is the largest and best-preserved imperial garden in China.**
A: What fun can I have there?
B: You can boat, watch the lilies and climb Longevity Hill.

| 1. The Summer Palace is the largest and best-preserved imperial garden in China. |
| 2. The Hyde park is one of the Royal Parks in central London. |
| 3. Fragrant Hills Park is an imperial garden and is well-known for its autumn red leaves. |
| 4. The Temple of Heaven was inscribed as a UNESCO World Heritage Site in 1998. |
| 5. Ocean Park Hong Kong is the World's Seventh Most Popular Amusement Park. |
| 6. Zhongshan Park was built in honor of Sun Zhongshan, who is considered by many to be the "Father of Modern China". |
| 7. There are many notable places in Beihai Park. The White Dagoba is a 40-meter high stupa built on Jade Flower Island. |
| 8. The Great Wall of China was built to protect the Chinese states and empire against the raids and invasions of the various nomadic groups. |
| 9. Glacier National Park has almost all its original native plant and animal species. |
| 10. The Grand Canyon is often considered one of the Seven Natural Wonders of the World. |

III. Focus Listening

A. Listen to the recording and choose the correct answer for each question.

1. In what way are theme parks different from traditional amusement parks?

A. They often want to teach visitors something

B. They have a collection of rides and exhibitions

C. They make every effort to attract visitors

D. They put visitors as the first consideration

2. From the article we know that China has _____ minorities.

  A. 50   B. 55   C. 56   D. 59

3. What is the common characteristic of theme parks?

A. They make sure that people know their themes

B. They have children learn about animals

C. They let people know customs and culture

D. They combine fun and learning together

4. Over _____ students visit Ocean Park every year.

  A. 15,000 B. 50,000 C. 60,000 D. 65,000

5. The purpose of the conservation centre in Ocean Park is to _____.

A. educate and entertain visitors visiting the park

B. prevent visitors from being injured

C. protect marine animals and their habitats

D. help visitors look for thrills and entertainment

B. Listen to the recording and complete the sentences below.

1. The Forbidden City is situated _____.

2. There are altogether _____ emperors lived and ruled here.

3. There are _____ buildings in all in the Forbidden City.

4. The layout of the Forbidden City adopted _____.

5. In 1987 the Forbidden City was listed by UNESCO as a _____.

Section 2 Reading

Yellowstone National Park

  Built in 1872 by the United States Congress "for the preservation of many wonders" and "for the enjoyment of the people," and spanning an area of 3,472 square miles, Yellowstone National Park is America's first and foremost National Park. The park got its name from the yellow rocks in the Grand Canyon of the Yellowstone. It is a deep gash in the Yellowstone Plateau formed by floods during previous ice ages and by river erosion from the Yellowstone

River.

Yellowstone National Park is the most important part in the Greater Yellowstone Ecosystem.

Located mostly in the state of Wyoming, the park extends into Montana and Idaho. Its great natural beauty has made it one of the most popular national parks. Within this park, you can find Old Faithful and a collection of the world's most extraordinary geysers, hot springs, and the Grand Canyon of the Yellowstone.

Most visitors like to see Old Faithful, the world's most famous geyser, although it is not the biggest or the most beautiful. It is one of the most unusual places in the world. Extremely hot water shoots out of the ground in several hundred places. Visitors can watch bubbles coming up through the boiling hot mud. They can see rocks that were once liquid and have cooled into strange shapes. Visitors gather around Old Faithful before each eruption. Experts at the park are able to predict when these will happen. The eruption lasts between two and five minutes. Old Faithful releases up to about thirty thousand liters of water into the air each time.

It was an ancient and extremely violent volcano that created the great beauty of Yellowstone. Scientists believe the major volcanic activity in the Yellowstone area began about two million years ago. This activity caused violent explosions and built mountains and valleys. The last eruption created the mountains and valleys that visitors can see today in Yellowstone. However, the ancient volcano that formed Yellowstone is not dead. It is dormant. And some experts say it could become very dangerous in the future.

The incredible geysers have brought Yellowstone its fame. Meanwhile, its wildlife population is just as popular. It is home to varieties of wildlife. The most controversial of these is Yellowstone's wolf population. Until recently, the wolf was almost extinct. Afraid of the threat wolves would pose to their livestock, hunters killed Yellowstone's grey wolves for the price of fifteen dollars a head in the early 1900's. They were hunted to near extinction. It was almost a century before an effort began to reverse this damage. In 1995, Douglas Smith went to Canada to capture fourteen of the animals in an effort to revive Yellowstone's wolf population. One of the transplanted wolves in particular, has had a lot to do with the park's wolf repopulation. This female wolf is one of the park's top breeders, and 70% of the wolves born in the park today have her genes.

Yellowstone has numerous recreational opportunities, including hiking, camping, boating, fishing and so on. Paved roads provide close access to the major geothermal areas as well as some of the lakes and waterfalls. During the winter, visitors often access the park by way of guided tours that use either snow coaches or snowmobile.

Vocabulary

access /ˈækses/ *n.* 通路,进入
bubble /ˈbʌbl/ *n.* 泡沫 *vi.* 冒泡,沸腾
controversial /ˌkɔntrəˈvəːʃəl/ *adj.* 有争议的,引起争论的
dormant /ˈdɔːmənt/ *adj.* 休眠的,静止的
erosion /iˈrəuʒən/ *n.* 腐蚀,侵蚀
eruption /iˈrʌpʃən/ *n.* 喷发,爆发
extinct /iksˈtiŋkt/ *adj.* 熄灭的,灭绝的,耗尽的
gash /gæʃ/ *n.* (大而深的)切口或伤口
gene /dʒiːn/ *n.* 因子,基因

geothermal /dʒiəu'θə:məl/ adj. 地热的
incredible /in'kredəbl/ adj. 难以置信的
preserve /pri'zə:v/ vt. 保护,保存;腌制(食物)
release /ri'li:s/ vt. 释放,公布(新闻消息),发行(电影或唱片)
reverse /ri'və:s/ v. 倒车;倒转,改变
revive /ri'vaiv/ vt. (使)苏醒,(使)康复;复兴
span /spæn/ vt. 跨度,一段时间
violent /'vaiələnt/ adj. 暴力的,猛烈的,极端的

Phrases & Expressions

first and foremost 首先,首要地
be located in 位于
pose threat to... 对……构成威胁
in particular 特别
have sth to do with 与……有关系

Notes to the Text

1. the Grand Canyon 大峡谷
2. Old Faithful 老忠实间歇泉
3. Afraid of the threat wolves would pose to their livestock...形容词短语作原因状语。其中,wolves would pose to their livestock 为定语从句,修饰 the threat。

Exercise 1 Reading Comprehension

Answer the following questions according to the text.
1. For what purpose did the United States Congress build Yellowstone National Park?
2. In what way do we say the Old Faithful is one of the most unusual places?
3. How was the great beauty of Yellowstone formed? Is the ancient volcano still very dangerous?
4. Why was the wolf almost extinct?
5. Why do we say the female wolf is one of the park's top breeders?

Exercise 2　Word Training

Fill in the blanks with the words given below. Change the form where necessary.

| location | preserve | incredible | reverse | populate |
| pose | extinction | violence | release | explode |

1. We were anxious to _____ the original character of the village.
2. The islands were gradually _____ by settlers from Europe.
3. The _____ and bad language in the program shocked many of the viewers.
4. The bomb was timed to _____ during the rush-hour.
5. Their language is faced with the threat of _____.
6. He indicated the _____ of the Persian Gulf with a pen on the map. ?
7. The _____ of the coin was stamped with an eagle.
8. He is always talking about his deep interest in literature, but it's just a _____.
9. The latest developments have just been _____ to the media.
10. It's _____ that Julia can behave with such stupid lack of feeling.

Section 3　Translation

Ⅰ. *Translate the following sentences into Chinese.*
1. Situated at the heart of Beijing, the Forbidden City, known as the Palace Museum, was the imperial palace of the Ming and Qing Dynasties.
2. You can hike down into the depths on foot or by mule, hover above in a helicopter or raft through the whitewater rapids of the river itself.
3. Nearly 160 million people a year go to amusement parks in Europe and a recent survey found that nearly half of them are adults who go there without children.
4. The American people have experienced the happiness of Disney theme parks for over 50 years. Disney has a big name and it will definitely attract people and be a big success.
5. The layout of the park is based on an ancient Chinese legend.

Ⅱ. *Translate the following sentences into English.*
1. 北海位于北京城的中心,是北京最受人欢迎的公园之一。

2. 不可思议的天然喷泉给黄石公园赢得了名声。
3. 象征着中国古老文明的长城是世界最著名的建筑之一。
4. 在世界五个迪士尼主题公园中,香港迪士尼乐园是最小的。
5. 天坛占地面积273公顷,是紫禁城的三倍。

Section 4   Classified Word Bank

Read the following words and expressions aloud and then learn them by heart：

1.	Amusement park	游乐场
2.	Beijing World Park	世界公园
3.	China Century Altar	中华世纪坛
4.	Chinese Ethnic Culture Park	中华民族园
5.	Imperial Gardens	御花园
6.	Liulichang Cultural Street	琉璃厂
7.	Palace of Heavenly Purity	乾清宫
8.	Palace of Nations	万国宫
9.	Shanhaiguan Pass	山海关
10.	Suzhou Gardens	苏州园林
11.	The Echo Wall	回音壁
12.	The Fragrant Hills	香山公园
13.	The Lama Temple	雍和宫
14.	The Mansion of Prince Gong	恭王府
15.	The Ming Tombs	十三陵
16.	The Summer Palace	颐和园
17.	The Temple of Heaven	天坛
18.	Theme parks	主题公园
19.	The Hall of Prayer for Good Harvest	祈年殿
20.	The Imperial Summer Mountain Resort	避暑山庄

Part V

Food & Drinks

Unit 1 Chinese Cuisine

Section 1 Listening and Speaking

I. Listen and Repeat

Dialogue 1 Going out for Dinner

Mark is a tourist from England. He is talking with his tour guide Miss Wang about Chinese food.

Wang: Hi, Mark. Sorry to keep you waiting.
Mark: Not really. Actually I was a little late myself.
Wang: Oh, let's go. Today I'm going to take you to a Chinese restaurant nearby. It's famous for its dishes of traditional Beijing style.
Mark: I'm looking forward to it! I hear that Chinese Cuisine is delicious and has a long history.
Wang: Yeah. Actually there are eight culinary cuisines of China. They are Anhui, Cantonese, Fujian, Hunan, Jiangsu, Shandong, Sichuan, and Zhejiang cuisines.
Mark: Wow! There are so many of them.
Wang: Yeah, China is a country with 56 ethnic groups. Because of differences in geographical positions, climates, products, customs and culture, there are a variety of dishes in the land, and their flavors are quite distinct. For instance, Cantonese Cuisine is light and crisp while Sichuan food is very spicy. Actually when Westerners speak of Chinese food, they usually refer to Cantonese cuisine.

Mark: I see. I'd like to try Cantonese food next time.
Wang: No problem. There are lots of Cantonese Restaurants here.
Mark: Could you tell me why Sichuan Cuisine is very hot, Miss Wang?
Wang: Yeah. People there like spicy food because of the humid climate in Sichuan Province. They will sweat after eating hot dishes and the dampness in the body will be driven away.
Mark: Oh, that's interesting. Just like Russians drink vodka to drive away the cold.
Wang: Exactly!

Dialogue 2　In the Restaurant

Mark and Miss Wang have got to the restaurant where they will have their dinner.

Mark: Oh, the environment here is very special. It's just like home. The courtyard here is truly fantastic.
Wang: You're right. It's the traditional Beijing style. It's called Siheyuan or Beijing Quadrangle. I'm sure you've heard of this.
Mark: Yeah. What cuisine is served here?
Wang: It serves traditional Beijing Cuisine. Since you're in Beijing, I think you'd better try some local food first.
Mark: Okay.
Wang: Here's the menu, Mark. Every dish has its English name, which tells about the ingredients used in the dish
Mark: It's very thoughtful of them. I'm sure the restaurant will become more and more popular with foreigners.
Wang: You said it. As you have tried Beijing Roast Duck, let's have something different today.
Mark: That's good. What shall we have today?
Wang: We'll have "Jing Jiang Rou Si" and "Jiao Liu Wan Zi".
Mark: What are they?
Wang: "Jing Jiang Rou Si" is the shredded pork in sweet bean source while "Jiao Liu Wan Zi" is the crispy fried meat balls with brown sauce.
Mark: Sounds good. But Miss Wang, my Chinese friend told me that there is a food quite popular in Beijing. It's kind of pot-stewed lamb spine.
Wang: Oh, that's "Yang Xie Zi" or Lamb Spine Hot Pot. It's very popular in Beijing, especially in winter. We can order some now.
Mark: Okay. Miss Wang, can you tell me something about Beijing snacks?

Wang: Sure. There are many kinds of snacks in Beijing. For example, there is a snack called "Lu-Da-Gun", or "donkey roll". But remember that it has nothing to do with the donkey. It is a glutinous rice roll with sweet bean flour.

Mark: But why is it called Lu-Da-Gun?

Wang: That's because the last process of making the food is to roll it in the bean flour, just like the donkey rolls on the ground, hence the name "Lu-Da-Gun".

Mark: Oh, it's so interesting. I like it.

Wang: Here's our dish. Try it, Mark.

Mark: Oh, yummy.

Ⅱ. Act Out

1. Listen to the dialogue. Then practice it with your partners using the words and expressions below to help you.

Wang: Temptation of Spicy, famous, Sichuan restaurant, in Beijing, tell, face, customers, want, try, yourself, let, see, menu, Kung Pao Chicken, Mapo Tofu, then, Spicy Fish, fish filets, hot chili oil, spicy but tasty.
Mark: from the name, know, dishes, must, very hot, yes, that's, why, here, already try, China Town, home country, what is it, let's try it.

2. Study the following sample dialogue. Then strike up a conversation with your partners using the sentences listed in the chart.

A: What would you like to order, Madam?

B: Oh, there are so many dishes on the menu, let me see. Er... What would you recommend?

A: The West Lake Fish in Vinegar Gravy is worth trying. It tastes wonderful.

B: OK.

1. The West Lake Fish in Vinegar Gravy is worth trying.
2. Peking Duck is a famous duck dish from Beijing.
3. Chinese chicken salad is very popular both at home and abroad.
4. Beef ball is a commonly cooked food in southern China.
5. Beggar's Chicken is a dish from Changshu, Jiangsu province. The chicken is stuffed, wrapped in clay, and roasted.

6. The mouth feel of Dongpo pork is oily but not greasy.
7. Kung Pao Chicken is a spicy stir-fried dish made with chicken, peanuts, vegetables, and chili peppers.
8. The Chinese hot pot has a history of more than 1,000 years.
9. Crispy fried chicken is standard Cantonese cuisine. The skin of the chicken is extremely crunchy, but the white meat is relatively soft.
10. Twice cooked pork is a well-known Sichuan-style Chinese dish.

III. Focus Listening

A. *Listen to the recording and choose the correct answer for each question.*

1. The Chinese cooking style is characterized by a wide diversity of _____.
    A. ingredients   B. cooking methods
    C. starchy foods   D. both A and B
2. _____ is always present with traditional Chinese meals in the south of China?
    A. Rice   B. Fish   C. Meat   D. Seafood
3. What are always present with traditional Chinese meals in the north of China?
    A. Poultry and fish
    B. Wheat products
    C. Noodles and meat
    D. Potatoes and breads
4. _____ are generally considered supplementary food in daily Chinese meals?
    A. Beef and mutton
    B. Pork and fish
    C. Meat, poultry and fish
    D. Chicken, beef and seafood
5. To be more exact, the Chinese diet is basically a _____ diet.
    A. rice and vegetable
    B. meat and rice
    C. wheat and vegetable
    D. poultry and soybeans

B. *Listen to the recording and complete the sentences below.*

1. Hunan Province has a hot _____ summer and an extremely cold winter.
2. This region has some of the _____ and tastiest dishes in the Chinese diet.

3. Hunan people flavor so many dishes with chilies is to open the _____ and keep cool in the summer.
4. Most people associate spicy _____ with Hunan cooking.
5. Spicy does not necessarily mean "hot", it can also mean "just _____".

Section 2　Reading

Chinese Cuisine

No one can understand the culture of a country without first experiencing its food and drink. Chinese culinary traditions have adapted freely and changed with time. Over the course of 5,000 years, these culinary traditions have been devised and perfected and have withstood the test of time. For example, steaming, the basic kitchen technique, was used extensively long before the foundation of the first dynasty. Through trade, foreign ingredients made their way to the kitchens of the court mingling with the homegrown bounty to produce exceptional, unusual and marvelous dishes.

Under the last truly Chinese Imperial Dynasty (Ming 1368—1644 A. D.), the modern cuisine developed. Next came the Manchus, who established the Qing Dynasty and brought with them well earned peace and prosperity. They are said to have become more Chinese than the natives and enjoyed a life of luxury and leisure. The food consumed everyday by gourmets was developing into what is now considered authentic Chinese cuisine. A combination of many centuries of love of good food, a tradition of open hospitality and endless experimentation with nature's bounty has gone into making the rich and vibrant feast that is the colorful culinary heritage of China.

Throughout the years, the Chinese learned the importance of creatively treating food with respect. Also, they learned how to make anything edible taste good. The chefs were constantly challenged to create dishes with harmonious exciting combinations of flavors, textures and colors that centered on a love and respect for food.

   A well prepared Chinese dish is expected to appeal to more senses other than just one of taste. Its colors should be pleasing to the eye, the ingredients should be of uniform size and it should be fragrant. There should be contrasting tastes and textures within the meal; if one dish is crisp, it should be offset by another one that is smooth. A bland dish is paired with a spiced one, thereby always trying to create a balance. It is important to have this balance of yin and yang.

   To the Chinese, food is life but it is also health and a symbol of other good things such as luck and prosperity. The Chinese developed their genius for cooking due to the antiquity of their civilization. This savory and complex cuisine is full of exquisite flavors as well as fiery and subtle seasonings that have been perfected over thousands of years. From China's earliest days, food has been an integral part of the culture. Hence, there is truth in the saying "for people, food is heaven!"

Vocabulary

antiquity /æn'tikwiti/ *n.* 古代,古老,古物,古迹
authentic /ɔː'θentik/ *adj.* 正宗的,原汁原味的
bland /blænd/ *adj.* 平和的,温和的;(食品)清淡无味的
bounty /'baunti/ *n.* (尤指食物)丰盛,大量
culinary /'kʌlinəri/ *adj.* 烹饪的,厨房的
decadent /'dekədənt/ *adj.* 浪荡的,堕落的,颓废的
devise /di'vais/ *v.* 装置,器具,方法,手段
edible /'edibl/ *adj.* 可食用的
exceptional /ik'sepʃənl/ *adj.* 例外的,异常的
exquisite /'ekskwizit/ *adj.* 精致的,精美的,细腻的
feast /fiːst/ *n.* 宴会,酒席
fiery /'faiəri/ *adj.* 有火的,失火的;引发强烈情感的
gourmet /'guəmei/ *n.* 美食家,讲究饮食的人
ingredient /in'griːdiənt/ *n.* 原料;成分,因素
mingle /'miŋgl/ *v.* 混合,(在社交场合)相交往,来回应酬
offset /'ɔːfset/ *v.* 抵销,补偿
savory /'seivəri/ *adj.* 风味极佳的,可口的,味香的

season /ˈsiːzn/ v. 给(食品)调味
texture /ˈtekstʃə/ n. 质地,纹理
withstand /wɪðˈstænd/ v. 耐得起,承受得住

Phrases & Expressions

make one's way 前进,进行
go into 成为,进入
be worthy of 值得……的,应……的
appeal to 对……有吸引力
due to 因为,由于

Notes to the Text

1. Ming：明朝(中国古代朝代 1368—1644 A.D.)。1368 年,朱元璋在应天称帝,定国号为明,史称明朝,朱元璋就是明太祖。同年秋天,攻克元大都,结束了元朝在全国的统治。此后,他又用近 20 年的时间,完成了统一大业。
2. Manchus：满族人。1644 年,满族人入关占领北京,建立大清王朝。
3. Qing：清朝。(中国古代朝代 1644—1911 A.D.)它是中国历史上最后一个帝制王朝,统治者为出身建州女真的爱新觉罗氏。
4. Yin and Yang：阴阳。阴阳五行学说,是中国古代朴素的唯物论和自发的辩证法思想,它认为世界是物质的,物质世界是在阴阳二气作用的推动下兹生、发展和变化。

Exercise 1 Reading Comprehension

Answer the following Questions according to the text.
1. What kind of cooking style was used extensively before the establishment of the first dynasty?
2. Who founded the Qing Dynasty?
3. What did the Chinese learn throughout the years?
4. What can be regarded as a well prepared Chinese dish?
5. What is the Chinese saying mentioned in the text?

Exercise 2 Word Training

Fill in the blanks with the words given below. Change the form where necessary.

| offset | edible | decadent | authentic | savory |
| exceptional | mingle | ingredient | exquisite | devise |

1. The slowdown in domestic demand was _____ by an increase in exports.
2. The little boy showed _____ bravery in face of danger.
3. Can you tell me if these berries are _____?
4. She accepted the money with _____ feelings.
5. Many conservatives in the early 1900's thought impressionistic art was _____.
6. There is a list of _____ on the side of the packet.
7. The girl came up with a set of _____ stamps.
8. I don't know if the painting is _____.
9. Testing yourself through the use of computers is a useful _____ for studying.
10. He consumed a large plateful of the very _____ stew.

Section 3 Translation

Ⅰ. *Translate the following sentences into Chinese.*
1. From China's earliest days, food has been an integral part of the culture.
2. There is an awesome variety of chilies and peppers that range from the familiar harmless green bell pepper to the tiny red pepper known as the "delayed action bomb".
3. If the ingredients are truly fresh and prepared properly, MSG is not only unnecessary; it can actually spoil the dish for the diner.
4. A fundamental difference between the European and Chinese style of cooking is found in sauce making.
5. Waving your chopsticks around as if it was an extension of your hand gestures is considered unrefined, as is poking around your bowl looking for food and poking through food to pick it up.

Ⅱ. *Translate the following sentences into English.*
1. 人们只有在真正品尝到当地饮食之后才能真正了解这个国家的文化。
2. 中国人有句谚语："民以食为天。"
3. 开席之后先给长辈夹菜是礼貌的标志。
5. 中国菜具有色、香、味俱全的特点。
6. 中国人喜欢用筷子吃饭,两根筷子传达了和谐与平衡的智慧。

Section 4　Classified Word Bank

Read the following words and expressions aloud and then learn them by heart.

1.	Shredded Pork in Garlic Sauce	鱼香肉丝
2.	Fried Sweet and Sour	糖醋里脊
3.	Tenderloin Double Cooked Pork	回锅肉
4.	Moo Shu Pork	木须肉
5.	Mapo Tofu	麻婆豆腐
6.	Stewed Pork Hock	水晶肘
7.	Crispy Duck	香酥鸭
8.	Smoked Tea Duck	樟茶鸭
9.	Braised Pork Balls in Soy Sauce	红烧狮子头
10.	Hot and Spicy Yabbies	麻辣小龙虾
11.	Beef Seasoned with Soy Sauce	酱牛肉
12.	steamed corn bread	窝头
13.	slightly fried dumpling	锅贴
14.	Soft-Fried Pork Filet	软炸里脊
15.	Noodles, Sichuan Style	担担面
16.	Fried Prawns	酥炸大虾
17.	Kung Pao Chicken	宫保鸡丁
18.	Bitty Melon Beef	凉瓜炒牛肉
19.	Cashew Chicken	腰果鸡球
20.	Oyster Sauce Broccoli	豪油芥蓝

Unit 2 French Cuisine

Section 1 Listening and Speaking

I. Listen and Repeat

Dialogue 1   In a French restaurant

Susan and Franc have gone to a French restaurant to have dinner.

Waiter: Bonsoir, avez-vous des réserves?
Franc: I'm sorry, but we don't speak French.
Waiter: It doesn't matter. So there are two of you?
Franc: That's right.
Waiter: Would you like to follow me, please? There's a table free by the window.
Susan: Okay.
Waiter: Shall I take your coat, madam?
Susan: OK. Thank you.
Waiter: And here's the menu. Would you like something to drink before your meal?
Susan: Good idea. What have you got?
Waiter: Martini, kir, Coke, etc.
Susan: What is kir?
Waiter: It is white wine with a blackcurrant liqueur.
Susan: I'll have a glass of kir. What about you, Franc?
Franc: I'll have the same.
Waiter: Oh, two kirs.

(*The waiter goes to get the wine.*)

Susan: Have you ever been here before?
Franc: No, actually it's John who recommends this restaurant to me. But I've never been here myself.
Susan: But it is really very nice. I'm not entirely sure but I have a feeling that I came here for a working lunch a few years ago.

Dialogue 2   Order in the French restaurant

(*A few minutes later the waiter comes with wine.*)

Waiter: Here is your wine.

Susan: Oh, thank you.

Franc: Thank you.

Waiter: Are you ready to order?

Susan: I think so, but could you tell me what the soup today is?

Waiter: Certainly. Today we're serving coquille with onion. This is French onion soup cooked with coquilles and cheese.

Susan: Sounds good to me. I'll have that. What about you, Franc?

Franc: I think I'll have the snails. After all we're in France.

Waiter: Right you are. Is there anything else I can get for you?

Susan: Yeah, I'll have a rack of lamb. But could you do it without the mint sauce please? I'm allergic to it.

Waiter: No problem.

Franc: Oh, the lamb looks good on the menu. But could you tell me what Choron sauce is?

Waiter: Yes, of course. Choron sauce was created by a man called Alexandra Choron, a famous French chef of the 19 century. The Choron sauce is delicious béarnaise sauce with tomato puree.

Franc: Oh, very interesting. I'll have that, too.

Waiter: And what would you like to drink?

Susan: Do you have any recommendations?

Waiter: I certainly recommend Cabernet Sauvignon, madam.

Franc: So, we'll have a bottle of that please.

Waiter: Is there anything else?

Franc: No, thank you.

Waiter: OK. So that's one soup of the day, one plate of snails, two racks of lamb, and one bottle of Cabernet Sauvignon.

Franc: That's right.

Ⅱ. Act Out

1. Listen to the dialogue. Then practice it with your partners using the words and expressions below to help you.

Susan: wonderful, meal, with a smile, so nice, sure, I've heard, French restaurants, savory, ice cream, chocolate-flavored, mean, vanilla flavor,

Franc: it's true, try, dessert, what, have, a bottle of, mineral water, Waiter, have the bill, take credit card, include, tip, pay you or the cashier, pay you, keep the change, all right.

Waiter: would, some desserts, of course, so a vanilla-flavored, ice cream, mineral water, only accept cash, no, both will do, thank.

2. Study the following sample dialogue. Then strike up a conversation with your partners using the sentences listed in the chart.

A: Good evening, Sir. Have you a reservation?
B: Oh, yes. I'm Bruce. I reserved a table for 2 at 8 p.m..
A: Ok, would you follow me please? Your table is near the window.
B: Great.

1. Good evening, Sir. Have you a reservation?
2. Could I have the menu, please?
3. The meat is too fatty. Could you change it for me?
4. Could I have a doggie bag, please?
5. Do you have vegetarian dishes?
6. Can I have the receipt, please?
7. What are the specialties in your restaurant?
8. Would you like something to drink before dinner?
9. Could you recommend some good wine?
10. How do you like your steak?

III. Focus Listening

A. *Listen to the recording and choose the correct answer for each question.*

1. All of the following contribute to today's French cuisine except _____.
   A. research   B. elaboration
   C. perfection   D. encouragement
2. French cuisine is an integral part of their _____.
   A. culture   B. interest
   C. palate   D. tradition

3. Who once made great contribution to the success of French cuisine?
   A. The queen of Italy   B. Catherine de Medicis
   C. French chefs   D. The king of France
4. From the passage we know that French chefs _____ in 1533.
   A. were less experienced than Italian chefs
   B. gave Italian cooking a real boost
   C. introduced new dishes to Italy
   D. introduced sophisticated techniques to Italy
5. French cuisine is based on _____ according to the passage.
   A. cooking techniques
   B. prices of dishes
   C. local and high-quality products
   D. famous chefs and their reputation

B. Listen to the recording and complete the sentences below.

1. The food is usually good and often excellent; the prices are _____.
2. A number of restaurants call themselves "_____".
3. These restaurants may also serve smaller and cheaper children's _____.
4. The _____ books say that you should leave tips for dinner.
5. The tip is calculated on the basis of the total before the addition of _____.

Section 2 Reading

French Cuisine

French cuisine is one of the most famous cuisines in the world. Traditional French cooking is butter-based and centers on meat, poultry and fish. Today, however, the chefs of many Parisian restaurants are becoming more interested in regional food and in simple, home-style fare which relies on fresh, seasonal ingredients. French cooking tends not to be highly spiced, although fresh herbs like chives and parsley are essential ingredients in the sauces that accompany most savory dishes.

One of the most enjoyable aspects of Paris is the

diversity of places to eat. *Bistros* are small, often moderately-priced restaurants with a limited selection of dishes. *Brasseries* are larger, bustling eateries with immense menus, and most serve food throughout the day and are open late. Cafés (and some wine bars) open early and the majority close by 9 p. m.. They serve drinks and food all day long from a short menu of salads, sandwiches and eggs. At lunch most offer a small choice of hot daily specials.

The waiter usually takes your choice of *entrée* (first course), then the *plat* (main course). Dessert is ordered after you have finished your main course unless there are some hot desserts which have to be ordered at the start of the meal. In most restaurants you will be asked if you would like a drink before ordering food. A typical Apéritif is kir (white wine with a blackcurrant liqueur). Spirits are not generally drunk before a meal in France.

The first course generally includes a choice of salads or vegetables or pâté. Small fish dishes like smoked salmon, frilled sardines, herring, shellfish or oysters are also on offer. Main dishes usually include a selection of meat, poultry or fish served with French fries and vegetables. Highly recommended are *moules marinières* (mussels steamed in wine), and *chèvre tiède* sur un lit de salade (grilled goat's cheese with a mixed-leaf salad).

Prices vary from extremely economical to astronomical. Many places offer a *formule* or fixed-price menu, especially at lunch, and this will almost always offer the best value. If you want a greater choice of dishes, go for the à la carte menu. Remember that a bottle of wine will increase the size of your bill significantly and that coffee usually carries an extra charge.

Prices usually include service. Although you do not have to leave a tip, it is common to do so and is based on 5% ~ 10% of the total.

Vocabulary

accompany /əˈkʌmpəni/ *v.* 陪伴,陪同;为……伴奏
astronomical /ˌæstrəˈnɔmikəl/ *adj.* 天文学的,天文数字的
blackcurrant /blækˈkʌrənt/ *n.* 黑醋栗
bustling /ˈbʌsliŋ/ *adj.* 熙熙攘攘的, 忙乱的
chef /ʃef/ *n.* 厨师

chive /tʃaiv/ n. 细香葱
entree /ˈɔntrei/ n. 主菜,正菜
essential /iˈsenʃəl/ adj. 必要的,重要的,本质的
fare /fɛə/ n. 票价,食品
grill /gril/ v. 烧,烤,炙
herring /ˈheriŋ/ n. 青鱼,鲱
immense /iˈmens/ adj. 极广大的,无边的
ingredient /inˈɡriːdiənt/ n. 原料;要素,因素
moderate /ˈmɔdərit/ adj. 适度的,稳健的,温和的,中等的
mussel /ˈmʌsl/ n. 贻贝
oyster /ˈɔistə/ n. 牡蛎
parsley /ˈpɑːsli/ n. 荷兰芹
poultry /ˈpəultri/ n. 家禽
regional /ˈriːdʒənəl/ adj. 地区的,局部的
sardine /sɑːˈdiːn/ n. 沙丁鱼
savory /ˈseivəri/ adj. 芳香开胃的,美味可口的
special /ˈspeʃəl/ adj. 特殊的,特价的 n. 特价,特价菜

Phrases & Expressions

center on 集中在,着重在
rely on 依靠
tend to 倾向于(有助于,易于,引起,造成,势必)
vary from 不同于
based on 以……为基础

Notes to the Text

1. Cafés:(法语)小餐馆
2. entrée 和 plat:(法语)开胃菜和主菜。在法国,或法式餐厅点菜时,首先点的是主菜前的开胃菜。之后才是主菜。
3. Apéritif:(法语)餐前的开胃酒
4. pâté:混有肉类、肝脏、蔬菜、香料等其他原料的加工熟的细面团。常见法式鹅干酱,鸡肝酱等。
5. formula:(法语)套餐

6. kir：(法语)干白葡萄酒

Exercise 1   Reading Comprehension

Answer the following Questions according to the text.

1. Do you think French cuisine is changing today? Why or why not?
2. Many French people drink whisky as an aperitif, right?
3. What is the typical drink before meals in French restaurant?
4. What do cafés serve in France?
5. Should we leave a tip before we leave the restaurant in France?

Exercise 2   Word Training

Fill in the blanks with the words given below. Change the form where necessary.

| poultry | accompany | essential | regional | special |
| bustling | astronomical | moderate | ingredient | immense |

1. The menu features roast meats and _____.
2. His wife was astonished at the _____ sum of money he had spent
3. _____ is a dish or meal given prominence in a restaurant.
4. While a _____ amount of stress can be beneficial, too much stress can exhaust you.
5. I like this text book, because every text in it is _____ by illustrations.
6. It's almost impossible to find him in the _____ ocean.
7. There is a list of _____ on the side of the packet
8. Food and water are _____ elements to our life.
9. This district is getting more and more prosperous and _____.
10. The Hotel's menu is based on Hawaiian _____ cuisine.

Section 3   Translation

Ⅰ. *Translate the following sentences into Chinese.*
1. Noisettes d'aneau (法式烤羊排) are small, tender lamb cutlets fried in butter and served

with a variety of garnishes.
2. Chawanmushi（日式蒸蛋）is a thick egg custard steamed in a small lidded pot and served with vegetables, shrimp and other seafood.
3. Gefüllte Forella（德式鳟鱼）is wild trout steamed and served with a salad and mushrooms.
4. These sausages made from pork intestines are grilled or fried and served with onions.
5. This dish is served with a delicious white wine sauce.

Ⅱ. *Translate the following sentences into English.*
1. 你的蔬菜怎么做？是煮还是炒？
2. 在法国用餐后我要留多少小费？
3. 麻烦您能告诉我今天的例汤是什么吗？
4. 这样做蜗牛美味极佳。
5. 这个有草药味道的土豆奶油浓汤要和厚片香肠一起吃。

Section 4   Classified Word Bank

Read the following words and expressions aloud and then learn them by heart.

French Cuisine	法国菜
1. Braised Chicken with Cream Sauce	束法鸡
2. Chicken Meat Ball Soup	鸡肉丸子汤
3. Chicken Meat Salad	鸡肉色拉
4. Cold Grilled Chicken	冷烤鸡
5. Cucumber Salad	黄瓜色拉
6. Eel and Egg Roll	烤鳗鱼鸡蛋卷
7. Eggplant Salad	茄子沙拉
8. Fish Roll	鱼卷
9. Fried Fish with Egg	蛋煎鱼
10. Fried Pig Chop	煎猪排
11. Fried Prawn Meat	煎龙虾肉
12. Fried Snail and White Wine	白酒田螺
13. Grilled Mutton	烤羊肉
14. Onion Soup	洋葱汤

15.	Prawn Salad	龙虾色拉
16.	Savory Fish Soup	多味鱼汤
17.	Spiced nails	五香蜗牛
18.	Stewed beef with Red Wine	红酒炖牛肉
19.	Stewed Veal	炖小牛肉
20.	Thin Beef Steak	薄牛排

Unit 3 Muslim Cuisine

Section 1 Listening and Speaking

I. Listen and Repeat

Dialogue 1 Turkish Breakfast

Cora is from Turkey. She is now working in China. She meets her colleague Mr. Gao in a restaurant in the morning.

Cora: Hi, Mr. Gao. It's really a surprise to meet you here!

Gao: Hi, Cora. What a coincidence! I'm having breakfast here. Would you like to join me?

Cora: I'd love to. I like Chinese food. There are a lot of varieties to choose from.

Gao: So, what do you Turks have for breakfast?

Cora: Well, breakfast is very important to our Turkish people. At breakfast we usually have Turkish tea, olives, white cheese, etc.

Gao: I hear Turkish tea is very famous. Can you say something about it?

Cora: Well, Turkish Tea is an unmissable drink at breakfast. We call it "Cay". It is drunk in a thinly small tea glass.

Gao: Oh, do you add something to the tea?

Cora: Many people drink with sugar and in most cases the sugar is cut in rectangular pieces. At people's homes, tea is prepared in a special pot called "Caydanlik". You can drink either light or dark tea though many Turks do prefer the dark. If you can't drink the dark you need to mention it. The best way to tell this is "Açlk Çay lutfen", which means "Light tea please" in Turkish.

Gao: Thank you for telling me that. But can you tell me something about cheese?

Cora: OK. There are many kinds of cheese in Turkey. The white cheese is mostly a product from the cow or lamb. The rare ghost cheese has a salty taste and is similar to the feta cheese of the Greek. Eski Kaşar is a kind of old yellow cheese produced all around Turkey. And there is the east cheese which is of the top quality.

Gao: I like cheese. If I have a chance to go to Turkey, I'll try them.

Cora: They are really worth trying.

Dialogue 2   Turkish and Chinese Breakfast

After breakfast, the conversation continued on the way to their company.

Cora: In big cities as both men and women have to work, they do not spend much time for breakfast and prefer to buy a "simit", "poğaca" or "börek" on their way to work.

Gao: Oh, Cora. I don't understand Turkish.

Cora: I'm sorry. Those are the names of food. Simit is the famous round sesame bread. Many people eat it as breakfast with a piece of cheese and tea. Poğaça is kind of pastry filled with either white cheese, minced meat, potatoes or spinach. Börek is the famous pastry which has several sorts, just like different kinds of bread.

Gao: Oh, breakfast is really important in Turkey.

Cora: Yes. And bread is the main and most consumed product in Turkey. Bread is eaten with every meal and many people even eat it with macaroni or rice. Although there are different sorts of bread produced, the main one is the white bread.

Gao: But in China, people seldom have bread for breakfast.

Cora: I know that. As a matter of fact, we have a lot of other food and dishes for breakfast. Miss Gao, can you tell me something about Chinese breakfast?

Gao: OK. Sometimes we eat sandwiches and hamburgers at McDonal's or Kentucky Fried Chicken. Of course, that is the western style breakfast. For our traditional one, we would like to have deep-fried twisted dough sticks or steamed stuffed buns with soybean milk or jellied beancurd. Actually there is a large variety for us to choose from.

Cora: Oh, it's wonderful.

Gao: How about going to a Chinese restaurant for breakfast tomorrow morning?

Cora: Great! I'd love to.

Gao: Then, I'll search on the internet for a good Chinese restaurant. I'll call you this evening.

Cora: Okay, thank you very much.

Gao: That's all right.

II. Act Out

1. Listen to the dialogue. Then practice it with your partners using the words and expressions below to help you.

> **Cora**: like the food, I ordered, so glad, you enjoy, it's like, Chinese dumplings, do you like, Hamsi, yes, we, eat, a lot, at least, 40 dishes, made of, hamsi, include, dessert, have a try, next time, typical Turkish Cuisine.
> **Gao**: yes, all tasty, especially, Manti, you are right, you mean, little fish, similar to, anchovy, interesting, imagine, dessert, little fish, also, like Turkish Pizza, dishes, cheese and yogurt, Chinese restaurant, introduce, cuisine.

2. Study the following sample dialogue. Then strike up a conversation with your partners using the sentences listed in the chart.

A: For those gastronomists, Turkish cuisine is worthy of exploration.
B: I think so. Turkish cuisine is palatable and tempting.
A: Yeah, One of the most famous dishes is Kebap.

1. For those gastronomists, Turkish cuisine is worthy of exploration.
2. Turkish cuisine is very rich in flavor with influences from Central Europe and Southern Arabia.
3. The Italian pasta and the French sauce are very famous.
4. French cuisine was heavily influenced by Italian cuisine.
5. Oriental cuisine, needless to say, is represented by Chinese cuisine.
6. Turkey is known for an abundance and diversity of foodstuff.
7. Authentic Muslim Cuisine is based on delicious Turkish Cuisine.
8. Italian cuisine is well known for its use of a diverse variety of pasta.
9. The main ingredients of Turkish cuisine are meat, vegetables and beans.
10. Contrary to the prevalent Western impression of Turkish food, spices and herbs are used very simply and sparingly.

III. Focus Listening

A. *Listen to the recording and choose the correct answer for each question.*

1. Who is starving and wants to eat out?

A. Mary   B. Fred   C. Mark   D. Susan
2. Who hasn't got much money?
   A. Alison   B. Anne   C. Felix   D. Fred
3. To what food is Fred allergic?
   A. Beef   B. Mutton.   C. Seafood   D. Pork
4. Which of the following food doesn't Fred like to eat?
   A. Fish   B. Mutton   C. Beef   D. Chicken
5. What kind of restaurant will they have to go to?
   A. A vegetarian restaurant   B. A carnivore restaurant
   C. A French restaurant   D. A Thai restaurant

B. Listen to the recording and complete the sentences below.

1. The meat of Turkish cuisine includes beef, mutton and _____.
2. Turkish chefs like to use tomatoes, _____, yoghurt and spices.
3. The delicious flavor with fresh materials is generally not _____ though the well-made dishes seem very simple.
4. There are many kinds of cooking methods, such as roast, _____ and cook in clay ovens.
5. Turks sometimes string pieces of mutton or chicken together with tomatoes and green peppers and grill on the _____.

Section 2   Reading

Turkish Cuisine

There are three major world cuisines—Oriental cuisine, the European cuisine and Muslim cuisine. Oriental cuisine, needless to say of course, is represented by Chinese cuisine. And the French cuisine with high reputation around the world is the prolocutor of the European cuisine. As for Muslim cuisine, it is not Malan Noodles we can see everywhere in China. Actually the authentic Muslim cuisine is based on delicious Turkish cuisine.

The evolution of this glorious cuisine was not

an accident. Similar to other grand cuisines of the world, it is a result of the combination of three key elements.

Firstly, a nurturing environment is irreplaceable. Turkey is a country across the Eurasian continent and the soil is fertile. The climate is more moderate than the European continent, and also not as hot as other countries in Western Asia. It is known for an abundance and diversity of foodstuff due to its rich resources and regional differentiation.

Secondly, the legacy of an Imperial Kitchen is inescapable. Hundreds of cooks, all specializing in different types of dishes, and all eager to please the royal palate, no doubt had their influence in perfecting the cuisine as we know it today. The Palace Kitchen, supported by a complex social organization, specialization of labor, worldwide trade, and total control of the Spice Road, all reflected the culmination of wealth and the flourishing of culture in the capital of a mighty Empire.

Finally, the longevity of social organization should not be taken lightly either. The Turkish State of Anatolia is a millennium old and so, naturally, is its cuisine.

A survey of the types of dishes according to their ingredients may be helpful to explain the basic structure of Turkish cuisine. Otherwise there may appear to be an overwhelming variety of dishes, each with a unique combination of ingredients and its own way of preparation and presentation. All dishes can be conveniently categorized: grain-based, grilled meats, vegetables, seafood, desserts and beverages.

The foundation of the cuisine is based on grains (rice and wheat) and vegetables. Each category of dishes contains only one or two types of main ingredients. Turks are purists in their culinary taste, that is, the dishes are supposed to bring out the flavor of the main ingredient rather than hiding it under sauces or spices. Thus, the eggplant should taste like eggplant, lamb like lamb, pumpkin like pumpkin, and so on.

Contrary to the prevalent Western impression of Turkish food, spices and herbs are used very simply and sparingly. For example, either mint or dill weed are used with zucchini, parsley is used with eggplant, a few cloves and garlic has its place in some cold vegetable dishes, and cumin is sprinkled over red lentil soup or mixed in ground meat when making "köfte" (meat balls). Lemon and yogurt are used to complement both meat and vegetable dishes as well as to balance the taste of olive oil or meat. Most desserts and fruit dishes do not call for any spices. So their flavors are refined and subtle.

Vocabulary

categorize /ˈkætigəraiz/ vt. 把……进行分类；把……列作
clove /kləuv/ n. 丁香
culmination /ˌkʌmiˈneiʃən/ n. 顶点，极点，最高潮
cumin /ˈkʌmin/ n. 莳萝，土茴香子
differentiation /ˌdifərənʃiˈeiʃən/ n. 辨别，区别，区分
dill /dil/ n. 莳萝，小茴香
glorious /ˈglɔːriəs/ adj. 光荣的，辉煌的，壮丽的
longevity /lɔnˈdʒeviti/ n. 长寿，寿命
Muslim /ˈmuzlim/ n. 穆斯林，伊斯兰教信徒
nurture /ˈnəːtʃə/ n. 养育，培育
overwhelming /ˌəuvəˈwelmiŋ/ adj. 势不可挡的，压倒一切的
prolocutor /prəuˈlɔkjutə/ n. 代言人，发言人，主持会议者
refined /riˈfaind/ adj. 精炼的，精制的；举止文雅的
represent /ˌrepriˈzent/ v. 代表，象征
reputation /ˌrepjuˈteiʃən/ n. 名誉，名声
sparingly /ˈspɛəriŋli/ ad. 节俭地，节约地
sprinkle /ˈspriŋkl/ v. 喷洒，洒（小液滴）
subtle /ˈsʌtl/ adj. 微妙的，细微的，含蓄的，狡猾的

Phrases & Expressions

be known for 因……而众所周知
specialize in 专攻，专门从事于（某一科目），专门研究
be eager to 渴望做……
be helpful to 有助于……
appear to 看来像是，看来似乎

Notes to the Text

1. Muslim cuisine：穆斯林菜系，世界三大菜系之一。

2. Malan Noodles：马兰拉面,清真面馆连锁店,在中国有很多家。
3. Eurasian continent：欧亚大陆。
4. Anatolia：安纳托利亚,亚洲西部半岛,小亚细亚的旧称。
5. "köfte"：一种土耳其肉丸。

Exercise 1 Reading Comprehension

Answer the following Questions according to the text.

1. What are the three major world cuisines?
2. What cuisine is the prolocutor of the European cuisine?
3. What may help explain the basic structure of Turkish cuisine?
4. What does the sentence "Turks are purists in their culinary taste" mean?
5. What is the main function of Lemon and yogurt used in Turkish cuisine?

Exercise 2 Word Training

Fill in the blanks with the words given below. Change the form where necessary.

| reputation | longevity | glorious | sprinkle | subtle |
| nurture | represent | refined | overwhelming | sparingly |

1. The general secretary may _____ the president at official ceremonies.
2. Somehow the restaurant has a very bad _____.
3. They won a _____ victory in the campaign.
4. The villagers in this area enjoy good health and _____.
5. The _____ majority of small businesses went broke during the economic crisis.
6. His speech and manner are _____.
7. _____ the meat with salt and place in the pan.
8. I have noticed the _____ gradation in color in this painting.
9. Use the milk _____, there's not much left.
10. Parents want to know the best way to _____ and raise their child to adulthood

Section 3   Translation

Ⅰ. *Translate the following sentences into Chinese.*
1. Authentic Muslim cuisine is based on delicious Turkish cuisine.
2. It is not easy to discern a basic element or a single dominant feature, like the Italian "pasta" or the French "sauce".
3. Early Turks cultivated wheat and used it liberally, in several types of leavened and unleavened breads baked in clay ovens, fried on a griddle, or buried in embers.
4. Contrary to the prevalent Western impression of Turkish food, spices and herbs are used very simply and sparingly.
5. Most desserts and fruit dishes do not call for any spices. So their flavors are refined and subtle.

Ⅱ. *Translate the following sentences into English.*
1. 总体上来说,土耳其人吃早餐的时间都比较长。爱吃土耳其茶、橄榄和白乳酪做的早餐。
2. 在这些天里,手工艺品、纺织品、玻璃制品和其他家庭用品都在这儿以最合算的价格摆卖。
3. 土耳其菜就像它的肚皮舞一样,无拘无束,自由式的,充满了热情还带有一点点神秘。
4. 你会发现,土耳其菜并不仅仅是你印象里的烤肉,而是有各种各样的烹饪方法,比如烤、炖和炉烤。
5. 东方菜系不用说,当然以中国菜为代表。

Section 4   Classified Word Bank

Read the following words and expressions aloud and then learn them by heart.

Turkish Cuisine	土耳其菜
1. Ahtapot Salatas	小章鱼沙拉
2. Baklava	果仁蜜饯点心/千层酥
3. Cerkes Tavugu	加入调味料的鸡肉冷盘
4. Cig Kofte	土耳其肉丸子
5. Doner Kebap	旋转烤肉

6. Ekmek	土耳其面包
7. Gozleme	包馅煎饼
8. Kebap	土耳其烤肉
9. keskek	土耳其特色餐
10. Manti	土耳其饺子
11. Meusim Salatasi	土耳其式季节沙拉
12. Meze	开胃菜
13. Pancar Tursusu	腌甜菜
14. Pide	土耳其比萨饼
15. Piyaz	菜豆沙拉
16. Porsiyon Doner	烤鸡夹面包
17. Sade Pilav	土耳其炒饭
18. Sigara Boregi	土耳其炸起司春卷
19. Vegetaren Meze	果蔬小点
20. Yaprak Dolmasi	土耳其香叶包米饭

Unit 4 Tea and Coffee

Section 1 Listening and Speaking

Ⅰ. Listen and Repeat

Dialogue 1   In the Teahouse

Mr. Wang is talking about Chinese Tea with Amanda.

Wang: Amanda, you've been in China for a long time. Do you like Chinese tea?

Amanda: Yes, of course. And I've even taken a course about it.

Wang: Really? What have you learnt from the course?

Amanda: Quite a lot, such as tea growing, processing, brewing, drinking, etc. I've also learned something about the tea set, tea manners and tea ceremony.

Wang: Sounds interesting.

Amanda: Yes, after the course I know Chinese tea has multiple health care functions. It lowers blood pressure, protects the heart, helps to prevent obesity and tooth decay, boosts immunity, etc. Sounds like a TV commercial but it has been working on more than billions of Chinese people over thousands of years.

Wang: Maybe I should also offer courses about tea in my teahouse here. It would attract a lot of foreigners like you here.

Amanda: Yes, you really should do that. It's announced in November 2001 that research has found scientific evidence that Chinese tea can actually help to prevent cancer. It's more than just empty talk now. I'm sure that people would pay attention to this and enjoy drinking tea.

Wang: Yes. Tea is a beverage that can not only quench one's thirst, but also make people healthy.

Amanda: It's true. And when I get home after a busy day, I make myself a cup of tea and drink it while sitting comfortably on the sofa. A sip of hot tea down the throat, the whole world loosens up. The feeling is so wonderful.

Wang: It is because Chinese tea's impact on one's psychological health is immediate.

Amanda: Yes. A cup of tea in the morning sets the pace of the day. Sitting and chatting with a few good friends over cups of tea makes life worth living. Brewing Chinese tea calms me down. Chinese tea is more than just something to drink. It has in fact become a way of life for me.

Wang: Oh, you are a Chinese now and you've been assimilated into the Chinese tea culture.

Amanda: I'm happy to hear that. You're an expert on Chinese tea. Could you tell me something about tea manners?

Wang: Oh, there're quite a lot. But one thing is a must. You may see in the teahouse here that after the waiter pours a cup of tea for a customer, the customer will tap on the table with his bended index and middle fingers. This is just a gesture of thanks.

Amanda: It's so interesting.

Wang: Yes. And younger generation greets elder generation with a cup of tea. That is a way to show their respect. But please note that in the old days only people of lower rank serve tea to the people with higher rank. Today, the society is more liberal. Parents may pour tea for his kids at home, and bosses may do it for his subordinates at restaurants. But in formal occasions, it is still inappropriate for lower rank people to expect their seniors to pour tea for them.

Amanda: Oh, It's so complicated. Mr. Wang, there is a tea ceremony over there. Let go and have a look.

Wang: Okay.

Dialogue 2　In the Starbucks

Alvin and Linda have come to the Starbucks during lunch break.

Waiter: Welcome to Starbucks. What can I do for you?
Alvin: I think I'm going to have a cup of decaf mocha.
Waiter: Medium or Large.
Alvin: Large please.
Waiter: We've used up all the mugs here. Shall we put your coffee in a paper cup?
Alvin: OK.
Waiter: Thank you. Do you want to add topping or syrup?
Alvin: Mocha syrup please.
Waiter: That's $ 5.5.
Linda: I'd like to order the same coffee without extra syrup.
Waiter: Oh, a large decaf mocha without extra syrup. It's $ 5, please.
Alvin: Linda, let's go and sit on the sofa over there. There are so many people here.
Linda: OK. Most of them are having a rest here. But some are talking about their business.
Alvin: Yes, some Chinese businessmen like to discuss their business in the café. The other day I saw an officer even having a meeting here.
Linda: This is my first time in the Starbucks. I like the atmosphere, but it's a little noisy.
Alvin: You'll get used to it.
Linda: Oh, maybe. The coffee tastes good. It stays in my mouth for quite a long time. The overall flavor is fantastic.
Alvin: That's high quality coffee.
Linda: I see. I know nothing about coffee except coffee beans. Can you tell me something about it?
Alvin: No problem. The history of coffee can date back to thousands of years ago.
Linda: Wow!
Alvin: The first coffee plants are said to have come from the Horn of Africa. Originally, coffee beans were taken as a food and not as a beverage.
Linda: That's interesting. How could they eat it?
Alvin: East African tribes would grind the coffee cherries together, mix them with animal fat and make them into little balls, which were said to give warriors much-needed energy for battle. Later, around the year 1000 A.D., Ethiopians concocted a type of wine by fermenting the dried beans in water. Coffee also grew naturally on the Arabian

Peninsula, and it was there, during the 11th century that coffee was first developed into a hot drink.

Linda: You are really an expert on it.

Alvin: I like coffee, so I learn something about it. According to one story, a goatherd noticed that his herd became friskier than usual after consuming the red cherries of a wild coffee shrub. Curious, he tasted the fruit himself. He was delighted by its invigorating effects. It's the origin story of coffee.

Linda: Very interesting.

Alvin: Yes, nowadays one third of the world's population starts the day with coffee.

Ⅱ. Act Out

1. Listen to the dialogue. Then practice it with your partners using the words and expressions below to help you.

> **Waiter:** welcome, coffee bar, medium, large, want, add, topping, syrup, anything else, $4.5, what, madam, coffee for the week, anything else, OK, $8, thank, change.
> **James:** think, decaf Caramel Macchiato, small, syrup, no.
> **Lisa:** order, decaf black coffee, chocolate biscuits, here you are.

2. Study the following sample dialogue. Then strike up a conversation with your partners using the sentences listed in the chart.

A: Coffee is conducive to refresh ourselves and eliminate drowsiness.

B: I agree. But drinking too much coffee will do harm to people's health.

A: That's true.

1. Coffee is conducive to refresh ourselves and eliminate drowsiness.
2. Coffee has stimulating effects and makes people wide awake.
3. Coffee could lift your mood and might stop your headaches.
4. Coffee can help people maintain a clear mind.
5. Drinking too much coffee will make people irritable and absent-minded.
6. Caffeine interrupts the brain hormone that sends people into sleep.
7. For most people, very little bad comes from coffee drinking, but a lot of good.

8. Having a cup of coffee late in the day will affect your sleep.
9. Overall, the research shows that coffee is far more healthful than it is harmful.
10. Excessive intake of coffee will lead to melanoma accumulation in the body, which will cause bad complexion.

III. Focus Listening

A. Listen to the recording and choose the correct answer for each question.

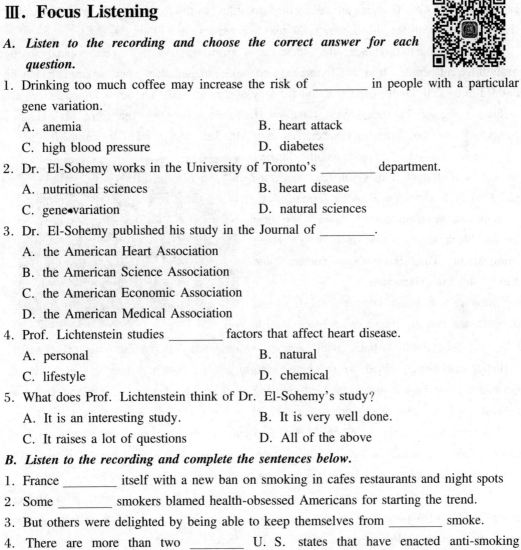

1. Drinking too much coffee may increase the risk of _____ in people with a particular gene variation.
   A. anemia B. heart attack
   C. high blood pressure D. diabetes
2. Dr. El-Sohemy works in the University of Toronto's _____ department.
   A. nutritional sciences B. heart disease
   C. gene·variation D. natural sciences
3. Dr. El-Sohemy published his study in the Journal of _____.
   A. the American Heart Association
   B. the American Science Association
   C. the American Economic Association
   D. the American Medical Association
4. Prof. Lichtenstein studies _____ factors that affect heart disease.
   A. personal B. natural
   C. lifestyle D. chemical
5. What does Prof. Lichtenstein think of Dr. El-Sohemy's study?
   A. It is an interesting study. B. It is very well done.
   C. It raises a lot of questions. D. All of the above

B. Listen to the recording and complete the sentences below.
1. France _____ itself with a new ban on smoking in cafes restaurants and night spots
2. Some _____ smokers blamed health-obsessed Americans for starting the trend.
3. But others were delighted by being able to keep themselves from _____ smoke.
4. There are more than two _____ U. S. states that have enacted anti-smoking restrictions.
5. _____ became the first U. S. state to ban smoking in restaurants and bars.

Section 2 Reading

Chinese Tea

There are hundreds of varieties of Chinese tea. They can mainly be classified into five categories. The classifications are determined according to the method of tea processing. The five types are green tea, black tea, brick tea, scented tea, and Oolong tea.

With its natural fragrance, the oldest tea is green tea, which is very popular among many different people. It is not fermented and baked immediately after picking. It can be divided into many kinds, depending on the way it is processed. The most famous green tea includes Longjing Tea from West Lake of Hangzhou, Maofeng Tea from Mt. Huang, Biluochun Tea from Jiangsu, Yinzhen Tea from Mt. Jun, and Yunwu Tea from Mt. Lu.

Black tea is favored mainly among foreigners. Different from green tea, black tea is a kind of fermented tea. After fermentation, its color changes from green to black. The most famous black tea in China includes Qi Hong from Anhui, Dian Hong from Yunnan, and Ying Hong from Guangdong.

Oolong tea, which combines the freshness of green tea and the fragrance of black tea, is becoming increasingly popular with people. Oolong tea has various medical benefits, including anti-aging, blood fat reducing, weight losing, health promoting, etc. Fujian, Guangdong and Taiwan are the major producing areas of this kind of tea. Oolong tea grows on cliffs, which makes it difficult to harvest. Therefore it becomes very precious.

Scented tea, popular in North China, is a mixture of green tea with flower petals of roses, jasmines, orchids and plums. The combination is through an elaborate process. The most famous scented tea is Jasmine tea produced in Fujian Province.

Brick tea, or compressed tea, is shaped like a brick, and is mainly produced in Hunan, Hubei, Sichuan, Yunnan and Guangxi Zhuang Autonomous Region. Brick tea is made from black or green tea and pressed into blocks, which makes it easier to transport. This kind of tea is popular with the ethnic minority people in border regions. The most famous brick tea is "Pu'er Tea" made in Yunnan Province.

There are other kinds of tea. Among them is the white tea, which is special but not very familiar to most people. Just as its name suggests, this type of tea is as white as silver. It is mainly produced in Zhenhe and Fuding in Fujian Province, but popular in Southeast Asia. Famous varieties include "Silver Needle" and "White Peony".

The Chinese people attach great importance to the act of "savoring tea", which is not only a way to discern good tea from mediocre tea, but also a way to take delight in their reverie and in tea-drinking itself. Snatching a bit of leisure from a busy schedule, making a kettle of strong tea, securing a serene space, and serving and drinking tea by yourself can help banish fatigue and frustration, improve your thinking ability and inspire you with enthusiasm. You may also imbibe it slowly in small sips to appreciate the subtle allure of tea-drinking, until your spirits soar up and up into a sublime aesthetic realm. Buildings, gardens, ornaments and tea sets are the elements that form the ambience for savoring tea. A tranquil, refreshing, comfortable and neat locale is certainly desirable for drinking tea. Chinese gardens are well known in the world and beautiful Chinese landscapes are too numerous to count. Teahouses tucked away in gardens and nestled beside the natural beauty of mountains and rivers are enchanting places of repose for people to rest and recreate themselves.

Vocabulary

aesthetic /i:s'θetik/ adj. 美学的,审美的,有美感的
allure /ə'ljuə/ v. 引诱,吸引
banish /'bæniʃ/ v. 驱逐,放逐
cliff /'klif/ n. 悬崖,峭壁
elaborate /i'læbərit/ adj. 精心制作的,详尽的,复杂的
enchanting /in'tʃɑ:ntiŋ/ adj. 令人喜悦的,迷人的,可爱的
ethnic /'eθnik/ adj. 民族的,种族的,具有民族特色的
fatigue /fə'ti:g/ n. 疲劳,十分劳累
imbibe /im'baib/ v. 喝,饮(尤指烈酒)
jasmine /'dʒæzmin/ n. 茉莉

kettle /ˈketl/ n. 水壶
locale /ləʊˈkɑːl/ n. (某事发生的)现场,场所
mediocre /ˌmiːdiˈəʊkə/ adj. 平庸的,一般的,不好不坏的
nestle /ˈnesəl/ v. (使)舒适地安顿下来,(使)偎依,(使)依靠
petal /ˈpetl/ n. 花瓣
process /ˈprəʊses/ v. n. 加工,处理
realm /relm/ n. 王国,领域
scented /ˈsentid/ adj. 有香味的,有气味的,芬芳的
snatch /snætʃ/ n. 强夺,攫取,抓住(机会)
sublime /səˈblaim/ adj. 卓越的,超群的,令人赞叹的
tranquil /ˈtræŋkwil/ adj. 安静的,宁静的

Phrases & Expressions

classify into 把……分类为
be favored among 在……中受到欢迎
be originated in 起源于
be popular with 受欢迎
inspire sb. with sth. 用……激励某人

Notes to the Text

1. Longjing Tea:龙井茶,盛产于杭州西湖龙井村,著名绿茶。
2. "Qi Hong"(which originated in Anhui), "Dian Hong"(which originated in Yunnan), and "Ying Hong"(which originated in Guangdong):安徽祁红、云南滇红和广东瀛红三种著名红茶。
3. Oolong tea:乌龙茶。半发酵茶,以本茶的创始人而得名。
4. Brick tea, or compressed tea:砖茶。内蒙古地区用以煮奶茶。

Exercise 1　Reading Comprehension

Answer the following Questions according to the text.

1. How many types can Chinese tea be classified into? What are they?
2. Can you list some famous green tea?

3. Which places are very famous for brick tea?
4. What are the elements that form the ambience for savoring tea?
5. What kind of locale is desirable for drinking tea in the text?

Exercise 2   Word Training

Fill in the blanks with the words given below. Change the form where necessary.

> snatch   sublime   nestle   fatigue   enchant
> elaborate process   banish   allure   tranquil

1. Your application for a mortgage is being _____ now.
2. She almost _____ the letter from my hand.
3. Her children had the best, most _____ birthday parties in the neighborhood. elaborate
4. The spy was dishonorably _____ from the land.
5. Rewards _____ men to brave danger.
6. Interrupting an opera on television for a pet-food commercial is going from the _____ to the ridiculous.
7. Coca is well-known for reducing hunger, thirst and _____.
8. Both my husband and I love the _____ life in the country.
9. If you do not mind my saying so, your smile is quite _____.
10. I _____ down on the big sofa and began to read novels.

Section 3   Translation

I. *Translate the following sentences into Chinese.*

1. It lowers blood pressure, protects the heart, helps to prevent obesity, prevents tooth decay and increases immunity, etc.
2. Starbucks has about ten thousand stores in the United States.
3. When we take a sip of the hard-earned tea, we realize that the process itself is what tastes the best.
4. Tea drinkers had lower levels of the stress hormone after exposure to stress.
5. It was suggested that coffee lovers drink decaf instead of caffeinated coffee.

Ⅱ. *Translate the following sentences into English.*
1. 巴西被称为咖啡的王国。
2. 咖啡的历史可以追溯到 9 世纪。
3. 经常喝茶可以预防某些疾病。
4. 绿茶只是经过加热制成的，没有经过任何发酵工艺。
5. 中国人喜欢喝茶，并且经常用茶来款待朋友和客人。

Section 4　Classified Word Bank

Read the following words and expressions aloud and then learn them by heart.

1.	Jasmine Tea	茉莉花茶
2.	Black Tea	红茶
3.	Chrysanthemum Tea	菊花茶
4.	Osmanthus Tea	桂花茶
5.	Tibetan Tea	酥油茶
6.	Alishan Mountain Tea	阿里山茶
7.	Emei Green Tea	峨眉竹叶青
8.	Fuan Silver Needle	福安银针
9.	Baihao Silver Needle	白毫银针
10.	Dongting Green Tea	洞庭碧螺春
11.	Pu'er Tea Bricks of Seven Pieces	普洱七子饼茶
12.	Osmanthus Oolong	桂花乌龙
13.	Rose Tea	玫瑰茶
14.	Ginseng Tea	人参茶
15.	Espresso	浓缩咖啡
16.	Cappuccino	卡布基诺
17.	Black Coffee	黑咖啡
18.	Blue Mountain Coffee	蓝山咖啡（牙买加）
19.	Mocha	摩卡咖啡
20.	Latte	拿铁咖啡

Part V
Food & Drinks

Unit 5 Wine

Section 1 Listening and Speaking

I. Listen and Repeat

Dialogue 1 In the Bar

Tom, John, Mary and Sally come to the bar together.

Waiter: May I help you, ladies and gentlemen?
Mary: I don't know what I want. I'm not really a drinker.
Waiter: An aperitif or some white wine?
Mary: Um… A Sunrise Beer.
Waiter: I don't believe I know that one. How about our special cocktail?
Mary: That sounds good. How about you, Sally?
Sally: I don't drink at all. Do you serve soft drinks?
Waiter: Of course, ma'am. But What about a non-alcoholic cocktail?
Sally: Sounds interesting. I'll take that.
Waiter: What would you like to drink, gentlemen?
Tom: Well, none of that stuff they're drinking, eh John?
John: No, Tom. We'll have the usual beer, I suppose.
Tom: Okay.
Waiter: Any special brand, sir?
Tom: What about your local brew? I hear it's good.
Waiter: It is Five Star Beer. Bottled or draught?
John: Let's try the draught.
Waiter: Fine. A special cocktail and one non-alcoholic cocktail for the ladies, and two draught Five Star Beer for the gentlemen.
Sally: Can we have some snacks?
Waiter: Certainly, I'll get a fresh supply. Just moment, please.

Dialogue 2 In a Bar of the Hotel
Bartender: Good evening, sir! What'll you have?

Guest: I'll have a Scotch.

Bartender: We have Chivas Regal, Johnny Walker Blue Label, Queen Ann. Which would you like?

Guest: Give me a Chivas Regal.

Bartender: Royal Salute or 12 years?

Guest: Royal Salute.

Bartender: One Chivas Regal Royal Salute. And How would you like your Scotch, straight up or on the rocks?

Guest: On the rocks.

Bartender: Here you are, sir. A Scotch on the rocks.

Guest: Thank you. Now how much do I owe you?

Bartender: A Chivas Regal Royal Salute is 50 yuan plus 10% service charge. So the total is 55 yuan. But you don't have to pay right now. You can hold the payment of the bill until you decide to leave

Guest: Really? In American bars you pay drink by drink as you get it.

Bartender: But isn't that too much trouble?

Guest: Yes, but it is much safer. You see, American bars can be very crowded and it is very hard to keep an eye on everyone. Besides you can never know what may happen when people are drunk.

Bartender: I see. But we've never had the experience of a guest sneaking out on us without paying his bill.

Guest: Well, the way I see it, you've been pushing your luck and you've been lucky so far. That's all. OK, here is 60 yuan and you can keep the change.

Bartender: That's very kind of you, sir. But we don't accept tips. Here is your change.

Guest: Sorry. I don't know that. You see, I just got here from America. No tipping. That's good. But how can you survive without tips.

Bartender: You know, people in service industries in China can get almost the same wage as employees in other businesses.

Guest: Oh, I see. But in America it is customary to tip taxi drivers, waiters and waitresses, hotel boys, doormen, barbers, because people working at these jobs usually receive a low basic salary, Tips are quite necessary to supplement their income.

Bartender: I see. But how much should people tip them?

Guest: Well, that depends. But in America it is customary to tip anything from 10% to 20%. But today most people decide the size of tip according to the quality of the service. If the service is good, people will leave a big tip, if not, a small tip or possibly no tip at all.

II. Act Out

1. **Listen to the dialogue. Then practice it with your partners using the words and expressions below to help you.**

> **Waiter**: What'll it be, sir, Tequila, Vodka, Rum, Beer, of course, Bourbon whisky, famous in America, no problem, 60 yuan, plus, 10 percent, service charge, 66 yuan, yes, pay me, thank.
>
> **John**: What wine, you, have, do you have, whisky, sound, good, make, on the rocks, how much, include, gratuity, pay you, or pay at the register, here, money, pleasure.

2. **Study the following sample dialogue. Then strike up a conversation with your partners using the sentences listed in the chart.**

A: What will you have, sir?
B: **A gin martini, please.**
A: Here you are.
B: Thank you.

1. **A gin martini, please.**
2. Two alcoholic cocktails, please.
3. One vodka martini, please.
4. Double tequila sunrise, please.
5. Do you have brandy Alexander?
6. Scotch up, please.
7. I'd like a whisky with soda.
8. I'll have a draft beer.
9. I'll have a Scotch on the rocks and my friend will have a perfect Manhattan.
10. I hear the best Chinese liquor is Maotai. I'd like to try it.

III. Focus Listening

A. **Listen to the recording and choose the correct answer for each question.**

1. According to the passage it is _____ to give a description of American laws concerning

185

alcohol?

  A. easy   B. hard   C. necessary   D. positive

2. What kind of beer is known as "three-two" beer?

  A. It is rather weak beer.

  B. It is extremely strong beer.

  C. It contains 3 percent alcohol.

  D. It contains 2 percent alcohol.

3. Which of the following statements is not true?

  A. Some places don't allow the sale of alcohol on Sundays.

  B. The alcohol shelves in some bars are locked over on Sundays

  C. Some places permit alcohol to be sold on Sunday mornings and evenings.

  D. You are not allowed to drink beer in public places in some parts of America.

4. What does the sentence "Some bars are allowed to sell 'Mixed drinks'" mean?

  A. Some bars can sell the mixture of wine and beer.

  B. Some bars can sell both beer and wine.

  C. Some bars can sell not only beer and wine, but also spirits

  D. Some bars can sell only beer, wine and soft drinks.

5. The period when many bars sell drinks at lower-than-usual prices is called _____.

  A. low hour   B. usual hour

  C. discount hour   D. happy hour

B. Listen to the recording and complete the sentences below.

1. _____ drinking age varies from place to place but is generally between 18 to 21.

2. Some places permit the _____ of beer at 18 but spirits only at 21.

3. Young people therefore often drive from one place to another with more _____ drinking laws.

4. In most places these drinking laws are fairly _____ enforced.

5. On such occasions Americans often show their driving _____, which have their date of birth written on them.

Section 2 Reading

Wine: How Much Is Good for You?

  Glass of wine a day keeps the doctor away. Could this be true? Experts will tell us how we can get the health benefits of wine or alcohol while keeping our weight in check below.

The French diet is often used as an example of how wine can improve heart health. The French have a fairly high-fat diet but their heart disease risk is relatively low. And some have attributed this to red wine.

But there are so many differences between the lifestyle of the French and the other nationalities from their activity levels to the foods they eat. You cannot isolate red wine as the magic bullet for disease prevention. Choose whichever alcoholic beverage you enjoy, drink it in moderation and try to have it with meals, and that would be good to your health.

Alcohol can stimulate the appetite, so it is better to drink it with food. When alcohol is mixed with food, it can slow the stomach's emptying time and potentially decrease the amount of food consumed at the meal. However, researchers agree that any alcohol in limited quantity will provide the same health benefit.

There is a misunderstanding that red wine is abundant in antioxidants. It does contain some, but they are not always well absorbed. If you want antioxidants, you are better off eating a spinach salad with vegetables than drinking a glass of red wine.

Lower Your Cholesterol

Alcohol can also have a very powerful effect and increase HDL, the "good" cholesterol, by 20% if used moderately and in the context of a healthy diet along with regular physical activity. Higher HDL levels are linked to lower risks of heart disease. The research evidence points to ethanol, or the alcohol component, of beer, wine, or spirits as the substrate that can help lower cholesterol levels, increase "good" HDL cholesterol, expert says.

Boost Your Brain

A recent study shows a boost in brain power for women who enjoy a little alcohol. The study evaluated more than 12,000 women aged 70-81. Moderate drinkers scored better than teetotalers on tests of mental function. Researchers found a boost in brainpower with one drink a day. Moderate drinkers had a 23% reduced risk of mental decline compared with nondrinkers.

Vocabulary

abundant /əˈbʌndənt/ adj. 丰富的,充足的,充裕的
alcohol /ˈælkəhɔl/ n. 酒精,酒
antioxidant /ˌæntiˈɔksidənt/ n. 抗氧化剂
attribute /əˈtribjuːt/ v. 把……归功于,把……归咎于
benefit /ˈbenifit/ n. 利益,好处,益处
beverage /ˈbevəridʒ/ n. (热或冷的)饮料
boost /buːst/ v. 增加,提高,促进,增强
cholesterol /kəˈlestərɔl/ n. 胆固醇
component /kənˈpəunənt/ n. 零件,成分,组成部分
ethanol /ˈeθənɔl/ n. 乙醇
isolate /ˈaisəleit/ vt. (使)隔离,(使)孤立
moderate /ˈmɔdərit/ adj. 适度的,温和的,中等的
nationality /ˌnæʃəˈnæliti/ n. 国籍,民族
prevention /priˈvenʃən/ n. 阻止,妨碍,预防
spinach /ˈspinidʒ/ n. 菠菜
stimulate /ˈstimjuleit/ vt. 刺激,促进,激发,鼓励
substrate /ˈsʌbstreit/ n. 酶作用物,(生物)基层
teetotaler /tiːˈtəutələ/ n. 滴酒不沾的人,禁酒主义者

Phrases & Expressions

keep sth. in check 控制……,抑制……
attribute sth. to sb. or sth. 归功于,归咎于
be good to 有益于
be abundant in 富有……

be better off（比以前）更富裕,境况更好
be linked to 与……有关

Notes to the Text

1. Glass of wine a day keeps the doctor away："每天一杯酒,医生远离我。"这是根据西方常用的一句保持健康的句子 An apple a day, keeps the doctor away.（每天一苹果,医生远离我）改写而成,这在英语修辞中称作仿拟辞格（Parody）。它把人们所熟知的一些习语、谚语格言、名言名句等进行巧妙的修改,以达到令人耳目一新的效果。
   仿拟辞格被广泛使用于文学作品、广告语、文章或报纸的标题等当中。又如：Not all cars are created equal.（不是所有的汽车都生来平等）它的含意是：我们的汽车才是出身高贵,质量是一流。这是日本三菱汽车公司开拓美国市场的广告语。该句仿拟的是美国独立宣言中的句子：All men are created equal.（人人生而平等）。
2. HDL—high density lipoprotein：高密度脂蛋白。
3. teetotaler：绝对禁酒主义者,即滴酒不沾的人。包括含酒精饮料。

Exercise 1   Reading Comprehension

Answer the following Questions according to the text.

1. Which diet is always used as an example of how wine can improve heart health?
2. In what way can you make wine beneficial to your health?
3. Why should wine be drunk with food?
4. What effect does alcohol have on HDL?
5. Which group of people is better on tests of mental function, moderate drinkers or teetotaler?

Exercise 2   Word Training

Fill in the blanks with the words given below. Change the form where necessary.

| check | isolate | stimulate | cholesterol | component |
| attribute | prevention | spinach | benefit | boost |

1. Edward is not very cheerful. He needs a holiday to _____ him up.
2. Although high _____ will do harm to people's health, it is essential for children, especially those under two.
3. I hope my warning will _____ her to greater efforts.
4. They both _____ financially from the arrangement.
5. Enriched uranium is a key _____ of a nuclear weapon.
6. I don't like _____ even though I know it's good for me.
7. Scientists have _____ the virus causing the epidemic.
8. He is studying the branch of medicine that deals with tumors, including study of their development, diagnosis, treatment, and _____.
9. They _____ their success to their teacher's encouragement.
10. If I hadn't kept myself in _____, I might have said something that I would have regretted later.

Section 3　Translation

Ⅰ. *Translate the following sentences into Chinese.*

1. Experts will tell us how we can get the health benefits of wine or alcohol while keeping our weight in check below.
2. The French have a fairly high-fat diet but their heart disease risk is relatively low.
3. You cannot isolate red wine as the magic bullet for disease prevention.
4. However, researchers agree that any alcohol in limited quantity will provide the same health benefit.
5. If you want antioxidants, you are better off eating a spinach salad with vegetables than drinking a glass of red wine.

Ⅱ. *Translate the following sentences into English.*

1. 每天一杯酒,医生远离我。
2. 法国人和其他民族的生活方式有很大区别。
3. 酒精可以刺激食欲。所以酒最好和食物搭配食用。
4. 高水平的高密度蛋白可以降低罹患心脏病的概率。
5. 适量饮酒的人和滴酒不沾的人比起来脑力退化的概率降低了百分之二十三。

Section 4　Classified Word Bank

Read the following words and expressions aloud and then learn them by heart:

Wine and Place of Origin　酒及产地	
1. Martell Cordon Blue	蓝带马爹利（法国）
2. Remy Martin	人头马（法国）
3. Hennessy	轩尼诗（法国）
4. Gin	杜松子酒（荷兰）
5. Whisky	威士忌酒（苏格兰）
6. Chivas	芝华士（酒名）
7. Martini	马提尼酒（法国）
8. Tequila	龙舌兰酒（墨西哥）
9. Vodka	伏特加（俄罗斯）
10. Rum	朗姆酒（牙买加）
11. Cider	苹果酒（英国）
12. Stout	烈性啤酒（爱尔兰）
13. Ale	清淡啤酒（英格兰）
14. Bock	烈性黑啤（德国）
15. Bourbon whisky	波旁威士忌（美国）
16. Brandy	白兰地（法国）
17. Campari	金巴利（意大利）
18. Amarula	爱玛乐（南非）
19. Frangelico	意大利榛子酒（意大利）
20. Grand marnier	柑曼怡（法国）

Part VI

Shopping

Unit 1 Tourist Souvenirs

Section 1 Listening and Speaking

I. Listen and Repeat

Dialogue 1　At the Handcrafts Department

Mr. Zhang is a salesman of the Handicrafts Department and Anne is an American tourist who wants to buy some souvenirs for her friends.

Zhang: Good morning, madam. Can I help you?

Anne: I'm looking for some souvenirs for my friends.

Zhang: How about the vase? It is a traditional Chinese design, made in Jingdezhen, a place famous for porcelain.

Anne: It's extremely beautiful. I'll take it. Do you have any tablecloth to go with it?

Zhang: Yes. What about this one? It's hand-embroidered, with the bamboo design.

Anne: (*Looking at the price tag*) But it's too expensive. Have you got anything cheaper?

Zhang: Please consider the fine craftsmanship. It's worth the price.

Anne: Really? Then I'll take it.

Zhang: Shall I wrap the vase together with the tablecloth or wrap them separately?

Anne: Separately, please.

Zhang: OK. Your total is 2,300 yuan.

Anne: Here is the money.

Zhang: Thank you, madam. Here is your change.

Dialogue 2　Bargaining and Making Purchases

Mr. Liu is a tour guide and Susan is a British tourist. They enter an arts and crafts store. They are rehearsing how to bargain with vendors.

Susan: Can we bargain here, Mr. Liu?

Liu: Yes, of course.

Susan: I am not good at bargaining. How does it work?

Liu: Well. How about rehearsing it? Suppose you are the vendor and I am the buyer.

Susan: Good idea. Let's go about it. (*Their rehearsal begins*)

Liu: How much is this jade bracelet?

Susan: It's 200 Yuan.

Liu: That's too steep for me! Could you go down a little? I can only give you 100 Yuan.

Susan: No way. It cost me more than that. How about 160 yuan?

Liu: Don't try to rip me off! I know what this is worth. 120 Yuan, okay?

Susan: I cannot let it go for that price. It is a high quality jade. 150 yuan, take it or leave it.

Liu: It is only a simple bracelet without any decoration on it. That's too expensive! (*starts to leave*)

Susan: Wait! Wait! OK. 140 yuan. Final price.

Liu: If that's the final price, I'll leave. 130 yuan. Final offer.

Susan: Well, you drive a hard bargain. I'll let you have it for 130 yuan.

Liu: Thank you very much.

Susan: You are welcome.

Ⅱ. Act Out

1. Listen to the dialogue. Then practice it with your partners using the words and expressions below to help you.

Saleslady: help, anything, particular, how about, folklore dolls, like, silk fabrics, what about, lacquer-ware, local specialty, look, elegant, attractive, certainly, workmanship, surely, wonderful present, on sale, 200 yuan, sorry, cheapest, in stock.

Customer: looking, not really, buy, presents, no thanks, something personal, look around, show, jewelry box, so beautiful, hand-made, how much, too expensive, something cheaper, take it, wrap up.

2. Study the following sample dialogue. Then strike up a conversation with your partners using the sentences listed in the chart.

A: How do you like this silk cheongsam?

B: Oh, it is very nice. But the color is too bright.

A: What about this blue one?

B: Elegant.

1. **How do you like this silk cheongsam?**
2. What about this cloisonné vase with a light blue background?
3. Could you show me that one on the top shelf?
4. Do you like this pearl necklace? It's in fashion now.
5. I advise you to buy a bottle of Maotai. It is the most famous brand of wine.
6. I think this embroidered tablecloth is chic. It is hand-made.
7. You'd better get some Chinese tea. It is very famous in the world.
8. What about this Chinese painting by Zhang Daqian?
9. How about this pair of jade bracelets?
10. What about this Four Treasures of Study? It will add more Chinese flavor to your study.

Ⅲ. Focus Listening

A. Listen to the recording and choose the correct answer for each question.

1. All of the following are good souvenirs mentioned for travelers to buy in China except _____.

    A. handicrafts　　B. antiques　　C. jades　　D. roast ducks

2. Beijing is the right place to buy _____.

    A. fresh water fish　　　　B. real cloisonné

    C. Chinese Qipao　　　　D. calligraphies

3. What is Shanghai famous for?

    A. Silk carpets　　　　B. Sea pearls

    C. Fine paintings　　　D. Tea sets

4. Which of the following is not a specialty in Xi'an?

    A. Replicas of the terracotta warriors　　B. Tie-dyed fabric

    C. Antique furniture　　　　　　　　　　D. Tangsancai

5. From the passage we know that travelers can buy _____.
   A. high quality carpets in Tibet
   B. first-class Tangka in Xinjing
   C. Pu'er tea in Yunnan province
   D. fine china in Hangzhou

B. Listen to the recording and complete the sentences below.
1. Shanghai is a "_____ paradise"!
2. However, in boutiques, you will not find _____ on high fashions and imports.
3. Shanghai is one of China's most important regions for _____.
4. Chinese silk is famous throughout the world for its _____.
5. Jade has different colors and can be _____ in many styles.

Section 2 Reading

Major Styles of Chinese Embroidery

Chinese embroidery is an exquisite craft, famous for its long history, and is internationally loved. It appeals to the people at home and abroad. Some four thousand years ago, there was a rule that on ceremonial occasions, people should wear dresses with embroidered designs; thus, embroidery became very important in china. The embroidery of the Warring States Period shows that the lockstitch was the principal stitch used during that period. In the Ming and Qing dynasties, the art of embroidery had its heyday, and the embroidered works began to be exported. Household embroidery was also developed greatly.

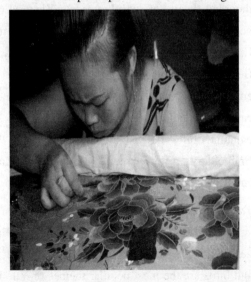

Chinese embroidery has four major traditional styles: Su, Shu, Xiang, and Yue.

Su Embroidery

Su is the short name for Suzhou. A typical southern water town, Suzhou and everything from it reflects tranquility and elegance. So does Su Embroidery. Embroidery with fish on one side and kitty on the other side is a representative of this style. Favored with the advantageous climate, Suzhou with its surrounding areas is suitable for raising silkworms and planting mulberry trees. As early as the Song Dynasty, Su Embroidery was already well known for its elegance and vividness. In history, Su Embroidery dominated the royal wardrobe and walls.

Shu Embroidery

Originated from Shu, the short name for Sichuan, Shu Embroidery, influenced by its geographic environment and local customs, is characterized by a refined and brisk style. The earliest record of Shu Embroidery was during the Western Han Dynasty. At that time, embroidery was a luxury enjoyed only by the royal family and was strictly controlled by the government. During the Han Dynasty and the Three Kingdoms, Shu Embroidery and Shu Brocade were exchanged for horses and used to settle debts. In the Qing Dynasty, Shu Embroidery entered the market and an industry was formed. Government supports promoted the development of the industry.

Xiang Embroidery

Xiang Embroidery, an art from Hunan, is a witness of the ancient Hunan and Hubei culture. Xiang Embroidery was a gift to the royal family during the Spring and Autumn Period. Through over two thousand years of development, Xiang Embroidery became a special branch of the local art. Xiang Embroidery has been gaining popularity day by day. Besides the common topics seen in other styles of embroidery, Xiang Embroidery absorbs elements from calligraphy and painting. The uniqueness of Xiang Embroidery is that it is patterned after a painting draft, but is not limited by it. Perhaps because of this technique, in Xiang Embroidery, a flower seems to give off fragrance, a bird seems to sing, a tiger seems to run, and a person seems to breathe.

Yue Embroidery

Yue Embroidery includes Guangzhou Embroidery and Chaozhou Embroidery. People generally agree that Yue Embroidery started from the Tang Dynasty. Portraits and flowers and birds are the most popular themes of Yue Embroidery as the subtropical climate favors the area with birds and plants. In addition, Yue Embroidery uses rich colors for strong contrast. Since Cantonese are very superstitious, red and green, and auspicious patterns are widely used. The most famous piece of Yue Embroidery is Hundreds of Birds Worshiping the Phoenix.

Vocabulary

auspicious /ɔː'spiʃəs/ *adj.* 吉兆的,幸运的
brocade /brə'keid/ *n.* 织锦
Cantonese /ˌkæntə'niːz/ *n.* 广东人,广东话
embroidery /im'brɔidəri/ *n.* 刺绣品,粉饰,刺绣
exquisite /'ekskwizit/ *adj.* 精致的,细腻的,敏锐的
elegance /'eligəns/ *n.* 高雅,典雅,优雅
geographic /ˌdʒiə'græfik/ *adj.* 地理的,地理学的
heyday /'heidei/ *n.* 全盛期
lockstitch /'lɔkstitʃ/ *n.* 双线连锁缝法
mulberry /'mʌlbəri/ *n.* 桑树,深紫红色
phoenix /'fiːniks/ *n.* 凤凰,长生鸟
representative /repri'zentətiv/ *n.* 代表,代理(人)
silkworm /'silkwəːm/ *n.* 蚕
stitch /stitʃ/ *n.* 线步,针脚,针步
subtropical /'sʌb'trɔpikəl/ *adj.* 亚热带的
superstitious /ˌsjuːpə'stiʃəs/ *adj.* 迷信的
tranquility /træŋ'kwiliti/ *n.* 宁静
wardrobe /'wɔːdrəub/ *n.* 衣柜

Phrases & Expressions

give off 发出,放出(气体,气味,光和热)
Warring States Period 战国时期
Southern and Northern Dynasties 南北朝
the Three Kingdoms 三国时期
Spring and Autumn Period 春秋战国时期
Hundreds of Birds Worshiping the Phoenix 百鸟朝凤

Notes to the Text

1. the lockstitch：双线连锁缝纫法。它一种传统的刺绣方法，是在战国时期的刺绣作品中主要应用的一种方法。
2. Shu Embroidery, influenced by its geographic environment and local customs, is characterized by a refined and brisk style. 蜀绣因为受到当地地理环境和当地文化习俗的影响，具有优雅而活泼的特性。refined and brisk style：优雅伙伴的类型
3. Portraits and flowers and birds are the most popular themes of Yue Embroidery as the subtropical climate favors the area with birds and plants. 粤绣最流行的主题是肖像和花鸟。因为亚热带气候给这个区域带来丰富的鸟类和植物。the most popular themes of Yue Embroidery：粤绣最流行的主题

Exercise 1   Reading Comprehension

Answer the following Questions according to the text.

1. When did embroidery become very important in china?
2. When did the art of embroidery come into its heyday?
3. What is the most famous representative of Su Embroidery?
4. What is the uniqueness of Xiang Embroidery?
5. What is the most famous piece of Yue embroidery?

Exercise 2   Word Training

Fill in the blanks with the words given below. Change the form where necessary.

establish	embroidery	dominate	reflect	auspicious
heyday	raise		representative	superstitious	influence

1. I need one more spool of thread before finishing the _____.
2. The general overthrew the last emperor of that country and _____ a republic.
3. In its _____, the studio's boast was that it had more stars than there are in heaven.
4. Her sad looks _____ the thought passing through her mind.

5. The tiger is a _____ of the cat family.

6. His long absence _____ fears about his safety.

7. He has authority, but he doesn't try to _____ others.

8. Mary was extremely _____ and believed the color green brought bad luck.

9. No one can avoid being _____ by advertisements.

10. Michael Grimm found himself on a more _____ path.

Section 3 Translation

Ⅰ. *Translate the following sentences into Chinese.*

1. I'd like to try something in grey, in traditional Chinese style with hand-made embroidery.
2. The rarity of the raw material is the deciding factor of both the value and the mystery of silk.
3. Despite scientific and technological development, a silkworm can only produce 1,000 meters of silk in its lifespan.
4. In the past, many families south of the Yangtzi River raised silkworms and did embroidery.
5. Lockstitch was a traditional technique of Chinese embroidery.

Ⅱ. *Translate the following sentences into English.*

1. 明代和清代是我国丝绸工艺的鼎盛时期。
2. 蜀锦因为大量使用金线和银线而得名。
3. 在古代刺绣的图案中，经常使用凤凰图案来象征吉祥。
4. 苏绣以工艺精湛、图案精美、颜色雅致而闻名。
5. 湘绣是来自湖南的刺绣工艺，是古代两湖文明的良好佐证。

Section 4 Classified Word Bank

Read the following words and expressions aloud and then learn them by hear

1. brooch	胸针
2. clay figure modeling	泥塑
3. cloisonné	景泰蓝
4. crystal glass	水晶玻璃

5. diamond ring　　　　　　　　钻戒
6. dough modeling　　　　　　　面塑
7. embroidery　　　　　　　　　刺绣品
8. emerald　　　　　　　　　　绿宝石
9. handcraft　　　　　　　　　手工艺品
10. Hunan embroidery　　　　　湘绣
11. Jade carving　　　　　　　玉雕
12. lacquer ware　　　　　　　漆器
13. painted pottery　　　　　彩陶
14. porcelain　　　　　　　　瓷器
15. pottery　　　　　　　　　陶器
16. ruby　　　　　　　　　　　红包石
17. Shoushan Stone carving　寿山石雕
18. silk fabrics　　　　　　　丝织品
19. Suzhou embroidery　　　　苏绣
20. wood carving　　　　　　　木雕

Unit 2 Jewelry

Section 1 Listening and Speaking

I. Listen and Repeat

Dialogue 1　At a Jeweler's

Tina is a tourist who wants to buy her mother a gift at Laoyinjiang Jeweler's. Mr. Qian is a shop assistant there.

Qian：Hello. Is there anything I can do for you?
Tina：I'd like to buy my mother a silver bracelet for her 60th birthday. I'd like something in a traditional Chinese style.

Qian: Well, here is one with a very traditional design. Do you want to have a look?

Tina: Sure. What does the pattern mean? Is it a sort of a bird?

Qian: Yes. It's a phoenix, the queen of birds in Chinese legends. The design is most suitable for middle-aged women.

Tina: Oh, it's very beautiful. But will you show me some other designs?

Qian: No problem. This one has a lotus flower, the symbol of purity. And this is a dragon, an imaginary animal, a symbol of auspiciousness.

Tina: OK. I prefer the lotus flower. It looks like a lily, and lily is my mother's favorite flower. Can I try it on?

Qian: Yes. Let me help you.

Tina: Oh, it's a bit too tight.

Qian: This is the largest one we have. But don't worry. We can make it larger for you if you decide to buy it. Just a minute, please.

Tina: It's all right now. Mom wears almost the same size as me. How much does it cost?

Qian: 500 Yuan.

Tina: That's reasonable. Could you please wrap it up for me?

Qian: OK. Just a moment, please.

Dialogue 2   At a Pearl Shopping Center

Mr. Smith is a tourist from New York and Mrs. Huang is a shop assistant who is receiving him.

Smith: Can you recommend something for an anniversary present?

Huang: I'd like to. How about this natural pearl necklace?

Smith: It's nice but too expensive. Do you have a cultured one?

Huang: Yes, we do have cultured pearl necklaces, but there is not much choice. Would you like to have a custom-made one?

Smith: No, thanks. Can I have a look at that pair of earrings?

Huang: Here you are. They are the most beautiful ones in our shop. They are 24K gold and inlaid with pearls.

Smith: Are they real natural pearls?

Huang: Yes, of course, sir. Everything sold here is genuine. We have very good reputation in this field.

Smith: How much is it?

Huang: Six hundred dollars.

Smith: I'll take it. Do you accept credit card?

Huang: Yes, we do.

Smith: Could you please gift-wrap it for me?

Huang: Would you like a ribbon on it?

Smith: Yes, please. Thank you very much.

Huang: You are welcome.

Ⅱ. Act Out

1. Listen to the dialogue. Then practice it with your partners using the words and expressions below to help you.

> **Gao**: what, do, for you, which, prefer, natural, cultured, higher value, equal luster, just beautiful, certainly, reputation, assure, wares, genuine, how, like, 200 yuan, ivory bracelets, 1200 yuan, welcome.
>
> **Rich**: look, pearl necklace, wonder, better, I see, genuine, wife, present, 16th wedding anniversary, look, beautiful, how much, quite reasonable, take it, by the way, what, these, how much, quite deer, leave, moment, thanks a lot.

2. Study the following sample dialogue. Then strike up a conversation with your partners using the sentences listed in the chart.

A: Good morning. **I'd like to have a look at the cloisonné bracelet.**

A: How about this one? It's made by hand.

B: Very unique.

1. I'd like to have a look at the cloisonné bracelet.
2. What is this necklace made of?
3. Can I get a receipt for the earrings?
4. Do you have any other designs for me to choose?
5. Do you have emerald jade? I want to get one for my wife.
6. I'd like to get some genuine Chinese calligraphy and paintings.
7. Do you accept credit card?
8. Can I get some discount for the cloisonné bracelet if I take two?
9. I'd like to buy a pearl necklace. Could you give me some suggestions?
10. Could you please wrap up the cloisonné vase for me?

III. Focus Listening

A. Listen to the recording and choose the correct answer for each question.

1. Cloisonné is originated from _____.
   A. Beijing
   B. Shanghai
   C. World Expo
   D. the Qing Dynasty
2. When did cloisonné reach its peak development?
   A. In the period of Xuande
   B. The Qing Empire
   C. In 1904
   D. The Ming Empire
3. Cloisonné is also called Jingtailan because _____.
   A. it is made by hand
   B. cloisonné making is very complex
   C. the objects are mostly in blue color
   D. it is with unique national character
4. Cloisonné making needs to go through more than _____ procedures.
   A. 13
   B. 20
   C. 23
   D. 30
5. Which of the following statements is not true?
   A. Some cloisonné articles are designed for ornamental purposes
   B. The earliest cloisonné reserved till now were made in the Qing Dynasty
   C. Cloisonné objects have been exported to many countries
   D. Cloisonné won the first prize at the World Expo in 1904

B. Listen to the recording and complete the sentences below.

1. A department store is usually divided into several _____: men's wear, women's wear, kitchen ware, jewels, stationery, toys, shoes, etc.
2. There is such a great variety of goods that an elaborate department store may occupy _____.
3. Even if you don't want to buy anything _____, a department store is a good place to spend time at.
4. In some countries sales may come annually, seasonally, or even _____ because the shop-owners want to promote the sale of goods.
5. It is a delight to witness a great _____ in service at department stores in china now.

Section 2　Reading

Jade, the Stone of China

Many countries have jade culture, but none of them has as long a history as China does. China's jade culture has undergone a long process of development from the New Stone Age 10,000 years ago.

The earliest jade ware found in China was a piece of serpentine stoneware unearthed in Liaoning Province dating back to the New Stone Age, more than 12,000 years ago. The second was a small hanging jade article excavated in the site of Hemudu in Zhejiang Province dating back more than 7,000 years ago. Jade ware in that period was mainly used for personal decoration. A large number of exquisite jade objects were produced 4,000 years ago. Jade ware at that time was mainly used for witchcraft and as a symbol of power.

During the Shang Dynasty, craftsmen used metal tools to make new progress in jade ware models and sculpture. Round jade articles increased in number and jade ware was often given as gifts.

The jade-carving technique developed fast in the Spring and Autumn and Warring States Periods. The Spring and Autumn Period was known for its well carved and exquisite jade ware. The delicate patterns of dragon and phoenix on the jade decorations are still treasured today.

In the periods of the Qin and Han Dynasties, jade ware became more practical. At that time, people began to believe in the power of jade ware to give people a long life. They thought they would live forever if they had jade ware. Therefore, the practice of burying the dead with jade ware became common. Invaluable jade figures and clothes of jade pieces sewn with gold threads have been found in tombs dating back to the Han Dynasty.

During the periods of the Three Kingdoms to the Song and Yuan Dynasties, there was no great development in the jade-carving technique. This changed in the Ming Dynasty when many famous craftsmen emerged. White jade vessels with gold holders and white jade bowls with gold covers, which were unearthed in the Ming Tombs, reflected the dynasty's peak level in jade carving. The jade ware technique peaked in the Qing Dynasty with the support of Emperor Qianlong.

The patterns of China's jade ware have rich meanings. Bats and gourds were often used as a basis for more than 100 patterns because the Chinese words for bat and gourd sound like good fortune in the Chinese language. This reflected the ancient Chinese people's hope for a happy life and revealed the essence of China's traditional culture.

Jade in China varies and can be divided into two categories: hard and soft. Good materials provide strong basis for jade ware carving, but the value of a jade object depends on the skills and reputation of craftsmen, the dates of carving, peculiar modeling and the owner's status. Certainly, different people will have various views on the value of the same jade object. It is a special skill to exploit the natural color of a piece of jade to create an effective design. So the most expensive ones are not those of one single color, but those of multiple colors the carving skillfully enhancing the different colors in an object.

Vocabulary

category /ˈkætigəri/ n. 种类,类别
decoration /ˌdekəˈreiʃən/ n. 装饰,装饰物
enhance /inˈhɑːns/ v. 提高,加强,增加
essence /ˈesns/ n. 本质,精髓
excavate /ˈekskəveit/ v. 开凿,挖出,发掘
exploit /iksˈplɔit/ v. 开发,利用,开拓

exquisite /ˈekskwizit/ adj. 精致的,高雅的,细腻的
gourd /guəd/ n. 葫芦,脑瓜
multiple /ˈmʌltipl/ adj. 多样的,多重的
practical /ˈpræktikəl/ adj. 实际的,实用的
reputation /ˌrepjuˈteiʃən/ n. 名誉,名声
serpentine /ˈsəːpəntain/ adj. 曲折的,蜿蜒的
skillfully /ˈskilfuli/ ad. 巧妙地,技术好地
witchcraft /ˈwitʃkrɑːft/ n. 魔法,巫术

Phrases & Expressions

date back to 追溯到
believe in 信任,信赖,相信……的存在
be used for witchcraft 用于巫术
be divided into 被分为……
depend on 取决于

Notes to the Text

1. The jade-carving technique developed fast in the Spring and Autumn and Warring States Periods. 春秋战国时期玉雕发展得很快。Spring and Autumn Period 春秋时期,简称春秋。公元前 770 年—公元前 475 年。Warring States Period 战国时期。公元前 475 年—公元前 221 年。

2. the periods of the Three Kingdoms：三国时期,公元 220 到公元 280 年。三国时期是一个混乱和割据的时期,形成了以魏、蜀、吴三足鼎立的局面。

3. The patterns of China's jade ware have rich meanings. Bats and gourds were often used as a basis for more than 100 patterns because the Chinese words for bat and gourd sound like good fortune in the Chinese language. 中国玉雕图案有丰富的含义,蝙蝠和葫芦经常由 100 个以上的图形构图作为背景。因为在中国,蝙蝠和葫芦的发音和福禄的发音是类似的。

4. So the most expensive ones are not those of one single color, but those of multiple colors the carving skillfully enhancing the different colors in an object. 最昂贵的玉制品不是那些单色的,而是那些多种颜色的作品,精湛的雕刻技术突出了一件作品的多重颜色效

果。enhancing the different colors in an object.：突出了一件作品不同的颜色。玉器的价值就在于利用其天然的颜色进行创作。

Exercise 1   Reading Comprehension

Answer the following Questions according to the text.

1. When was the earliest jade ware found in China?
2. When did jade ware become more practical in the jade history?
3. When did jade ware technique reach the peak?
4. What does the value of jade objects rely on?
5. What patterns are often used in Chinese jade ware?

Exercise 2   Word Training

Fill in the blanks with the words given below. Change the form where necessary.

| fashion | witchcraft | practice | essence | excavate |
| enhance | treasure | mean | reputation | emerge |

1. On his 11th birthday, Harry Potter learned that he possessed magical powers and was admitted for training at the Hogwarts School of _____ and Wizardry.
2. Tina _____ the jade bracelet very much, which was a present of her marriage anniversary.
3. _____ measures must be taken to stop the negative effect of this fight.
4. The judge said that new evidence _____ during the trial.
5. The _____ of the pattern of dragon and phoenix is auspiciousness.
6. The two things are the same in outward form but different in _____.
7. The value of a jade object not only depends on the skills and _____ of craftsmen but also depends on the dates of carving.
8. The forest will _____ the attractiveness of the region.
9. Nowadays, wearing diamond ornaments was in _____ especially for the young people.
10. The Ming tombs were first _____ by some archaeologists in 1956.

Section 3 Translation

Ⅰ. *Translate the following sentences into Chinese.*

1. Jade is a gemstone of unique symbolic energy, and unique in the myths that surround it.
2. Jade is strictly speaking a generic term for two different gems, nephrite and jadeite.
3. In general, the value of jade is determined according to its color and the intensity of that color, the texture, and its clarity and transparency.
4. In Chinese traditional belief, jade is a kind of ornament, which could get rid of evil spirit.
5. In China, wearing jade as ornaments has a history of more than 4,000 years and till today a lot of people love jade decorations, especially ancient jade.

Ⅱ. *Translate the following sentences into English.*

1. 中国的玉雕作品在世界上享有很高的声誉。
2. 在过去,只有高官才能陪葬玉器。
3. 金缕玉衣是我国汉代出土的一件珍贵的玉器制品。
4. 在中国古代,玉不仅是财富的象征,也是权力的象征。
5. 在古代,不少孩子名字中有"玉"字,反映出父母对孩子的珍视。

Section 4 Classified Word Bank

Read the following words and expressions aloud and then learn them by heart:

1.	Gem	宝石
2.	Ruby	红宝石
3.	Emerald	绿宝石
4.	Sapphire	蓝宝石
5.	Synthetic cut stone	人造宝石
6.	Amber	琥珀
7.	malachite	孔雀石
8.	coral	珊瑚
9.	pearl	珍珠
10.	diamond	钻石
11.	crystal	水晶

12. ivory	象牙
13. gemstone	宝石坠子
14. bracelet	手镯
15. earring	耳环
16. engagement ring	订婚戒指
17. necklace	项链
18. neck ring	项圈
19. brooch	胸针
20. jadeite	翡翠

Unit 3 Clothing

Section 1 Listening and Speaking

I. Listen and Repeat

Dialogue 1   In a Clothing Shopping Arcade

Katherine is an American tourist who is attracted by the beautiful dresses in the shopping arcade. Mr. Chen, a shop assistant, is serving her.

Catherine: I'd like to buy a dress closely related to Chinese culture as a reminder of my trip to China. What do you think is the most suitable for me?

Chen: Well, madam, The Chinese cheongsam or Qipao is so popular with young ladies in China, so I strongly recommend you buy one.

Catherine: Qipao? Would you show me one, please?

Chen: Certainly. How do you like this one? It's made of velvet. Black is quite in fashion this year.

Catherine: Ah, that's my favorite color. I like it very much. May I try it on?

Chen: Sure. Please come with me to the fitting room.

Catherine: Oh, it's really elegant, but I'm afraid it's a little tight across the shoulders.

Chen: I see. Would you like to try that pink one, madam? It's made of brocade.

Catherine: I like the style very much and the size fits me nicely. But don't you think the color is too bright for me?

Chen: Yeah, pink is a little bit bright for you. How about that dark green one over there? It's so chic.

Catherine: Wow! It looks terrific on me. I'll take it. But I wonder if it's colorfast.

Chen: It Certainly is! The garments here are all colorfast.

Catherine: How much do you charge for this?

Chen: 820 yuan.

Catherine: All right.

Dialogue 2　Buying a T-shirt

Mrs. Smith is shopping for a T-shirt at the knitwear counter of a department store. Mr. Li, a shop assistant, is receiving her with a smile.

Li: Good afternoon, madam. Are you being attended to?

Smith: No, I'm trying to find some women's T-shirts.

Li: Well, we have a variety of types of the latest fashion.

Smith: Sounds great. Do you have T-shirts with Beijing scenic spots printed on them? I'd like to buy one for myself and two for my daughters.

Li: Yes, we do. Will you please tell me what sizes you need, madam?

Smith: I need a size 10. My daughter Marilyn needs a size 8 and Linda a size 6.

Li: Just a moment, please. Here you are, madam.

Smith: Wow! I think the pink one is too bright for me. Do you have this in dark colors?

Li: Yes, madam. How about this blue one?

Smith: Can I try it on?

Li: Yeah. Oh, that looks great on you. Is there anything else I can help you with, madam?

Smith: I also need a T-shirt printed with the Great Wall for my husband. He wears size 17.

Li: Let me see. Here you are, madam.

Smith: Oh, that looks nice. I'll take it. But I wonder if the color will fade.

Li: Never. As a matter of fact, all the T-shirts here are both colorfast and shrink-proof.

Ⅱ. Act Out

1. Listen to the dialogue. Then practice it with your partners using the words and expressions below to help you.

Zhou: morning, madam, help, look at, Tangzhuang, Chinese style jacket, pretty popular,

> of course, 100% silk, size, try on, middle, think, OK, worry, material, shrink-proof, colorfast, no problem, really, flatter, 320 yuan, here, jacket.
>
> **Helen**: buy, fashion clothes, may, look, red jacket, don't know, clothing sizes, decide, for me, shrink, fade, wash, tight fit, better, larger size, fit, perfectly, how much, take it, here, money.

2. *Study the following sample dialogue. Then strike up a conversation with your partners using the sentences listed in the chart.*

A: Is there anything I can do for you?
B: Yeah, **I'd like to buy a shirt. Do you have Size XL?**
A: Sure

1. I'd like to buy a shirt. Do you have Size XL?
2. I'm looking for something for my wife. Do you have any handbags for women?
3. I like the necktie very much. Do you have this in blue?
4. I'd like to try on the jeans. Where is the fitting room?
5. This shirt is very beautiful. Do you have a necktie to match?
6. Is this blouse made of 100% cotton?
7. I need the shoes and the belt. How much are they altogether?
8. May I have a look at the wedding ring?
9. I like the hat very much. May I try it on?
10. I am fond of this mink coat. But could you bring the price down?

III. Focus Listening

A. *Listen to the recording and choose the correct answer for each question.*

1. When was Coco Chanel born?
   A. In 1883   B. In 1913   C. In 1871   D. In 1920
2. Chanel spent her girlhood _____ .
   A. in the French Village of Saumur   B. with her mother
   C. in the Second World War   D. in orphanage
3. Which of the following about Chanel is not true?
   A. She became a mistress of a playboy when growing up

   B. She moved to Paris with the help of a playboy

   C. She founded "Chanel Fashion Shop" in 1913

   D. She led the fashion of the 1920s

4. When the Second World War broke out, Chanel had to _____.

   A. leave France   B. close her fashion shop

   C. return to Saumur   D. go to America

5. Coco Chanel died in _____.

   A. 1954   B. 1970   C. 1971   D. 1975

B. Listen to the recording and complete the sentences below.

1. In the Tang Dynasty, men's daily wear was _____.
2. The change of neckline was the biggest _____ of the women's clothes in the Tang Dynasty.
3. In addition to round, square, straight and V-neck shapes, there also appeared _____.
4. The dress of the Tang Dynasty has become a type of _____.
5. Tang Clothes are usually worn on festivals and _____.

Section 2 Reading

Chinese Qipao

    Qipao, the classic dress for Chinese women, combines elegance with elements of style. Qipao is one of the most versatile costumes in the world. It can be long or short, with full, medium, short or even no sleeves at all to suit different occasions, weather and personal tastes.

    Qipao can display all women's modesty, softness and beauty. Like Chinese women's temperament, Qipao is elegant and gentle, making wearers fascinating. Qipao can display the refined manner of a mature woman perfectly. The collar of Qipao is high and tight fitting, not just for preventing coldness but also for beauty. The collar of Qipao generally takes the shape of a semicircle, its right and left sides being symmetrical, making the soft and slender neck of a woman more attractive.

    For convenient movement and display of the slender legs of women, Qipao generally has two big slits at either side of the lower hem. The slits of Qipao expose a woman's legs indistinctly when she walks. Today you can get Qipao with different lengths and kinds of slits.

Qipao is usually made of excellent materials like silk, brocade, satin or velour. Nearly all colors can be used. Often Qipao gets a certain pattern, such as Chinese Dragons, different kinds of flowers, butterflies or other typical Chinese icons for prosperity and wealth.

Qipao comes from China's Manchu Nationality. There is a legend about its origin. A young fisherwoman living by the Jingpo Lake was not only beautiful, but also clever and skillful. When fishing, she often felt hindered by her long and loose fitting dress. Then an idea struck her: why not make a more practical dress for work? She got down to sewing and produced a long gown with slits, which enabled her to tuck in the front piece of her dress. The young emperor who ruled China at that time had a dream one night. In the dream, his dead father told him that a lovely fisherwoman in Qipao by the Jingpo Lake would become his queen. After awakening from his dream, the emperor sent his men to look for the girl. So she became the queen, bringing the long gown with her.

We do not know whether the story is true or not. But one thing is certain. Qipao came from the Manchus who grew out of ancient Nvzhen tribes. In the early 17th century, Nurhachi unified the various Nvzhen tribes and set up the Eight Banners System. Over the years, a collarless, tube-shaped gown was developed. That is the embryo of Qipao. The dress is called Qipao in Chinese or translated as "banner dress".

Qipao became popular among ladies of the royal family in the Qing Dynasty. At that time, Qipao fitted loosely and was so long that it would reach the insteps. In the 1920s, Qipao became popular throughout China but underwent a change. The arms grew narrower and were usually trimmed with thin lace. The dress was shortened as well. This new adaptation allowed the beauty of female body to be fully displayed. In the 1930s, wearing Qipao became a fashion among women throughout China. Various styles existed during this period. Some were short; some were long, with low, high or even no collars at all. Starting from the 1940s, Qipao became closer-fitting and more practical. In summer, women wore sleeveless dresses. Qipao of this period was seldom adorned with patterns. Qipao had become standard female attire by the 1960s. Following Western fashion, the tailors raised the lower hem, even to above the knee. Today, more and more women in China have come to appreciate its beauty. In fact, many people have suggested that Qipao should become the national dress for women in China. This shows that Qipao remains a vibrant part of Chinese culture.

Vocabulary

appreciate /ə'priːʃieit/ v. 欣赏,感激,赏识
banner /'bænə/ n. 旗帜,横幅
brocade /brə'keid/ n. 织锦,锦缎
classic /'klæsik/ adj. 一流的,经典的
costume /'kɔstjuːm/ n. 服装,剧装
elegance /'eligəns/ n. 高雅,典雅,优雅
embryo /'embriəu/ n. 胎,胚胎,雏形
fascinating /'fæsineitiŋ/ adj. 迷人的
hem /hem/ n. (衣服的)褶边
indistinctly /,indi'stiŋktli/ ad. 不明了地,朦胧地
instep /'instep/ n. 脚背,鞋面
modesty /'mɔdisti/ n. 谦逊,虚心
occasion /ə'keiʒən/ n. 场合,机会
symmetrical /si'metrikəl/ adj. 对称的
temperament /'tempərəmənt/ n. 性格,性情
velour /və'luə/ n. 丝绒,天鹅绒
versatile /'vəːsətail/ adj. 多才多艺的,多方面的
vibrant /'vaibrənt/ adj. 有活力的,精力充沛的

Phrases & Expressions

combine...with... 把……和……结合(混合)在一起
get down to 开始做(需要花费力气和时间的事情)
have a dream 做梦
grow out of 长大穿不进(原来的衣服);由……而来
be trimmed with 装饰,点缀

Notes to the Text

1. Qipao comes from China's Manchu Nationality. 旗袍起源于满族。Manchu Nationality 满族。历史上的"女真人",1635 年改族名为"满洲",满语中是"吉祥"的意思。1911 年辛亥革命前称"满洲族",辛亥革命后才改称"满族"。满族历史悠久,是唯一在中国历史上曾两度建立中原王朝的少数民族。
2. Qipao came from the Manchus who grew out of ancient Nvzhen tribes. 旗袍起源于由女真部落演变而来的满族。Nvzhen tribes 女真族。满族原名女真族,1635 年皇太极把族名改为满族,国名定为大清。
3. Nurhachi unified the various Nvzhen tribes and set up the Eight Banners System. 努尔哈赤统一了女真各个部落,建立了八旗制度。Eight Banners System 八旗制度。八旗制度,是清太祖努尔哈赤于明万历二十九年(1601 年)正式创立,初建时设四旗:黄旗、白旗、红旗、蓝旗。1614 年因"归服益广"将四旗改为正黄、正白、正红、正蓝,并增设镶黄、镶白、镶红、镶蓝四旗,合称八旗,统率满、蒙、汉族军队。

Exercise 1   Reading Comprehension

Answer the following Questions according to the text.

1. What kinds of temperaments of women can be displayed by Qipao?
2. Which nationality first began to wear Qipao?
3. What was Qipao like during the Qing Dynasty?
4. What change did Qipao undergo in the 1920s?
5. When did Qipao become closer-fitting and more practical?

Exercise 2   Word Training

Fill in the blanks with the words given below. Change the form where necessary.

versatile	elegance	popularity	fascination	adapt
display	appreciate	vibrant	fit	temperament

1. The carpet and paintings imparted an air of _____ to the room.
2. Now, with the advent and _____ of the home computer, its advantages and

disadvantages have been a subject of discussion.
3. The plot of the movie is intricate and _____.
4. The twin brothers have entirely different _____.
5. Beijing is China's _____ capital city. It is a combination of ancient and modern China.
6. With the spread of Chinese culture, the Chinese style clothes are _____ by more and more foreign people.
7. I am too fat, so I don't think Qipao _____ me very much.
8. This film was _____ from a famous novel written by T. E. Laurence.
9. The girl is _____ and loved by a lot of boys.
10. This industrial exposition will _____ the newest development and technology in every field of China's industry.

Section 3　Translation

Ⅰ. *Translate the following sentences into Chinese.*
1. I wonder if the color will fade in washing.
2. Please wash it in lukewarm soap water and rinse well.
3. As a matter of fact, all the T-shirts here are colorfast and shrink-proof.
4. I love all fashionable things, and my favorite brand is Chanel.
5. This material of the jacket is 80% wool and 20% polyester.

Ⅱ. *Translate the following sentences into English.*
1. 运动式的风格将在今年流行起来。
2. 劳驾，我想试试挂在橱窗里那件晚礼服。
3. 唐装有各种不同的颜色，最常见的是红色、深蓝色、金色、黑色和绿色。
4. 贵是贵了点，不过这是最好质量的，我们的做工也是这里最好的，非常值。
5. 除了丝绸质的上衣以外，具有鲜明中国特色的旗袍也越来越流行。

Section 4　Classified Word Bank

Read the following words and expressions aloud and then learn them by heart.

1. satin		缎子
2. silk		丝绸的

3.	cotton	棉质的
4.	wool	羊毛的
5.	cashmere	羊绒
6.	business suit	西装
7.	Chinese style slack	中式裤
8.	woolen garment	毛呢服装
9.	wedding gown	新娘礼服
10.	Chinese tunic suit	中山装
11.	down garment	羽绒服
12.	pleated skirt	百褶裙
13.	T'ang clothes	唐装
14.	blue jeans	牛仔裤
15.	mini-skirt	超短裙
16.	night-grown	睡袍
17.	pajamas	睡衣袍
18.	straight skirt	筒裙
19.	swallow-tailed coat	燕尾服
20.	trench coat	风衣

Unit 4   Perfume and Makeup

Section 1   Listening and Speaking

Ⅰ. Listen and Repeat

Dialogue 1   Buying Perfume

Jack is a tourist who wants to buy some perfume for his wife. Miss Wu is the shop assistant waiting on him.

Wu: Good afternoon, sir. Would you like some man's perfume?

Jack: No, I am looking for some perfume for my wife. Could you give me some recommendations?

Wu: Certainly, what do you have in mind?

Jack: I'd like softer smelling perfume.

Wu: OK, here are three different bottles of this kind.

Jack: I really have no idea about them. Could you give me some introductions?

Wu: Okay. This is a bottle of Parisian perfume. It is very fragrant and the quality is unequalled.

Jack: How about this one?

Wu: This scent is really soft and alluring. It is a famous brand, Chanel No. 5.

Jack: Yes, I know it. I have seen its advertising on TV.

Wu: This bottle is also very famous with the name "Poison".

Jack: Poison? The name is really frightening. I don't think I dare to buy this for my wife.

Wu: Then I advise you to buy Chanel No. 5? It is a well-known make.

Jack: OK. I'll take a bottle of Chanel No. 5.

Dialogue 2 A New Fashion for Men

Lucy and Mr. Yang are talking about perfume, lipsticks, foundation makeup and so on.

Yang: Wow! Look at the perfume, Clinique, Chanel, Dior, Joy, Lancome, they've got all the world's famous brands here. Lucy, what is your favorite one?

Lucy: I love all of these brands, but my favorite is Lancome.

Yang: Oh, Lancome is very famous and has a series of products.

Lucy: Yeah. Each style of Lancome is specially designed by world's top designers. So they can always make you enthralling.

Yang: Right on. For example, Tresor, designed by Lancome in 1990, has flowery fragrance and has been quite popular ever since, especially with young girls.

Lucy: Oh, Mr. Yang. Come and have a look at the lipsticks. They look terrific!

Yang: Wow! There are so many colors, red, pink, orange, peach, brick read, apricot pink…

Lucy: Which color do you like best?

Yang: I like pink best.

Lucy: Mr. Yang, do you think this foundation makeup matches me well?

Yang: Yes, very tasteful.

Lucy: Oh, there are so many French perfumes. Oops, perfumes for guys? So strange!

Yang: Come on. Fashion is not only for women. It's a new fashion for men to wear

perfumes,

Lucy: Oh, that's really something new. I'm afraid not everyone can accept it.

Yang: It takes time for that. But people's consuming attitudes are changing nowadays.

Lucy: That's true.

II. Act Out

1. *Listen to the dialogue. Then practice it with your partners using the words and expressions below to help you.*

> **Angela**: excuse me, show, nail-polish, great, hard to say, white, light purple, nice, friends, like, pink nail-polish, still, prefer, mascara, eye cream, very nice, sunshine-resistant cream, I see, take, bottle, pink eye cream.
>
> **Ding**: yes, all kinds, colors, famous brand, Maybelline, favorite color, don't, understand, pink, match, skin, production date, expiry date, yes, pink eye cream, sells very well, foundation, makeup, resist, sunshine,

2. *Study the following sample dialogue. Then strike up a conversation with your partners using the sentences listed in the chart.*

A: Good morning, what can I do for you?

B: I'd like to buy some new eyebrow pencils. Do you have any good brands?

A: Yeah.

1. I'd like to buy some new eyebrow pencils. Do you have any good brands?
2. My skin is very sensitive. Do you have any trial samples of the perfume?
3. Do you have night cream for middle-aged women?
4. If my skin is allergic to the face mask, can I bring it back for a refund?
5. With this membership card, could you give me a 15% discount for purchasing this night cream?
6. Do you sell anything that can prevent freckles?
7. My complexion is a little dark. What is the best color foundation I should use?
8. Can I apply the powder blush to brighten my face?
9. I have dark circles under my eyes. How can I conceal them?
10. Do you have the same color lipsticks as the one in the gift package?

III. Focus Listening

A. Listen to the recording and choose the correct answer for each question.

1. How many reasons does the writer give for men to wear makeup?
    A. 4 B. 5 C. 6 D. 7
2. Which of the following was not the makeup that men from Egypt to England wore?
    A. Face powder   B. Lipstick   C. Eye shadow   D. Eyeliner
3. Which of the following statements is not true?
    A. Makeup can provide sun protection.
    B. Makeup can help actors fit their roles.
    C. Makeup can sometimes fluster you
    D. Makeup can help you boost your confidence
4. Actors and musicians often wear makeup as part of their _____.
    A. daily routine   B. self-esteem
    C. roles   D. characters
5. The most important reason for men wearing makeup is that _____.
    A. they find it saintly
    B. they think it ridiculous
    C. they want to look strange and different
    D. they like the way they look with it on

B. Listen to the recording and complete the sentences below.

1. The conversation probably took place at _____.
2. A bottle of 100 ml rose foundation costs _____.
3. Besides the foundation cream the customer needs some _____ too.
4. The shop assistant said they also had mascara that could _____ the eyelashes.
5. The customer needs to clean off her own _____ before trying the sample mascara.

Section 2   Reading

How to Use Perfume in the Right way

  "Ladies and gentlemen, have you ever used perfume before?" Someone said: "The art of perfume is the art of romance." Statistics show that 23% of the people in the world always use perfume, 27% use it when they leave the house, 21% use it at social occasions, only 18% rarely use it and 12% never does. If you have no idea about perfume, I'm afraid you're a bit out. But never mind, because "it's never too late to learn!" You can know some ideas about how to use it properly according to different weather, skin, places, occasions, etc. Nowadays, Loyalty to a single perfume is out. Wearing the scent that goes with the occasion and the look is definitely in!

Different weather use different perfume

Spring: in spring the temperature is a little bit low, the climate tends to be damp, the fragrance is not easy to volatilize, so we'd better try some fresh flower, fruit or some light, refreshing fragrance.

Summer: the climate is hot and wet during summer and people can easily perspire, so perfume of high volatility and fresh fragrance are your right choice.

Autumn: in autumn the climate is dry, and the autumn wind is quite strong, so we can try a little bit strong fragrant perfume.

Winter: the weather is very cold in winter and people always wear thick clothes, so the strong fragrance is absolutely necessary.

Different places use different perfume

Closed room: in the carriage, bus, car or theatre, try not to use the strong fragrant perfume, otherwise it may affect others. Restaurants: when you are eating, don't use strong fragrant perfume, water or oceanic type is good. Because the strong smell may influence the

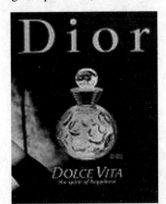

good smell of food. Hospital: not every situation suits for perfume. When you are in the hospital, you'd better say goodbye to your perfume. When the medical smell and perfume's fragrance mixes together, the smell can be terrible!

Different occasions use different perfume

Wedding ceremony: in this situation, good scent may increase the happiness feeling, and you can use the fresh smell in the daytime and strong fragrance in the night! Appointment: using fruit and flower fragrance may increase your attractiveness and hormone. Rainy day: during the rainy day, the wet weather may make your perfume hard to volatilize, so the weak and fresh fragrant perfume is suitable. Sports: when the smell of sweat mixes with your perfume, it smells terrible, so we should choose the sport perfume or no alcohol perfume when we do some sports.

Different skin use different perfume

Diet, acid balance, medication, skin oil, mood, and environmental factors will influence how a fragrance develops on the skin as well as its staying power. Blondes or people with light skin have a tendency towards dry skin, and perfumes are basically oils that will be absorbed by the skin like moisturizers. To help your fragrance last longer use a matching body lotion or unscented body lotion。

You may notice a change in the way your favorite fragrances smell if you have changed your diet, moved to a new climate, began taking a new medication, or if you are under more stress than usual. Perhaps you have become so accustomed to your regular perfume that you simply can't detect it. This is called olfactory fatigue. If so, ask friends before you put more on, it may already be strong enough. It might also be time to experiment with new fragrances.

If you use perfume in a right way, it is likely to perform some magic. So, I hope all of you know how to use your perfume properly according to different weather, skin, places, occasions, etc. I hope all of you can be an amazing attractive people after using it in a right way.

Vocabulary

alcohol /ˈælkəhɔl/ *n.* 酒精,酒
attractive /əˈtræktiv/ *adj.* 吸引人的,有魅力的
attractiveness /əˈtræktivnis/ *n.* 魅力,吸引力
definitely /ˈdefinitli/ *ad.* 肯定地,明确地,确切地
diet /ˈdaiət/ *n.* 饮食 *v.* 照规定饮食
fatigue /fəˈtiːg/ *n.* 疲乏,疲劳,劳累
fragrance /ˈfreigrəns/ *n.* 香味,芳香
hormone /ˈhɔːməun/ *n.* 荷尔蒙,激素
influence /ˈinfluəns/ *v. & n.* 影响

loyalty /ˈlɔiəlti/ n. 忠诚，忠心
magic /ˈmædʒik/ n. 魔法，魔术，戏法
moisturizer /ˈmɔistʃəˌraizə/ n. 润肤霜
occasion /əˈkeiʒən/ n. 场合，机会
oceanic /ˌəuʃiˈænik/ adj. 海洋的，大洋的
olfactory /ɔlˈfæktəri/ adj. 嗅觉的
perfume /ˈpəːfjuːm/ n. 香水，香味，芳香
scent /sent/ n. 气味，香味，香水
tendency /ˈtendənsi/ n. 趋势，倾向

Phrases and Expressions

have no idea about perfume 对香水一无所知
a bit out 有点过时了
suit for 适合……
get along with 相处，进展
become accustomed to 习惯了……

Notes to the Text

1. Wearing the scent that goes with the occasion and the look is definitely in! 使用和场合装扮相配的香水是非常时尚流行的做法。在这个句子中 that goes with the occasion and the look 是定语从句修饰先行词 scent。be definitely in 意思是 be definitely fashionable.
2. To help your fragrance last longer use a matching body lotion or unscented body lotion. 为了让你的香水能延长持续的时间，使用相配的乳液或者无香型的身体乳液。unscented body lotion：无香型洗涤液或乳液，很多高档的护肤品都是没有香味的就是为了在使用香水的时候不会和香水的味道相冲突。

Exercise 1   Reading Comprehension

Answer the following Questions according to the text.
1. According to the statistics what percent of people never use perfume?
2. What kind of perfume should be used in winter?

3. Where shouldn't people use perfume?
4. What kind of perfume is a good choice when you go to an appointment?
5. If you can't detect your perfume, what should you do?

Exercise 2 Word Training

Fill in the blanks with the words given below. Change the form where necessary.

| fragrant | occasion | loyal | tendency | attractive |
| fatigue | influence | smell | mix | romantic |

1. It is said that Frenchmen are among the most _____ people in the world.
2. People should learn how to wear properly on different social _____.
3. Perfume can not only make you _____ good but also make you feel more confident.
4. The _____ soldiers gave up the lives of themselves for the benefits of their country.
5. My brother displayed artistic _____ at an early age.
6. There are a lot of _____ recreational activities, so every child would like to play at the Disneyland.
7. She put the sugar into the coffee and _____ them up with a spoon.
8. She was pale with _____ after a sleepless night in the desert.
9. Don't let your parents or friends _____ your decision.
10. This kind of fruit, which is grown in many parts of the world, is _____ and sweet.

Section 3 Translation

Ⅰ. *Translate the following sentences into Chinese.*

1. I have oily skin. What is the best foundation for me?
2. Do you have any anti-wrinkle products?
3. My T-zone gets oily easily, but my cheeks are dry in the winter.
4. You can use a gentler, cream-based facial cleanser, and remember to follow that with a thick moisturizer.
5. The eye cream I bought last time was too greasy.

Ⅱ. *Translate the following sentences into English.*
1. 胭脂会使你的脸颊红润。
2. 这种口红有没有深一点颜色的？
3. 玛丽选择的唇膏很适合她的肤色。
4. 您有没有听说我们这个月的特别促销活动啊？
5. 这个香水太浓了，我对香味非常敏感。

Section 4 Classified Word Bank

Read the following words and expressions aloud and then learn them by heart：

1.	Avene	雅漾
2.	Avon	雅芳
3.	Biotherm	碧欧泉
4.	Burberry	巴宝莉
5.	Calotine	歌宝婷
6.	Chanel	香奈儿
7.	Clarins	娇韵诗
8.	Dior	迪奥
9.	Elizabeth Arden	伊丽莎白·雅顿
10.	Estee Lauder	雅诗兰黛
11.	Gucci	古姿
12.	Guerlain	姣兰
13.	L'Oreal	欧莱雅
14.	Lancome	兰蔻
15.	Lolita	洛丽塔
16.	MaryKay	玫琳凯
17.	Revlon	露华浓
18.	SK Ⅱ	SK Ⅱ
19.	Versace	范思哲
20.	Vichy	薇姿

Unit 5 Antiques

Section 1 Listening and Speaking

I. Listen and Repeat

Dialogue 1 Shopping in an Antique Market

A tourist named Thomas comes into an Antique Market with his tour guide Mrs. Wang. Mr. Qiao, the shop assistant, is receiving them.

Qiao: Hello. What can I do for you?

Thomas: What's this cabinet made of?

Qiao: Mahogany, real mahogany. It's been handed down in the family. It's at least four or five hundred years old.

Thomas: Four or five hundred years old? From the Qing Dynasty?

Qiao: No, from the Ming Dynasty. Look at the craftsmanship. Only furniture from the Ming Dynasty is this well made.

Thomas: How much will you part with it for?

Qiao: One hundred thousand yuan.

Thomas: That's too expensive

Qiao: It's a family heirloom. We could never bear to sell it before.

Thomas: I'll think about it.

Qiao: Sure, the price is still negotiable.

Wang: Think it over before you pay! I suggest you just remember the price and make your final decision after you see some other stores of this kind. And you can bargain with the shop assistant.

Thomas: Thank you for your advice. Would the shop assistant feel unhappy that we just look around and buy nothing?

Wang: Well, he should understand it. It needs time and patience to look for real antiques.

(*Going into another store*)

Dialogue 2　Packaging and Shipping

Thomas wants to send a set of porcelain to his friend. Ms. Wang is serving him.

Thomas: Where is the parcel counter, please?

Wang: What is it you are sending?

Thomas: A set of porcelain that I've bought for a friend.

Wang: Will you open it for inspection?

Thomas: But I have just packed it up nicely. I don't want to spend the next hour repacking it.

Wang: I'm sorry, but it is a question of security. That is the rule. We will just look into the box and will be very careful with it.

Thomas: Okay, if that's the rule. I'll abide by it.

Wang: There is some embroidery here as well as the porcelain set.

Thomas: Right. They go with the set.

Wang: You'll have to put them both on the form. Do you want to send it by air or surface mail?

Thomas: Airmail please. How much is it?

Wang: That will be 72 yuan. Anything else?

Thomas: No, thank you.

Ⅱ. Act Out

1. **Listen to the dialogue. Then practice it with your partners using the words and expressions below to help you.**

> Su: what, do, for you, seal cutting, engravers, typical traditional Chinese arts, briefly speaking, by colors, brush touches, by lines and strokes, reproduction, which, like best, artistic eyes, imitation, Xubeihong, famous, modern China, 1000 yuan, take, together with.
>
> Aaron: feel puzzled, stones, interested, traditional Chinese painting, difference, western oil painting, Chinese ink painting, original, reproduction, ancient beauties, galloping, landscapes, very nice, how much, reasonable, thank.

2. **Study the following sample dialogue. Then strike up a conversation with your partners using the sentences listed in the chart.**

A: May I help you?

B: Yes, I'd like to buy something that is closely connected with Chinese culture.

A: Okay. **These cloisonné products are so beautiful. Cloisonné is a unique art form of Beijing.**

B: Oh, they're so nice.

1. These cloisonné products are so beautiful. Cloisonné is a unique art form of Beijing.
2. These ancient coins can often remind you of your visit to China.
3. Paper cutting is a traditional Chinese art. You can buy some for your families and friends.
4. Calligraphy is a good choice. It is the traditional art of Chinese character writing.
5. What about this tea set? It is made in Jingdezhen, a famous place for Chinese porcelain.
6. I think kites are very good gifts. They were invented by the Chinese people 2000 years ago.
7. Bianzhong or chime bells is a kind of percussion musical instrument. We have some replicas to sell.
8. Jade has been treasured by the Chinese people for thousands of years. How about this jade beast?
9. Chinese fans are good gifts for friends and families. They have been carrying artistic and unique national style since old ages.
10. I suggest you buy some Chinese paintings? Chinese paintings can be divided into three types, figure painting, landscape painting, and flowers and birds painting. Which do you prefer?

III. Focus Listening

A. Listen to the recording and choose the correct answer for each question.

1. The tri-colored glazed pottery of the Tang Dynasty was developed _____ years ago.
   A. 1,100   B. 1,200   C. 1,300   D. 1,400

2. The three main colors of the tri-colored glazed pottery are _____.
   A. yellow, green and white
   B. green, white and red
   C. blue, white and brown
   D. white, green and orange

3. The tri-colored glazed pottery was used by the nobles during the 8th century as _____.
   A. dragonhead cups
   B. pillows for females
   C. funeral objects
   D. marriage portions

4. Which of the following statements about the tri-colored glazed pottery is not true?

   A. It drew on the skills of Chinese painting and sculpture.

   B. It flourished during a long period of time in the Tang Dynasty.

   C. It is valued for its brilliant colors and life-like shapes.

   D. it is limited in number now and considered to be a rare treasure.

5. Which of following excavated tri-colored Tang Pottery have won greatest admiration?

   A. Female figurines   B. Figurines of acrobats

   C. Horses   D. Camels

B. Listen to the recording and complete the sentences below.

1. Nowadays many foreigners are able to _____ the unique Chinese art form of seal cutting.

2. Seal-cutting is a unique part of the Chinese cultural _____.

3. The materials for seals vary with different types of _____.

4. Compared with average persons, famous people usually use more _____ materials to make their own seals.

5. Today _____ is the most widely used material in seal engraving.

Section 2   Reading

Traditional Chinese Painting

Though Chinese painting has much in common with Western painting as an important part of the country's cultural heritage, it still possesses its unique national character. Chinese traditional painting seldom follows the convention of central focus perspective or realistic portrayal, but gives the painter freedom on artistic conception, structural composition and method of expression.

One of its main features is that it is painted on Xuan paper(or silk) with the Chinese brush, Chinese ink, mineral and vegetable pigments. Xuan paper is most suitable for Chinese painting. It can allow the writing brush wet with Chinese ink and held in a trained hand, to move freely on it, making strokes vary. These soon turn out to be human figures, plants and flowers, birds, fish and insects, full of interest and lift. To work on this art needs continual exercise, a good control of the brush, and a feel and knowledge of the qualities of Xuan paper and Chinese ink.

Before setting a brush to paper, the painter must conceive a well-composed draft in his mind, drawing on his imagination and store of experience. Once he starts to paint, he will normally have to complete the work at one go, and there is no possibility of any change of wrong strokes.

Chinese often consider a good painting a good poem, and vice versa. Hence the expression "painting is in poetry and poetry in painting". In the past, many great artists were also great poets and calligraphers. The inscriptions and seal on the paintings can not only help us understand the painter's ideas and emotions, but also provide decorative beauty to the painting.

In terms of technique, Chinese paintings are divided into two major categories: free hand brushwork (xieyi) and detailed brushwork (gongbi). The former is characterized by simple and bold strokes intended to represent the exaggerated likenesses of the objects, while the latter by fine brushwork and close attention to detail. Employing different techniques, the two schools try to achieve the same end, the creation of beauty.

According to subject matter, classical Chinese painting can be divided into three categories: landscapes, figures and birds-and-flowers. Throughout the course of Chinese painting, images of emperors, philosophers, and court ladies provide role models from the past; landscapes and bird-and-flower paintings demonstrate the central place of nature in Chinese thought. Religious paintings reflect both the Daoism philosophy native to China and Buddhism.

It is difficult to tell how long the art of painting has existed in China. Pots of 5,000—6,000 years ago were painted in color with patterns of plants and animals, reflecting various aspects of daily life of the past. These may be considered the beginnings of Chinese painting.

In 1949 from a tomb of the Warring States Period was unearthed a painting on silk of human figures, dragons and phoenixes. The earliest work on silk ever discovered in China, it measures about 30 centimeters long and 20 centimeters wide.

Paintings on paper appeared much later than those on silk for the simple reason that silk was invented long before the invention of paper.

In 1964, when a tomb dating back to the Jin Dynasty was discovered in Turpan, Xinjiang, a colored painting on paper was discovered. It shows, on top, the sun, the moon and the Big Dipper and, below, the owner with a fan in his hand. A vivid portrayal of a feudal land-owner, measuring 106.5 centimeters long and 47 centimeters wide, it is the only known painting on paper with such a long history in China.

Vocabulary

aesthetic /i:s'θetik/ *adj.* 美学的，审美的，有美感

bold /bəuld/ *adj.* 大胆的，粗体的，醒目的

composition /kɔmpə'ziʃən/ *n.* 结构，组成，作文；构图，布局

conceive /kən'si:v/ *v.* 想象出，构想出，设想

conception /kən'sepʃən/ *n.* 观念，概念，见解

convention /kən'venʃən/ *n.* 习俗，常规，惯例；大会

draft /drɑ:ft/ *n.* 草稿，草图，汇票

heritage /'heritidʒ/ *n.* 遗产

imagination /i,mædʒi'neiʃən/ *n.* 想象，想象力

perspective /pə'spektiv/ *n.* 角度，观点；透视画法

portrayal /pɔ:'treiəl/ *n.* 描述，描写，刻画

possess /pə'zes/ *v.* 拥有，具有；驱使

realistic /riə'listik/ *adj.* 现实的，现实主义的

stroke /strəuk/ *n.* （绘画等）一笔；中风

structural /'strʌktʃərəl/ *adj.* 结构上的

Turpan /'tuə'pɑ:n/ *n.* 吐鲁番

Phrases & Expressions

1. have sth. in common with 与……有共同之处
2. work on 致力于,专心干
3. at one go 一次,一气,一气呵成
4. and vice versa 反之亦然
5. in terms of 至于,关于,从……观点来看
6. native to 当地的,本地生产的
7. the Big Dipper 北斗七星

Notes to the Text

1. Chinese traditional painting seldom follows the convention of central focus perspective or realistic portrayal…中国传统绘画很少采用中心焦点透视,写实作品也很少见。the convention of central focus perspective or realistic portrayal:中心焦点透视和写实画法的惯例,这是西方绘画的一个基本原则。

2. Religious paintings reflect both the Daoism philosophy native to China and Buddhism. 宗教绘画反应的是中国的本土宗教道教和佛教。Daoism philosophy native to China:中国的本土宗教道教。道教是中国固有的一种宗教,距今已有1 800余年的历史。它的教义与中华本土文化紧密相连,深深扎根于中华沃土之中,具有鲜明的中国特色,并对中华文化的各个层面产生了深远影响。

3. In terms of technique, Chinese paintings are divided into two major categories:free hand brushwork (xieyi) and detailed brushwork (gongbi). 根据工艺不同,国画可分为写意画和工笔画。free hand brushwork (xieyi) and detailed brushwork (gongbi). 写意画法和工笔画法。前者用粗犷而简单的笔触夸张地展现物体的大概形象,而后者多用细腻的笔触来展现物体的细节。两种画派虽然使用不同的技法,但其目的都同样是创造美丽。

Exercise 1   Reading Comprehension

Answer the following Questions according to the text.

1. What is the unique national character of Chinese traditional painting?
2. According to subject matter, how many categories can Chinese painting be divided into?

3. What can be considered the beginning of Chinese painting?
4. Why did paintings on paper appear much later than those on silk?
5. When was the first colored painting on paper discovered?

Exercise 2   Word Training

Fill in the blanks with the words given below. Change the form where necessary.

| realistic | conceive | employ | unearth | exaggerate |
| portrayal | perspective | possess | bold | convention |

1. He's _____ enough to know he's not going to succeed overnight.
2. I heard that the _____ was cancelled.
3. The painting provides us with one of the earliest examples of the use of _____.
4. Many people still like to watch dramas, because they are a _____ of human conflict.
5. Whatever may occur, do what you _____ to be right.
6. Jennifer is an extremely _____ girl.
7. The seriousness of the situation has been much _____ by the press.
8. We must _____ all available means to save the boy.
9. Many _____ cultural relics were exhibited at the museum.
10. He _____ creative imagination and true scholarship.

Section 3   Translation

Ⅰ. *Translate the following sentences into Chinese.*

1. The play was an aesthetic success.
2. The composition of this picture is wrong at perspective.
3. Chinese calligraphy and Chinese painting are closely related because lines are used in both.
4. Before setting a brush to paper, the painter must conceive a well-composed draft in his mind, drawing on his imagination and store of experience.
5. Landscapes and bird-and-flower paintings demonstrate the central place of nature in Chinese thought.

Ⅱ. *Translate the following sentences into English.*
1. 温莎城堡确实是名副其实的古物宝藏。
2. 那幅中国传统风景画美丽得无法形容。
3. 窗帘上绘有精美的花卉图案。
4. 1987年,长城被联合国教科文组织列入《世界遗产名录》。
5. 永乐大钟最为绝妙之处在于钟身内外都铸有佛经、咒语,总计230,000多字。

Section 4　Classified Word Bank

Read the following words and expressions aloud and then learn them by heart.

1.	Antique	古董
2.	Blue and white porcelain	青花瓷
3.	Bronze ware	青铜器
4.	Calligraphy	书法
5.	Enamel decorate	珐琅彩
6.	Fake	赝品
7.	Food vessel	鼎
8.	Fresco	壁画
9.	Green ware	青瓷
10.	Guan Ware	官窑
11.	Hanging scroll	图轴
12.	Heirloom	传家宝
13.	Ink and wash	水墨画
14.	ink stone	砚台
15.	jade carving	玉雕
16.	paper-cut	剪纸
17.	reproduction	复制品
18.	Ru Ware	汝窑
19.	Screen set	屏风
20.	seal-cutting	印刻

Part VII

Entertainment

Unit 1　Peking Opera

Section 1　Listening and Speaking

I. Listen and Repeat

Dialogue 1　Enjoying Peking Opera

Kate is invited to see Peking Opera in the theater. Mr. Mei is telling her the play on the stage.

Mei: Do you enjoy it, Kate?
Kate: Yes, I've never seen anything like that.
Mei: Every facial makeup represents a different character.
Kate: Oh, what does that red face represent?
Mei: The red represents integrity and loyalty, the white stands for cunning, and the black there means valor and wisdom.
Kate: Here comes a gold face.
Mei: Gold and silver usually symbolize something super-natural, such as a ghost or a fairy. Each role has its own facial painting and decoration.
Kate: How fascinating! Look at the woman, please. She seems to be so sad.
Mei: Yes, she is wrapped up in her misery. See she is covering her face with a handkerchief? That means she is weeping.
Kate: What happened to her?
Mei: She's abandoned by her husband and she couldn't find a way to make a living.

Kate: Now she is making her hair a mess.
Mei: That means she is going crazy.
Kate: Can you tell me what the opera is all about?
Mei: Sure. It's a story about a deserted woman in the Ming Dynasty.

Dialogue 2　Talking about the Musical Cats

Brian has just come back to China with his mother. Now they are watching the world-famous musical Cats with their friend Mrs. Zhou in their box. They are talking about it while watching.

Zhou: This is my first time to watch the Broadway musical. I like the scene though I don't know much about the Western opera.
Mother: Well, the set is a dreamlike marvel. It is midnight, not a sound from the pavement. Here come the Jellicle cats from the darkened landscape for their ball.
Zhou: It is something like Peking opera. Their actions are large and colorful.
Brian: Peking opera is much more symbolic than the western opera. Every gesture is highly stylized. But our opera is much more realistic and psychological.
Zhou: I agree with you.
Mother: I first saw the musical in 1987. I'd read about this fantastic musical in which actors transformed themselves into Eliot's Jellicle cats. I was captivated by it.
Zhou: These are not cartoon cats. They are costumed cats with distinct personalities and emotions.
Mother: Yeah, they are all marvelous. But it's Grizabella that really touches my heart, especially when she is accepted back into the tribe and ascends to cats' heaven, a four handkerchief experience!
Brain: Anyone who knows what it is to feel like an outsider can easily identify with Griz. And the older I get, the more deeply the memory of Grizabella and of all the cats haunts me.
Zhou: Yes, when Grizabella sang the Memory again, I was really touched.

Ⅱ. Act Out

1. Listen to the dialogue. Then practice it with your partners using the words and expressions below to help you.

Vicky: what, first show, thank you, what snacks, I see, what, selling, musical instrument, clapping the bamboo, monkey, dressing, minister, why, used, at

> the end of the words, audience shouting, transformed into dance, rhythm, fast, turn ten somersaults, best show.
>
> **Chen**: Monkey King, playbill, offer, snacks, water melon seeds, candied fruit, specialty, candied haws on a stick, call, Kuaibanr, mandarin jacket, because, Peking Opera, dialect, cheering, martial arts, that's right, basic skill.

2. Study the following sample dialogue. Then strike up a conversation with your partners using the sentences listed in the chart.

A: How come the two men on the stage have white patches on the nose?

B: **The white patches characterize them as clowns.**

A: Why are their hands and body trembling?

B: That shows they are extremely angry.

1. The white patches characterize them as clowns.
2. Peking Opera is a combined art of singing, recital, acting and acrobatic fighting.
3. Peking Opera is the most popular opera in China with a history of more than 200 years.
4. Qimo is a general term for all kinds of stage properties and simple settings which are used in Peking opera.
5. The actor can make the scene of rowing a boat by using an oar, which is called imaginary performance.
6. A bridge in Peking Opera can be made up of two chairs standing on each side of a table.
7. The audience can enjoy the performance while tasting Beijing snacks.
8. There is no doubt that Peking Opera is really the treasure of Chinese culture.
9. If you want to enjoy real Peking Opera, Beijing Liyuan Theatre is your best choice.
10. The world-famous Beijing Opera Troupe puts on a performance every night.

III. Focus Listening

A. Listen to the recording and choose the correct answer for each question.

1. All of the following are characteristics of the costumes in Peking Opera except _____.
   A. graceful   B. magnificent   C. valuable   D. plain

2. It could be seen from _____ that people were strictly divided into different classes.
   A. mandarin jackets   B. robes of emperors
   C. dresses of ministers   D. clothes of officers

3. Military officers of the highest rank had _____ on their dresses.

   A. tigers   B. lions   C. bears   D. horses

4. As for styles and colors, ministers of lower rank dressed in _____.

   A. red or yellow   B. reddish color

   C. blue or green   D. simple colors

5. Which of the following statements about the costumes on the stage is not true?

   A. The stage costumes can help identify the age of the characters.

   B. People can guess something from the costumes of characters.

   C. Costumes of red are often dressed at the wedding ceremony.

   D. Costumes of black and white are usually worn at the funeral.

B. Listen to the recording and complete the sentences below.

1. The actors of Peking Opera give an imaginary _____ on the stage.
2. A flag with a wheel painted on makes people think the actor is sitting _____.
3. Dancing with an umbrella shows he is _____.
4. In the old days Chinese people were deeply influenced by _____ for a long time.
5. Mei Lanfang was famous for his beautiful finger technique expressing woman's _____.

Section 2 Reading

Peking Opera

Peking Opera is an art form most representative of traditional Chinese culture and it can date back to the year 1790. At that time four local opera troupes of Anhui province came to Beijing on a performance tour. After that they absorbed the tunes of Bang Zi, a local opera from Hebei province, Kun Qu, from Jiangsu province, Qin Qiang, from Shanxi province, and some other local operas. Through years of combination and integration of various kinds of opera there evolved the present Peking Opera. There are four main types of roles in Peking Opera: Sheng, Dan, Jing and Chou. Sheng is the male role, Dan is the female role, Jing, mostly male, is the face-painted role and Chou is the clown.

Sheng can be divided into Laosheng, Xiaosheng and Wusheng. Laosheng wear artificial beards and represent old men, Xiaosheng represents young men while Wusheng are skilled in acrobatic fighting and military action. These roles usually wear no facial makeup. Famous Sheng actors include Ma Lianliang, Zhou Xinfang, Ye Shenglan, Li Shaochun and so on.

Dan can be classified into Qingyi, Huadan, Wudan and Laodan. Qingyi are young or middle aged ladies in elegant costumes, Huadan represents lively young ladies, Wudan always wears short robes and has excellent fighting skills, Laodan usually represents aged women. Mei Lanfang, Cheng Yanqiu, Shang Xiaoyun and Xun Huisheng were the four major Dan roles in the 1920s.

Jing are the face-painted male roles who represent warriors, heroes, statesmen, adventurers, etc. Famous actors include Qiu Shengrong, Yuan Shihai and so on.

Chou can be male or female, loyal or treacherous, pretty or ugly, good or bad. They play the roles of wit, alert and humor. It is the characters of Chou that make audience laugh. The renowned actors include Xiao Changhua, Ma Fulu and Zhu Shihui.

Peking Opera is a synthesis of stylized action, singing, dancing, mime, acrobatic fighting and martial arts. The actors and actresses sing and cry in stylized voice. They use symbolic gestures in every movement such as dancing, drinking, eating; horse riding, opening the door and so on. They also use well-established movements, such as smoothing a beard, adjusting hat, playing the water-sleeves to express certain emotion and meaning.

The music of Peking Opera is played on wind instruments, percussion instruments and stringed instruments. The chief musical instruments are jinghu, yueqin, suona and drum etc.

Peking Opera is very important in China. Its repertoire includes many historical events and fairy tales of preceding dynasties in ancient China. Now Peking Opera has become more and more popular with people all over the world. There are a great many famous artists, excellent performance and well-known audiences. It also makes an excellent contribution to cultural exchanges for China. It is our national treasure.

Vocabulary

absorb /əb'sɔ:b/ v. 吸引,吸收
artificial /ˌɑ:ti'fiʃəl/ adj. 人造的,假的
beard /biəd/ n. 胡须
combine /kəm'bain/ v. (使)联合,(使)结合
contribution /ˌkɔntri'bju:ʃən/ n. 贡献,捐献
copy /'kɔpi/ n. 复制,副本 v. 复制,复印,模仿
evolve /i'vɔlv/ v. (使)发展,(使)进化
exchange /iks'tʃeindʒ/ n. v. 交换,交流
integration /ˌinti'greiʃən/ n. 结合,综合,同化
percussion /pə'kʌʃən/ n. 打击乐器
performance /pə'fɔ:məns/ n. 表演,表现,成绩
province /'prɔvins/ n. 省
release /ri'li:s/ v. 释放,放出;发行(电影,唱片)
repertoire /'repətwɑ:/ n. 全部节目
representative /ˌrepri'zentətiv/ adj. 有代表性的,典型的
robe /rəub/ n. 长袍
stylized /'stailaizd/ adj. 程式化的
synthesis /'sinθisis/ n. 合成,综合
treacherous /'tretʃərəs/ adj. 阴险的,不可信任的;暗藏危险的
troupe /tru:p/ n. 剧团,歌舞团
version /'və:ʃən/ n. 版本,译文,译本

Phrases & Expressions

date back to 追溯到……
to the delight of 令某人高兴的是
contrary to 恰恰相反
make a contribution to 为……做贡献
do the other way round 做的刚好相反

Notes to the Text

1. Peking Opera is an art form most representative of Chinese traditional culture. 京剧是最

代表中国传统文化的艺术形式。京剧的前身是徽班。清朝乾隆年间(1790年)四大徽班进京后大量吸收当时在北京流行的京腔、昆曲、秦腔等各种戏曲艺术的成就，同时又受到北京的语言、风俗等地方文化潜移默化的影响，经过数十年的融汇，演变成为现在的京剧。

2. The music of Peking Opera is played on wind instruments... 京剧的乐曲由管乐、打击乐、和弦乐演奏。京剧的主要乐器有京胡、乐琴、唢呐和鼓等。其中唢呐是管乐，月琴是弦乐，鼓是打击乐。

3. Mei Lanfang, Cheng Yanqiu, Shang Xiaoyun and Xun Huisheng were the four major Dan roles in the 1920s. 梅兰芳、程砚秋、尚小云和荀慧生是二十世纪二十年代的四大名旦。在他们中间，梅兰芳是最著名的花旦。梅兰芳生于北京京剧世家，是著名的梅派大师。梅先生1952年任中国京剧院院长。代表剧目有《贵妃醉酒》《宇宙锋》《打渔杀家》等。

Exercise 1 Reading Comprehension

Answer the following Questions according to the text.

1. When did Peking Opera start?
2. How many main types of roles are there in Peking Opera?
3. Who were regarded as the four major Dan roles in the 1920s?
4. What is the female role called in Peking Opera?
5. What kind of musical instruments does Peking Opera use?

Exercise 2 Word Training

Fill in the blanks with the words given below. Change the form where necessary.

| historical | combine | stylized | copy | contribution |
| ancient | exchange | release | treacherous | representative |

1. The police said that they had uncovered a _____ plot by terrorists to bomb the airport.
2. In _____ Rome there were many gladiators who fought other men or animals as a public event.
3. He is _____ an album of folk songs.
4. We need three _____ of this document, two for the committee, the other one for you

to keep.

5. You should _____ study and entertainment at school. Or you'll be bored.

6. She had a stressful job as a sales _____.

7. We need to promote an open _____ of ideas and information.

8. It was one of the most dramatic moments in British _____.

9. This book _____ little to our understanding of this poem.

10. We can see the highly _____ form of acting in Japanese theatre.

Section 3　Translation

Ⅰ. *Translate the following sentences into Chinese.*

1. You should put on your makeup under the guidance of a professional makeup artist.
2. Usually you have to spend 3 years at school learning makeup skills of Peking Opera.
3. Most stage costumes have water sleeves. They tend to be long, almost like robes.
4. The theatrical costumes can either be tied at the waist or left straight down.
5. Exaggerated designs are painted on each performer's face to symbolize a character's personality.

Ⅱ. *Translate the following sentences into English.*

1. 这些是丑角穿的平底鞋。
2. 画猴王的脸要花将近半个小时。
3. 画京剧脸谱用毛笔,这就像我们写毛笔字、画国画那样。
4. 在影楼,你可以照一张穿着京戏女装的照片。
5. 京剧是中国流行最广、影响最大的一个剧种,有200多年的历史。

Section 4　Classified Word Bank

Read the following words and expressions aloud and then learn them by heart:

1.	Peking opera	京剧
2.	facial makeup	京剧人物脸谱
3.	pantomime	哑剧
4.	comedy	喜剧

5. tragedy	悲剧
6. mime	滑稽动作戏
7. one-act play	独幕剧
8. monodrama	独角戏,单人剧
9. puppet show	木偶戏
10. shadow play	皮影戏
11. skit	小品
12. cross talk	相声
13. story-telling	说书
14. vocal imitation	口技
15. make up	化妆
16. scenery	舞台布景
17. stage effect	舞台效果
18. stage property	道具
19. lighting	舞台灯光
20. sound effects	音响效果

Unit 2 Acrobatics and Chinese Martial Arts

Section 1 Listening and Speaking

I. Listen and Repeat

Dialogue 1 Talking About Chinese Martial Arts

Ashley is a tourist from Australia. Mr. Guan is her Chinese friend whose grandpa is from Wuqiao.

Ashley: I hear your grandpa is a well-known acrobat, is that right?

Guan: Yes, he loves acrobatics very much. He was born in Wuqiao, Hebei Province.

Ashley: I know that. Wuqiao is known as the Cradle of World Acrobatic Art.

Guan: Right on! Have you heard the saying, "All the people in Wuqiao, be he an old man of 99 or a baby just learning to walk, can do tricks-playing"?

Ashley: Yeah, and Wuqiao Circus World is one of the first groups of National Grade AAAA Tourism Attractions.

Guan: Nowadays the Wuqiao International Acrobatic Art Festival is held every other year.

Ashley: Oh, marvelous. What do people do if they want to become an acrobat, Mr. Guan?

Guan: To be an acrobat, you have to receive basic training at school when you are four or five years old. And then get specific training in an acrobatic group by the age of eight.

Ashley: What do you mean by basic training?

Guan: Basic training includes balancing, tumbling, dancing, flexibility and strength, which are practiced in the first two years.

Ashley: And then they can do performances on the stage?

Guan: Not yet. Students will have to spend another three or five years perfecting specific acts.

Ashley: When will they be able to give their first performance?

Guan: Usually when they reach the age of sixteen or seventeen.

Ashley: It's really hard work!

Guan: You bet.

Dialogue 2 Watching the Acrobatic Show

Shaw is an American visiting scholar and Miss Wu is his tour guide. They are watching the Chinese acrobatic performance in a theater.

Shaw: This is the first time I've seen plate spinning near the stage.

Wu: Lovely show, isn't it?

Shaw: Yes, it's marvelous! What is the next performance?

Wu: It's foot juggling.

Shaw: What is it?

Wu: It is a very traditional form of acrobatics. The acrobats will juggle various objects with their feet.

Shaw: Do they have any magnets on their shoes?

Wu: Of course not. They are not doing magic tricks!

Shaw: Are you sure with that?

Wu: Yes, I'm sure with it.

Shaw: Listen, the Chinese music sounds very beautiful.

Wu: Oh, it is called "Full of Joy".

Shaw: Good. I wonder when they will give another performance. I want to see it again.

Wu: They put on a performance at weekends all the year round.
Shaw: Thank you.
Wu: You're welcome.

Ⅱ. Act Out

1. Listen to the dialogue. Then practice it with your partners using the words and expressions below to help you.

> **Sun**: acrobatics, Chaoyan Theater, district, ticket booking, 180 yuan, 680 yuan, Hong Theater, lie, 44 Xingfu Street, Dongcheng, order, call, 010-67142473, excellent show, matter, performers, include, Long Fist, Shadow Boxing, Spear Show, Double-Edged Sword Show, sometimes, do, I think so.
> **Marian**: where, located, price, where, see, traditional, martial arts, give, information, performing, Shaolin Kung fu, monks, temple, International Wushu Federation, tell, something, performance, do they, karate, judo, see, tonight, order tickets, in advance.

2. Study the following sample dialogue. Then strike up a conversation with your partners using the sentences listed in the chart.

A: You know **Chinese martial arts can be means of self-defense and mental training.**
B: Yeah, but where can I learn it?
C: You can learn it from a master or in a martial arts school.

1. Chinese martial arts can be means of self-defense and mental training.
2. Kung fu and Wushu are popular terms for Chinese martial arts.
3. Practicing Taichi is beneficial to physical health.
4. Weapons are considered as an extension of the body.
5. Circling wrist and kicking are Taichi techniques.
6. Shadow Boxing is regarded as one of the internal styles of Chinese martial arts.
7. Modern Wushu is composed of two disciplines, forms and sparring.
8. The trainings include Taichi Sword, Taichi Falchion and so on.
9. Chinese martial arts have become an important element of Chinese culture.
10. Among the Chinese martial artists, Jackie Chan and Jet Li are the most well-known.

Ⅲ. Focus Listening

A. Listen to the recording and choose the correct answer for each question.

1. We know from the passage that China is a country with _____.
   A. many ethnic groups   B. a history of 6,000 years
   C. many fighting sports   D. many warriors
2. Most of the warriors were supported by _____.
   A. the folks   B. the warlord
   C. the acrobats   D. ancient kings
3. Which of the following was not performed on the stage in the Song Dynasty?
   A. Acrobatics and dance   B. Body sculpturing acts
   C. Martial arts   D. Cross talk
4. The acrobatics reached its peak in _____.
   A. the Han Dynasty   B. the Tang Dynasty
   C. the Song Dynasty   D. the Yuan Dynasty
5. Which of the following statements is not true?
   A. Acrobatics flourished from the Song Dynasty
   B. The Silk Road appeared in the Tang Dynasty
   C. Today acrobatics are less flourishing than before
   D. Dun Huang body sculpturing was beautiful

B. Listen to the recording and complete the sentences below.

1. "Kung fu" actually means some _____ ability in any skill.
2. Formerly, Wushu was used for _____.
3. _____ created a set of exercises called Wuqinxi.
4. Hua Tuo's work has a _____ in the history of Chinese Wushu
5. Wushu is believed to have the effect of _____ and _____ some diseases.

Section 2

Chinese Martial Arts and Acrobatics

Traditional Acrobatic Acts

  China has a lot of traditional acrobatic acts. They have very long history and have gained great popularity among people. These acrobatics acts can be seen in almost every

Chinese big festival. The Lion Dance is one of them.

The Lion Dance is an extension of the Chinese martial arts. It needs more skills. It is usually performed by martial artists. All the movements are based on stances and positions of Kung Fu. For a proper lion dance, the movements must follow the music played by three instruments: the drum, the gong and the cymbal. Usually there are two performers who play the lion. One who is handling the lion's head leads the dance and shows the lion's emotions. The other plays the body and the tail. They hide themselves under a cloth imitating the movements of lions. By doing lion dancing they develop their body strength, flexibility and endurance as well as their ability to work in team and overcome obstacles in a group. The performers show their strength, coordination, agility and endurance.

Some other acrobatic shows can be seen at the temple fair or in the park, such as streamer balancing, diabolos play or juggling. There are also some other items of acrobatic acts which can only be seen in the circus or in the theater. They are plate spinning, pagoda of bowls, flying trapeze, cycle skills, jumping through hoops, contortionist acts, etc. Each and every one shows the beauty, flexibility and strength.

Chinese Martial Arts

Wushu is the general term for all the martial arts styles in China. It has been practiced in China for thousands of years. Since long ago Chinese martial arts have been created and developed for self-defense. In ancient time the warriors trained themselves in order to survive in fighting. The most well-known Wushu classifications include: Shaolin, Wudang, Emei, Northern Styles, and Southern Styles. There are hundreds of Wushu styles belonging to these classifications, with over one thousand bare hand and weapon training routines.

Practical Wushu training has included basic skills, such as strength training, fencing, spearing, etc. The training can help you improve your physical ability. It is also good for your health. And it gives you an excellent method of exercise. The martial training includes kicking, punching, throwing, controlling, thrusting and so on. Each style has its basic forms. There are various basic forms, such as offense and defense strategies, retreat, with or without weapons. There are also some training methods for strengthening your body either internally or externally, which will enable you to withstand strikes and blows. Generally speaking, the difference between internal and external styles can refer to whether the strength is from the torso (internal) or whether it is from training of the arm and leg muscles (external).

Today Chinese Wushu is becoming increasingly popular among the foreign visitors and the Chinese youth. They want to learn something or practice kung fu as well. If you want to get some experience you may come to the clubs in Beijing, for example, Beijing Heroes Wushu Club in Chaoyang District. You can find professional masters and amateurs; you can have Taichi class and watch the performance there.

Vocabulary

acrobatics /ˌækrəˈbætiks/ *n.* 杂技
agility /əˈdʒiliti/ *n.* (动作)灵活,敏捷
amateur /ˈæmətə/ *adj.* 业余(爱好)的; *n.* 业余爱好者
balance /ˈbæləns/ *v.* & *n.* 平衡
contortionist /kənˈtɔːʃənist/ *n.* 柔体杂技演员
cymbal /ˈsimbəl/ *n.* 铙钹
diabolo /diˈɑːbələu/ *n.* 空竹
endurance /inˈdjuərəns/ *n.* 忍耐力,耐久性
extension /ikˈstenʃən/ *n.* 延长,扩展;分机
festival /ˈfestəvəl/ *n.* 节日
flexibility /ˌfleksəˈbiliti/ *n.* 灵活性,弹性,适应性
gong /gɔŋ/ *n.* 铜锣

internally /in'tənəli/ *adv.* 在内部,在体内
juggling /'dʒʌglɪŋ/ *n.* 杂耍
obstacle /'ɔbstəkl/ *n.* 障碍(物),妨碍,阻碍
overcome /ˌəuvə'kʌm/ *v.* 克服,战胜
professional /prə'feʃənl/ *adj.* 职业的,专业的
punch /pʌntʃ/ *v.* 用拳猛击(某人,某物)
routine /ruː'tiːn/ *n.* 常规,惯例,例行公事
stance /stæns/ *n.* 站姿;态度,看法
strategy /'strætidʒi/ *n.* 战略,策略
torso /'tɔːsəu/ *n.* 人体的躯干
traditional /trə'diʃənəl/ *adj.* 传统的,习惯的
trapeze /trə'piːz/ *n.* 高空秋千
withstand /wið'stænd/ *v.* 经受住,抵挡住

Phrases & Expressions

gain popularity 赢得欢迎,受到欢迎
each and every 每个
belong to 属于
be based on 以…为基础
refer to 提到,参考,有关,涉及

Notes to the Text

1. The Lion Dance is an extension of the Chinese martial arts. 耍狮子是中国武术的延伸。
   The Lion Dance：耍狮子。中国人认为耍狮子是上天赐福人间的一种仪式。通常,不仅在阴历年祭祀庆典时耍,在诸如开业典礼,播种收获这些预祝兴旺的时节也耍狮子。人们认为耍得好会给人生活带来一切好运。

2. The difference between internal and external styles…内功和外功的区别……
   内功(internal styles)是指来自丹田的功力,外功(external styles)是指来自四肢和肌肉的力量。内功实际上是一种气功,是一种通过调身、调息、调心三结合的,以内练为主的自我身心锻炼功法,可以改善身体素质,发挥人体功能潜力,达到防病治病、保健康复、益智延年的目的。

3. Shaolin 少林武术。

   传说北魏孝明帝时(公元527年),生于南印度贵族的高僧菩提达摩来到嵩山少林寺,面壁九年静坐修心,创立了中国佛教的禅宗。同时,他也将一种古老的印度武术传播到中国。

Exercise 1   Reading Comprehension

Answer the following Questions according to the text.

1. What music instruments are played in the course of a lion dance?
2. How long has Wushu been practiced in China?
3. What kind of acrobatic items can only be seen in the circus or in the theater?
4. What is the difference between the internal and external styles?
5. Where can you go if you want to get some martial experience?

Exercise 2   Word Training

Fill in the blanks with the words given below. Change the form where necessary.

| withstand | tradition | acrobatics | festival | balance |
| overcome | endurable | internal | professional | flexible |

1. These buildings _____ earthquakes since 1975.
2. National Day is one of the most important _____ in China.
3. Having identified the problem, the question arises of how to _____ it.
4. The longer she lived, the more she felt that life was no longer _____.
5. Tourists often disturb the delicate _____ of nature on the island.
6. We can go there by train or by air; our plans are quite _____.
7. Most of the people who signed up for the course were _____ women.
8. He got _____ injuries in the traffic accident.
9. There is a _____ in our family that we throw a party on the eve of the lunar new year.
10. Items in Chinese _____ include lion dance, oral stunts, pagoda of bowls, juggling, wire walking, etc.

Section 3　Translation

Ⅰ. *Translate the following sentences into Chinese.*
1. Finger hitting at certain part of the body is called qigong.
2. Most of the competition forms can be used for self-defense and it is a kind of sport.
3. Wushu has become a truly international sport through the International Wushu Federation.
4. Modern Wushu is composed of two disciplines: forms and sparring.
5. I am so crazy about it that I have come to the stage of watching motion pictures every night.

Ⅱ. *Translate the following sentences into English.*
1. 我真钦佩那些有武功的人。
2. 下一个表演是晃梯顶技。
3. 我想多了解一些中国杂技的详情。
4. 来自中国的武术电影经常被称为"功夫片"。
5. 根据传说,中国武术起源于几乎是神话般的夏朝。

Section 4　Classified Word Bank

Read the following words and expressions aloud and then learn them by heart.

1.	flying rope	绳技
2.	hand juggling	手技
3.	foot juggling	蹬技
4.	cycling skills	车技
5.	ball skills	球技
6.	bar act	杠杆
7.	jar on the head	顶花坛
8.	cycle skills on a high terrace	高台定车
9.	kicking bowls on a unicycle	高车踢碗
10.	shadow boxing	太极拳
11.	three-section cudgel	三节棍
12.	nine-section whip	九节鞭

13.	fist position	拳法
14.	foot position	腿法
15.	pushing the palm	推掌
16.	traditional Chinese boxing	拳术
17.	saberplay	刀术
18.	swordplay	剑术
19.	spearplay	枪术
20.	cudgelplay	棍术

Unit 3 Movies

Section 1 Listening and Speaking

I. Listen and Repeat

Dialogue 1 Going to the Cinema

Miss Wang, with her friends Ray and Martin, plans to see a film this weekend. Now they are talking about it in their office.

Wang: Shall we go to the cinema this weekend? There is a new film on. It's a thriller, but I can't remember its name.

Ray: I've heard of the film. It is said to be the new scary film classic. It could make you hair stand on end.

Wang: Yeah, and the director is nominated for Oscar. It's his best film since 1997.

Ray: Will you be scared, Miss Wang?

Wang: No, I won't be scared. I've never been scared when watching movies.

Ray: What about you, Martin?

Martin: I won't, either. What's it about, Miss Wang?

Wang: It's about a young female cancer patient and her partner who experience supernatural occurrences after their relationship fails.

Martin: Actually I am not very interested in such films. Will there be any other films this

weekend?
Wang: Yeah, other films include: Painted Skin, Super Typhoon, Lust Caution, Wanted, etc.
Martin: Do they have English subtitles?
Wang: I think so. If they don't, I'll be your interpreter.
Martin: Thank you very much.
Wang: You're welcome.

Dialogue 2   Talking about the Award Winning Film
Miss Zhang and Max are talking about this year's award winning film, which concerns climate crisis and environmental protection.
Max: Have you seen the film An Inconvenient Truth, Miss Zhang?
Zhang: No, what's it about?
Max: It's about climate crisis.
Zhang: Do you have a video disc of it?
Max: Yes, here it is. The film is really wonderful. It won an Oscar.
Zhang: Won an Oscar! Are you kidding?
Max: No, it won two awards, one for best documentary and the other for best original song.
Zhang: I can't wait to see it.
Max: It's interesting that many of the movies nominated this year were shot guerilla-style, low tech, outdoors, natural light.
Zhang: Natural light is a challenge to the film makers, but the moviegoer likes to see it because it's real life.
Max: You said it.
Zhang: Is it perfect?
Max: Of course not. But it's better than having the same show without anything about "the climate crisis". I think it's high time that people did something about environmental protection. I wonder if I could buy it for all of my friends and relatives as a present.
Zhang: Good idea!

II. Act Out

1. Listen to the dialogue. Then practice it with your partners using the words and expressions below to help you.

Lisa: have a look, posters, movie, it's said, Academy Award winner, Peter, didn't like it, nor, anyone else, family, how long, last, it's long, I see, fancy, movie star, see the trailer.

> **Ann**: all right, right, best movie, shocked, movie, high-budget, great screenplay and acting, action-pack flick, an hour and 37 minutes, care, glued to the movie, happen, into their roles, real-life characters, don't get any better.

2. *Study the following sample dialogue. Then strike up a conversation with your partners using the sentences listed in the chart.*

A: What language is in the soundtrack of the film?
B: English.
A: Is it widescreen?
B: Yes, it is.

1. What language is in the soundtrack of the film?
2. What is the newly released documentary about?
3. Who acts in the film Die Hard?
4. Can you tell me the plot of A Perfect Murder?
5. What do you think of the sitcom that has a total of 166 episodes?
6. Why don't you like the heroine of the American movie the Hunger Games?
7. Is the hero of the film handsome?
8. It is the best picture of the year, isn't it?
9. The film tells the story of a millionaire romancing the world's most beautiful woman
10. The drama recounts the years of his life from the late 1920s through the 1940s.

Ⅲ. Focus Listening

A. *Listen to the recording and choose the correct answer for each question.*

1. What is the length of the movie described in the passage?
   A. 110 minutes　　　　　　　B. 120 minutes
   C. 125 minutes　　　　　　　D. 130 minutes
2. All of the following actors acted in the movie except _____.
   A. Jet　　　　　　　　　　　B. Andy
   C. Anthony Wong　　　　　　D. Jackie Chan
3. _____ people died during the chaos of the Qing Dynasty.
   A. 5 million　　　　　　　　B. 15 million
   C. 25 million　　　　　　　　D. 50 million

4. Which of the following statements is not true?

   A. General Pang was a man without any ambition and dreams.

   B. People suffered a lot under the rule of the corrupt government.

   C. His sworn brothers helped General Pang to achieve his goals.

   D. General Pang could have changed the course of history.

5. As General Pang grew more powerful he _____.

   A. made every effort to end the war

   B. tried to bring peace to the land

   C. did anything to eliminate his enemies

   D. was no long in the pursuit of power

B. Listen to the recording and complete the sentences below.

1. Before we tell you what movies to see we should advise you first which one you should _____.

2. Moreover, you'd better not put the Hong Kong martial arts and _____ on your list either.

3. The Box Office shows that the _____ are very popular.

4. There are also good _____ movies you can add to your collection.

5. Actually the public more like _____ with intriguing plots.

Section 2   Reading

To Be Informed of the Movies

Every year around a hundred motion pictures are released around the country. With the digital technology getting inexpensive and popular, there has been a tremendous increase in availability of videos through cable and internet. We can get sitcoms, TV dramas and feature movies from online or we can buy or rent the audio visual data such as DVDs of movies, games and televisions in specialist shops.

The best monthly magazine for movie fans is Kan Dian Ying. Before going to the cinema or buying the discs we can get the trailers or be informed of the movies of the week. It tells us the newly released, the gossips and headlines of the entertainment industry.

In China the movies are divided into different styles according to the plot. They are love stories, scary films, motion pictures, war films, documentaries and cartoon films for children. In addition to these, Chinese Kung Fu films are well-known in the world. Dragon

Inn in 1992 was one of the classic among them. The famous horror film is In Love with the Dead this year. The romance's film is The Summer's Tail.

This year Chinese director An Lee's Lust Caution, which opened in the UK on 4th January, is nominated for Best Film, Best Director, Best Leading Actress, Best Cinematographer and other 6 categories. The next one in Chinese movie poster gallery is the Warlords. It has raked in U.S. $14 million across Asia in its opening weekend. It faced no major Hollywood competition in mainland China.

Today more and more foreign films are available in China. Korean TV series sell well in the video shops. Japanese cartoon series and the ones produced in Walt Disney are children's most favorite. Most of the boys are fond of the Japanese monster-fighting hero—Ultraman while girls like their Barbie princess even better. Therefore, the toys, books and clothes of their idols are popular everywhere.

Hollywood movies alone constitute a large portion of this market. The film fans have an easier time to get what they want now than a few years ago. And it is good news to language learners. Friends' been used as the materials for listening comprehension in oral class at some school.

Vocabulary

available /ə'veiləbl/ *adj.* 可用的,可得到的
cable /'keibl/ *n.* 电缆,缆绳,钢索
cartoon /kɑː'tuːn/ *n.* 动画片,卡通片
competition /ˌkɔmpi'tiʃən/ *n.* 竞争
comprehension /ˌkɔmpri'henʃən/ *n.* 理解

constitute /ˈkɔnstitjuːt/ v. 组成，构成
feature /ˈfiːtʃə/ n. 特点，特色；正片，故事片
gossip /ˈgɔsip/ n. 闲言碎语，花边新闻
idol /ˈaidl/ n. 偶像，崇拜物
Internet /ˈintənet/ n. 因特网
oral /ˈɔːrəl/ adj. 口语的，口头的
plot /plɔt/ n. （电影，戏剧）情节；密谋，阴谋
portion /ˈpɔːʃən/ n. 一部分，一份
poster /ˈpəustə/ n. 布告，招贴（画），海报
rent /rent/ n. v. 租
scary /ˈskɛəri/ adj. 恐怖的，吓人的
trailer /ˈtreilə/ n. 预告片，新片预告；（用汽车拖行供度假使用的）活动房屋
tremendous /triˈmendəs/ adj. 极大的，巨大的
visual /ˈviʒuəl/ adj. 可视的，视觉的

Phrases & Expressions

be fond of 喜欢
in addition to 除了…以外
be nominated for 提名，推荐
rake in 赚得（许多钱），捞到（大笔收入）
sell well 卖得好，畅销

Notes to the Text

1. in mainland China 指在中国大陆。overseas 指在海外，如 overseas Chinese 即：海外华人。
2. We can get sitcoms, TV dramas and feature movies. 我们可以看情景喜剧，电视剧和故事片。
   Sitcoms 是情景喜剧。Sitcom 是 situation 和 comedy 两词的合成。又如：brunch, smog, motel, telecast 等。
3. Dragon Inn 是由李惠民导演执导，徐克监制的武打片《新龙门客栈》；Lust Caution 是由李安导演执导的电影《色戒》；Warlords 是由陈可辛导演执导的电影《投名状》。

Exercise 1 Reading Comprehension

Answer the following Questions according to the text:
1. In what year was the Dragon Inn shot?
2. What is the possible meaning of the word "gossip" in the 8th line?
3. According to the article, What has ever been used in some English class?
4. What is the good news to language learners?
5. What is the best monthly magazine for film fans?

Exercise 2 Word Training

Fill in the blanks with the words given below. Change the form where necessary.

scary	idol	competition	invisible	gossip
tremendous	constitute	nominate	available	plot

1. Blind worship of this _____ must be ended.
2. Practically every film he made _____ for an Oscar.
3. I'm sorry, sir, this type of T-shirt is not _____ in your size at the moment.
4. There is no intense _____ between the two companies in this field.
5. Most people love hearing _____ about movie stars.
6. Things like X-rays and germs are _____ to the naked eye.
7. The car was already traveling at _____ speed.
8. The _____ of "C. S. I." was so complicated that I could hardly follow it.
9. This is the _____ movie I have ever seen.
10. College students _____ the majority of the people in these restaurants.

Section 3 Translation

Ⅰ. *Translate the following sentences into Chinese.*
1. What is the title of the new television series?
2. Ann is an extremely talented actress.
3. The movie is currently being filmed and will be aired sometime in 2016.

4. I'd like to view the complete list of his works and characters he acts.
5. They play a young couple with children living in the suburb.

Ⅱ. *Translate the following sentences into English.*
1. 谁在给这部电影编写剧本？
2. 编剧帮助他将其所著的小说改编成电影。
3. 预计这部电影将在 2015 年首映。
4. 他是无数影迷所喜爱的金发碧眼的偶像。
5. 在一年一度的电影节上他获得了金星奖。

Section 4   Classified Word Bank

Read the following words and expressions aloud and then learn them by heart.

1.	adventure film	惊险片
2.	cartoon	动画片
3.	cartoon and puppet film	美术片
4.	costume film	古装片
5.	detective film	侦探片
6.	disaster film	灾难片
7.	documentary	纪录片
8.	epic film	史诗片
9.	ethical film	伦理片
10.	factual film	纪实性影片
11.	feature film	故事片
12.	horror film	恐怖片
13.	military film	战争片
14.	musical film	音乐片
15.	puppet film	木偶片
16.	science fiction film	科幻片
17.	soap opera	肥皂剧
18.	swordsmen film	武打片
19.	thriller film	惊悚片
20.	violence film	暴力片

Unit 4 Sports

Section 1 Listening and Speaking

I. Listen and Repeat

Dialogue 1 Watching Games

Miss Wang wants to see a match in the Bird's Nest, but she simply doesn't know which to watch. So she turns to Jason for advice.

Wang: I'd like to see a championship match of the Olympics. What event do you think I should watch?

Jason: I think you should watch the synchronized swimming or football. The venue is very close to where we are.

Wang: Which is the most awaited team for synchronized swimming?

Jason: Well, Russia has always been the strongest contender in this event.

Wang: Why is that?

Jason: Because their team grabbed a gold medal in the last Olympic Games.

Wang: Don't you think China will beat them?

Jason: It's hard to say. I think we'd better watch it together and see for ourselves.

Wang: How about football? Who are competing for the finals?

Jason: Argentina and Nigeria

Wang: Wow, really? Argentina? They have twice won the world cups.

Jason: Yeah. But Nigeria may have a chance. Anyway, they have been working hard for the Olympics.

Wang: Yeah, I think I should go and see the football match. It must be very exciting.

Dialogue 2 Hiking in the Mountains

Ms. Li is asking Larry what he usually does for his holidays and surprisingly finds that they share the same interests. So they both agree that they will go hiking in the mountain for the coming holiday.

Li: What do you usually do during your holidays, Larry?

Larry: I like outdoor sports, especially hiking in the mountains. Anyway, I hate being confined to the room studying.

Li: So do I. As the saying goes, all work and no play makes Jack a dull boy.

Larry: Absolutely right. We cannot work all the time if we are going to maintain good health and enjoy life. By the way, what sports do you like?

Li: I enjoy hiking, skating, mountain climbing, etc.

Larry: Great! Then what about hiking in the mountains together for the coming holiday?

Li: Sounds like a great idea! I like the experience of climbing steep and high mountains.

Larry: We can make a one-day trip. We'll keep going all the way to the top by noon and get to the foot of the mountain before dark.

Li: What preparations should I make?

Larry: You should prepare a pair of climbing shoes, some necessary clothes, alpenstock, sunglasses, etc.

Li: Do we need any backpacking gear? I don't know where to get it.

Larry: Don't worry. I can lend you some.

Li: Thanks. I'll make good preparations for it and I'm sure we'll have a wonderful time.

Larry: Surely we will.

II. Act Out

1. *Listen to the dialogue. Then practice it with your partners using the words and expressions below to help you.*

> **Oliver:** excuse me, know, venue, gymnastics, not so far, splendid, like, watching, gymnasts' performance, bars, from Romania, thank you, division, strong, not mistaken, Sydney Olympics, Yangwei from China, fan of gymnastics, since, young, following, events, China, getting stronger, thank, taking me here.
>
> **Yang:** Gymnastic Arena, yellow and white building, I, watch, All-around Exercise Elimination Match, from United States, Romanian gymnasts, famous, you're right, also performed, last Asian Games, Chinese gymnastic team, preparing rigorously, really, welcome, enjoy, good luck.

2. *Study the following sample dialogue. Then strike up a conversation with your partners using the sentences listed in the chart.*

A: *What's the score?*

B: It's 48 to 40. The Lakers takes the lead.

A: What a wonderful shot!

B: Yes, but Houston is too far behind to win the game now

1. What's the score?
2. Why was Paul given a red card?
3. What sports are called extreme sports?
4. What is your favorite gymnastic event?
5. Are you sure that Chinese contestants will set some new records?
6. Do you think Mike was a little overconfident there?
7. I think Charlie was standing too close to the table to return the ball.
8. I can't keep up with the ball. It's moving so fast.
9. I usually go snowboarding with my friends on weekends.
10. I've bought a new table tennis bat. I'm going to learn to play table tennis.

Ⅲ. Focus Listening

A. **Listen to the recording and choose the correct answer for each question.**

1. Wushu or martial arts can do all of the following except _____.

    A. defending yourself

    B. curing various diseases

    C. adjusting your mind

    D. building up your body

2. Shaolin Temple is located in _____ Province.

    A. Henan   B. Hunan

    C. Hebei   D. Hubei

3. Which of the following about Shaolin Wushu is not true?

    A. It is well-known not only at home but also abroad.

    B. It is one of the most influential types of Chinese martial arts.

    C. It is named after the Shaolin Temple located in Dengfeng County.

    D. It is the martial arts that you can only practice at Shaolin Temple.

4. Shaolin Wushu is a very convenient sport because it is regardless of _____.

    A. space   B. weather

      C. time   D. all of the above
5. Shaolin Wushu has become very popular among the _____.
   A. local people   B. foreigners
   C. common people   D. Chinese athletes

B. Listen to the recording and complete the sentences below.
1. People who work for bungee operators usually have a great deal of _____.
2. Ropes are chosen according to the jumper's _____.
3. You should remember that bungee jumping is not always _____ for everyone.
4. People who suffer from high blood pressure or _____ should not try bungee jumping.
5. Bungee jumping has become a popular _____ the world over.

Section 2   Reading

Brief Introduction to Sports

Sport is as old as human life, the history of which can date back to millions of years when people lived in caves. The first sports were mainly composed of hunting competitions where the person who killed the most animals was honored and given gifts. These first sports served a very immediate need—to find food. Gradually, however, sports changed from mainly being about hunting to simply playing for pleasure.

China is well known as an ancient country with a civilization of several thousand years. But few people know that sports in China claim a history as long as the country's civilization. There is evidence of Chinese people practising gymnastics as early as 4,000 B. C.. Even today China is famous for its very skilled gymnasts.

England is generally believed to be the first modern society to develop swimming as a sport. In 1837, swimming competitions were held in London's six artificial pools. In 1896, swimming became an Olympic sport for men with the 100-metre and 1500-metre freestyle competitions held in open water. Soon after, as swimming became popular, more freestyle events were added, followed by the backstroke, breaststroke, butterfly and finally, the individual medley.

For a variety of reasons, women were excluded from swimming in the first several

Olympic Games because the developer of the modern games held firmly to the assumption, common in the Victorian era, that women were too frail to engage in competitive sports. It was not until the 1912 Games that women's swimming made its debut.

As to the beginning of badminton, there are a lot of stories. But one thing is certain that badminton started in the U. K., in about 1800, which was developed from tennis. You may discover a lot of similarities between the two. In the year of 1870, a sort of ball made of feather and wood as well as a bat woven with strings were invented. Ever since 1873, the sport of badminton has become more and more prosperous.

Basketball, the world's greatest sport, was invented by James Naismith.

It all started in December of 1891. Naismith was teaching in Massachusetts and was asked by the headmaster of the school to make a new sport. The major idea of the sport was mainly to be played inside when it was too cold to go outside. Naismith began to work. The first baskets were peach baskets that Naismith cleverly thought of hanging on the wall. From there, the legacy of basketball began. Originally, there were 9 men to each team, but the object was still the same, to pass the ball to other players on your team and throw the ball into the opposing team's basket. Immediately, basketball caught on like a wildfire. The hoops we know today were invented in 1906. They are made of steel, with a net hanging from its rim.

Extreme sports or X-sports started as an alternative to more expensive sports such as golf. A city kid who couldn't afford expensive sports equipment could get a skateboard and have fun. But now it has become a whole new area of sports, with specialized equipment and high levels of skill. The new equipment is so much better that people can take more risks without getting hurt. Extreme sports are certainly not for everyone. But it is a fact that extreme sports are gaining in popularity.

Vocabulary

alternative /ɔːlˈtɜːnətɪv/ *adj.* 可替代的,可供选择的 *n.* 可供选择的事物
artificial /ˌɑːtɪˈfɪʃəl/ *adj.* 人工的,人造的,假的

assumption /ə'sʌmpʃən/ n. 假定,假设,认为,采取
claim /kleim/ v. 声称,要求,认领,索赔
evidence /'evidəns/ n. 证据,证明,证词
exclude /iks'klu:d/ vt. 不包括,排斥(某人)
extreme /iks'tri:m/ adj. 极度的,极端的,偏激的
frail /freil/ adj. 瘦弱的,易损坏的,不牢固的
hoop /hu:p/ n. 箍,铁环
individual /ˌindi'vidjuəl/ adj. 个人的,单独的;独特的
legacy /'legəsi/ n. (祖先传下来)之物,遗产,遗赠物
original /ə'ridʒənəl/ adj. 最初的,原始的;有独创性的
prosperous /'prɔspərəs/ adj. 繁荣的,发达的,兴旺的
rim /rim/ n. (圆形物的)外缘,边缘,边
similarity /ˌsimi'læriti/ n. 相似,相似性

Phrases & Expressions

date back to 始于,可以追溯到……
be composed of 由……组成
for a variety of reasons 由于各种各样的原因
engage in 使从事于,参加
make one's debut 初次登台

Notes to the Text

1. gymnastics 体操;breaststroke 蛙泳;individual medley 混合泳。
2. It was not until the 1912 Games that women's swimming made its debut.
   此句话使用了强调句型:It is/was...that...
3. The first baskets were peach baskets that Naismith cleverly thought of hanging on the wall.
   此处,that Naismith cleverly thought of 是定语从句,修饰 peach baskets;hanging on the wall 为现在分词短语作定语,修饰 peach baskets。
4. Extreme sports started as an alternative to more expensive sports such as golf.
   极限运动最初是作为诸如高尔夫球等一些较为昂贵运动的替代形式而出现。

Exercise 1 Reading Comprehension

Answer the following questions according to the text.

1. What were sports in their original forms intended to satisfy?
2. How long is China's history in sports?
3. What does the phrase "made its debut" in the last sentence of paragraph 4 mean?
4. What is the similarity between original basketball and modern basketball?
5. How did extreme sports start?

Exercise 2 Word Training

Fill in the blanks with the words given below. Change the form where necessary.

| legacy | assume | equip | evidence | competition |
| prosperous | various | popular | preference | exclusive |

1. Padua and Vicenza are _____, well-preserved cities, not overrun by tourists.
2. As Christmas Day is approaching, Christmas decorations have come to be _____ with local consumers.
3. Recently there are _____ kinds of new brand shoes coming up. We wish you to visit our website and choose your favorite!
4. _____ yourself well for the coming interviews.
5. A body of _____ emerged suggesting that smoking tobacco caused serious diseases.
6. Because there is so much unemployment, the _____ for jobs is very fierce.
7. A teacher should not show _____ for any one of his students.
8. This dining room is for the distinguished guests' _____ use.
9. I think we can safely _____ that this situation will continue.
10. Lucy received a large _____ from her uncle.

Section 3 Translation

Ⅰ. *Translate the following sentences into Chinese.*

1. Snowboarding is becoming a more and more popular winter sport throughout the world.

2. I once participated in an outdoor training course, which was very worthwhile.
3. Every year there are many matches played on the municipal, provincial or national level.
4. Women are more involved in sports than they used to be, and they are frequently beating their male counterparts in some events.
5. Bungee jumping is really a breathtaking sport.

II. *Translate the following sentences into English.*
1. 在溜冰时你得学会保持平衡。
2. 我昨天晚上在电视上看了极限运动，表演真是太精彩了。
3. 我的叔叔说我应该去体验一下蹦极，但是我就是不敢。
4. 体操通过使用各种各样的设备，考验着人体的能力。
5. 越来越多的人愿意参加各种各样的运动，比如滑冰、滑雪、潜水、打猎，甚至是更刺激的运动。

Section 4   Classified Word Bank

Read the following words and expressions aloud and then learn them by heart.

1.	high jump	跳高
2.	long jump	跳远
3.	shot put	推铅球
4.	discus throw	掷铁饼
5.	javelin throw	掷标枪
6.	100-metre sprint	100 米短跑
7.	relay race	接力赛跑
8.	gymnastics	体操
9.	weight-lifting	举重
10.	basketball	篮球
11.	football	足球
12.	table tennis	乒乓球
13.	badminton	羽毛球
14.	ice hockey	冰球
15.	rugby	橄榄球
16.	hockey	曲棍球

17. cricket	板球
18. skating	滑冰
19. skiing	滑雪
20. diving	跳水

Unit 5 Bars

Section 1 Listening and Speaking

I. Listen and Repeat

Dialogue 1 In a Bar

A foreign guest is in a bar and the bartender Ms. Zhang is serving him.

Zhang: Welcome to our bar, sir. May I take your order?

Guest: I can hardly decide what to drink. Could you recommend some?

Zhang: How about a glass of wine?

Guest: That's fine and do you have any draft beer?

Zhang: Yes, of course. Would you care for some?

Guest: OK. Two glasses of wine, two draft beer, please.

Zhang: Okay. Anything else?

Guest: I'd like some vegetable spring rolls and the Thai deep-fried shrimp patties.

Zhang: OK.

Guest: How much should I pay for them?

Bartender: The total is 256 yuan. You can hold the payment of the bill until you decide to leave.

Guest: Really? Thank you very much. By the way, do you have Chinese Maotai?

Zhang: Yes, would you like to have a try?

Guest: OK. Four Maotai, please.

Zhang: But remember that Chinese liquor is a bit stronger than the Western spirit.

Guest: I see. Thank you.

Zhang: Is there anything else I can get for you?
Guest: No, thank you.

Dialogue 2 Going for a Drink

Mrs. Huang wants to invite Kevin for a drink. They are discussing where to go and what to drink.

Huang: Would you like to have a drink with me?
Kevin: Great! But where shall we go?
Huang: What about Houhai Bar Street? There're lots of bars there. It's really nice.
Kevin: That would be a good place for a drink. It is one of the most famous bar streets in Beijing.
Huang: Yes. There are 137 bars built along the street. Thousands of overseas tourists, businessmen and women enjoy their nightlife there.
Kevin: It is the right place to drop by to enjoy a cup of drink in the great atmosphere after a day's hard work.
Huang: That's true. Besides drinking, we can also sing or ask amateur singers to sing for us.
Kevin: I really like the atmosphere there.
Huang: Have you anything in mind as to what to drink there?
Kevin: No. Do you have any suggestions?
Huang: Yeah, would you like to have some Maotai there? It never goes to the head.
Kevin: Frankly speaking, I don't like this wine. I like Shaoxing rice wine because it tastes better.
Huang: I can't agree with you more. Maotai is much stronger than Shaoxing rice wine.
Kevin: What about cocktails there?
Huang: I bet cocktails there are very nice. A bartender knows what to do to your taste.
Kevin: But it is already 11 o'clock. Isn't it a little late to go there now?
Huang: Don't worry. Most of the bars open until 1 or 2 a.m. or even later.
Kevin: Then let's go for a drink.

II. Act Out

1. Listen to the dialogue. Then practice it with your partners using the words and expressions below to help you.

Waiter: welcome, drink list, take your time, what, drink, care for, vodka, suggest, taste, Great Wall wine, read, China Daily, wait for, your drink, sorry, keep,

> waiting, enjoy, your drink, check, terribly sorry, taken the wrong wine, change, immediately, here is your wine, hope, right, this time, glad to hear it, apologize, carelessness, sure, do better.
>
> **Guest**: too strong, think, Chinese wine, good idea, that's fine, not, what, ordered, wine, I want, Great Wall, not Dynasty, have a look, you are right, this time, different tastes, like European wine, that's all right, hope, mistake, next time.

2. Study the following sample dialogue. Then strike up a conversation with your partners using the sentences listed in the chart.

A: May I help you, sir?

B: Yes, **I'd like a martini. Make it dry.**

A: Okay. Wait a minute, please.

1. I'd like a martini. Make it dry.
2. I'd like a glass of red wine.
3. I'd like a lager.
4. I'd like some champagne.
5. I'll have a draft beer.
6. I'd like a whisky with soda.
7. I'd like a Bud.
8. I'd like a gin and tonic.
9. I'd like an ale.
10. I'd like a scotch on the rocks.

III. Focus Listening

A. Listen to the recording and choose the correct answer for each question.

1. Beijing used to be considered a dull city because there was no _____.
   A. nightlife   B. bands   C. theaters   D. restaurants

2. One of the first and largest bar areas is _____.
   A. Yuandadu Bar Street   B. Houhai Bar Street
   C. Sanlitun Bar Street   D. Shichahai Bar Street

3. Sanlitun is a place where there are _____.

A. many foreign embassies

B. a lot of beautiful scenery

C. rich wine types

D. so many visitors

4. Which of the following about Houhai Bar Street is not true?

   A. It is one part of Shichahai Lake.

   B. It combines Chinese and western culture.

   C. It is a hot place and highly praised by visitors.

   D. It is another place to enjoy acrobatics in Beijing.

5. Yuandadu Bar Street is unique because_____.

   A. the little moon river cuts across it

   B. it has parking lots for 400 cars

   C. it is located in Yuandadu Relics Park

   D. it combines bar culture with the history

B. Listen to the recording and complete the sentences below.

1. You will feel puzzled that in British pubs people buy their drinks without _____.

2. While _____, you should try your best to attract the bartenders' attention.

3. It is no good manners to _____ simply because you cannot make up your mind.

4. In order to attract the bartenders' attention, the proper _____ are expectant, hopeful or even slightly anxious.

5. To show your thanks for the bartender, the proper way is to offer them a drink rather than _____.

Section 2 Reading

Bars

Life is stressful. So, what people may need is to find a quiet spot somewhere and sit down by the window, looking at the passers-by in the streets, listening to music, sipping beer and chatting randomly with some friends.

Bars, which attract many people in Beijing at night, provide people with the alternative to traditional Chinese restaurants and teahouses. Hanging out in bars is now a lifestyle for modern people. Many young people indulge themselves in pleasures in the bars at night, where they gather to exchange views and to relax.

Currently there are a great many bars with various characteristics all around Beijing. It is estimated that there are some 500 bars in the city, each bar having its own special theme, both musically and aesthetically, and customers can choose where to go according to their tastes.

Some famous and not famous bars are scattered at various corners in Beijing, especially around Shichahai and near some colleges and universities. Quiet, at ease and with an ancient color, these bars are places for people to be together with some close friends, to have intimate talks, and to enjoy the peaceful moment in the bustling city.

Nan Luo Gu Xiang is becoming a good place for local residents to go to in their spare time. The long, narrow lane is shaded by luxuriant trees where rows of Siheyuan built in traditional Beijing local style stretch far on both sides of the lane. The tranquil atmosphere inside the lane will make one forget about the hustle and bustle in the street and it also makes the lane different from most other bar streets that are usually noisy. The lane is now dotted with over 30 bars, cafés, restaurants and small handicraft shops, all attracting people with their unique style. While most bar streets in other places have become more and more commercialized, people cherish the cultural atmosphere here.

For many foreign visitors and young people, Sanlitun Bar Street in Chaoyang District is also a must. There have been some 200, or 40% of the bars in Beijing gathering here since its first bar was set up in 1989. Its good location has made it popular among foreigners, Beijing's artists and white-collar workers. Here you will find rock-and-roll, hip-hop, Jazz and many other activities. In addition, this is a good place to see the first-hand something of modern China.

Varieties of bars can be found in Beijing. A bus bar is built in a deserted bus. A football bar specializes in all things about football A movie bar is the place where people can not only watch domestic movies which they have hardly any opportunities to watch in other places but also play the DV they have shot themselves. There is also the artists' bar filled with artistic atmosphere, where you can watch on-the-spot performances of original music every night. With traveling as a theme, some bars provide information and equipment for outdoor sports and they also regularly hold lectures on tourism. Some bars have thousands of books on the shelves against the four walls. One can dawdle away a whole day there and have dinner with friends there in the evening.

Bars are really good places for relaxation and pleasure. More and more people would like to enjoy such nightlife in Beijing.

Vocabulary

aesthetically /iːsˈθetikli/ adv. 美学的,有美感的,有审美能力的
commercialize /kəˈməːʃəlaiz/ v. (使)商业化;(使)商品化
currently /ˈkʌrəntli/ adv. 当前,现在
domestic /dəˈmestik/ adj. 家里的,家庭的;本国的,国内的
handicraft /ˈhændikrɑːft/ n. 手工艺,手艺
indulge /inˈdʌldʒ/ v. 放任,放纵,(使)沉溺于
intimate /ˈintimit/ adj. 亲密的,亲近的,隐私的,个人的
luxuriant /lʌgˈzjuriənt/ adj. 茂盛的,浓密的,华丽的
original /əˈridʒinəl/ adj. 最初的,原始的;有独创性的
random /ˈrændəm/ adj. 任意的,随便的
resident /ˈrezidənt/ n. 居民,居住者
scatter /ˈskætə/ v. (使)散开,驱散;抛撒,撒
specialize /ˈspeʃəlaiz/ v. 专门研究,专门从事,专攻
tranquil /ˈtræŋkwil/ adj. 平静的,宁静的
unique /juːˈniːk/ adj. 独一无二的,独特的

Phrases & Expressions

hang out 停留、经常去
indulge (oneself) in 沉湎于,沉溺于
hustle and bustle 拥挤,喧闹
be dotted with 点缀着,星星点点散布着
on-the-spot 现场的
dawdle away 闲混

Notes to the Text

1. Bars provides people with the alternative to traditional Chinese restaurants and teahouses.
   除了中国传统的饭馆和茶馆外,酒吧又为人们提供了另外一个可供选择之地。

alternative to：……的替代物。例如：There is no alternative to your plan. 除了你的计划，别无选择。

2. bar：酒吧。bar 的原意是栅栏或障碍物，相传早期的酒吧经营者为了防止意外，在吧台外设一横栏，横栏的设置一方面起阻隔作用，另一方面又可以为骑马的饮酒者提供拴马或搁脚的地方，久而久之，人们把"有横栏的地方"专指饮酒的酒吧。在中国，"吧"的意思几乎扩展到所有的公共消费空间，于是，便有了各种各样的"吧"：茶吧、网吧、影吧、泥吧、陶吧、书吧、氧吧、聊吧、说吧等。

3. Shichaha Bar Street：什刹海酒吧街。是北京最著名的酒吧一条街之一。什刹海酒吧街最动人之处在于可以观景。市井的喜气与飘香的红酒相安无事，古老的院落与时尚的潮流各得其所，什刹海的确是一种"北京特色"。

4. Sanlitun Bar Street：三里屯酒吧街。三里屯酒吧街是北京最早的酒吧群落，它分为南街和北街。北街的酒吧非常密集，沿街道两旁几十个酒吧一家贴着一家。由于北街毗邻北京最大的使馆区，老外是这里的固定客人，于是这里的酒吧不约而同地显得非常都市化，并以聚集人气、喧闹艳丽为主题。相比之下，三里屯南街的酒吧就有更多的胡同、院落、树甚至艺术气息。

Exercise 1 Reading Comprehension

Answer the following questions according to the text.

1. What is the main purpose of people's going to the bar?
2. Why can customers choose where to go according to their tastes?
3. In what way do we say Nan Luo Gu Xiang lane is different from most other bar streets?
4. What has made Sanlitun Bar Street so popular?
5. In what way is a movie bar different from a movie theater?

Exercise 2 Word Training

Fill in the blanks with the words given below. Change the form where necessary.

| random | exchange | indulge | commercial | current |
| stress | shade | estimate | special | domestic |

1. I don't like so many _____ breaks on TV.
2. We received several answers, and we picked one at _____.

3. Some universities lay _____ on language study.
4. You may write down something important and _____ on your notes.
5. It is natural to man to _____ in the illusions of hope.
6. The _____ central leaders have been doing a good job.
7. The medicare cost _____ to be one billion dollars.
8. As the _____ market becomes saturated, firms begin to export the product.
9. We sat down to rest under the _____ of a tree.
10. I will give you a candy bar in _____ for your soda pop.

Section 3   Translation

Ⅰ. *Translate the following sentences into Chinese.*
1. It is one of the bars in Beijing providing the cheapest drinks. A small bottle of Qingdao beer sells for only four yuan.
2. It is a bar in the center of a lake, a kind rarely seen in Beijing.
3. The bands giving performances generally consist of seven or eight persons with actors playing reversed roles and imitation shows.
4. The Guoke Bar, which is located at the southern end of the lane, has now become a must for backpackers from home and abroad.
5. A waitress said the bar received some 150 guests every day on average.

Ⅱ. *Translate the following sentences into English.*
1. 我想要杯加冰块的苏格兰威士忌酒。
2. 我们有一瓶保存了 20 年的葡萄酒。
3. 酒吧现在客满,请稍等约 20 分钟好吗?
4. 我想再要一杯跟刚才一样的酒。
5. 他沉浸在酒吧演奏的乡村音乐当中。

Section 4   Classified Word Bank

Read the following words and expressions aloud and then learn them by heart.

1. aperitif	开胃酒
2. cocktail	鸡尾酒

3.	orange juice	橘子原汁
4.	lemon juice	柠檬原汁
5.	soda water	苏打水
6.	milk tea	奶茶
7.	jasmine tea	茉莉花茶
8.	chrysanthemum tea	菊花茶
9.	oolong tea	乌龙茶
10.	green tea	绿茶
11.	black coffee	黑咖啡
12.	white coffee	牛奶咖啡
13.	Martell Cordon Blue	马爹利蓝带
14.	Remy Martin	人头马
15.	Hennessy Paradis	轩尼诗
16.	Brandy	白兰地
17.	light beer	淡啤酒
18.	champagne	香槟酒
19.	vodka	伏特加
20.	Martini	马提尼

附录一

本书专有名词列表

Altai Mountain 阿尔泰山
A-Ma Temple 妈祖庙
A-Ma 妈祖
American Falls 美国瀑布
An Lee 李安
Angel Gabriel 天使加百利
Baima Temple 白马寺
Bang Zi 梆子
Barbie 芭比
Beggar's Chicken 叫花鸡
Beijing Heroes Wushu Club 北京群英武术俱乐部
Blessed Virgin 圣母玛利亚
Bodhisattva Guan-yin 观音菩萨
Bridal Veil Falls 新娘面纱瀑布
Broadway 百老汇
Buddhist Arhats 罗汉
Bund 外滩
Butuoluo Temple 补陀罗寺
Byzantium 拜占庭时期
Canadian/Horseshoe Falls. 马蹄瀑布
Caramel Macchiato 焦糖玛奇朵（咖啡的一种口味）
Cataratas 伊瓜苏大瀑布

Changbai Mountain 长白山
Chengyanqiu 程砚秋
Chongsheng Temple 崇圣寺
Chu State 楚国
Cixi 慈禧太后
Confucius Temple 孔庙
Constantinus 君士坦丁政权时期
Coronation Square 加冕礼广场
Crispy fried chicken 脆皮炸鸡
Dage 达戈
Dali Ancient City 大理古城
Daoism 道教
Dengfeng City 登封市
Dharma 达摩
Dian Hong 滇红
Dongba Characters 东巴文字
Dongpo pork 东坡肉
Dragon Inn《新龙门客栈》
DUI 在酒精和药物影响下驾驶
DWI 醉酒时开车
Emei 峨眉
Famen Temple 法门寺
Feicui Spring 翡翠泉
Flying Trapeze 空中飞人

Friends 六人行
Fuding 福鼎白毫
Fufeng County 扶风县
Giant Red Fish 大红鱼
Golden Rooster Award 金鸡奖
Great Court 大中庭
Guanyu Pavilion 观鱼亭
Guihua Temple 桂花寺庙
Gulangyu 鼓浪屿
Guozijian 国子监
Hagia Sophia Church 圣索菲亚大教堂
Haitong 海通大师
Halls of Benevolence 仁寿殿
Hei Longtan 黑龙潭
Hohhot 呼和浩特
Houhai Bar Street 后海酒吧一条街
Huanglong Natural Scenic Area 黄龙风景区
Huangshan Maofeng 黄山毛峰
Huigen 慧根
In Love with the Dead 《冢爱》
Yinzhen 银针
Jade Buddha Temple 玉佛禅寺
Jinghu 京胡
Jingpo Lake 镜泊湖
Jiuzhaigou 九寨沟
Jumping Through Hoops 钻圈
Justinian 查士丁尼大帝
Kanas Lake 喀纳斯湖
Kun Qu 昆曲
Kung Fu 功夫
Kung Pao Chicken 宫保鸡丁
Lantern Festival 元宵节,灯节
Lantern Riddle Games 猜灯谜游戏
Leshan Giant Buddha 乐山大佛

Library of Mahmud 马哈茂德图书馆
Lijiang Ancient Town 丽江古城
Lijiang Naxi Autonomous County 丽江纳西族自治县
Lingyun Temple 凌云寺
Lintong County 临潼县
Long Hua Temple 龙华古寺
Longevity Hill 万寿山
Longjing 龙井
Lost Horizon 《失去的地平线》
Lotus Flower Stone 莲花峰
Lu-Da-gun 驴打滚
Luofeng Hill 螺峰山
Lust Caution 《色戒》
Macao 澳门
Mahavira Hall 大雄宝殿
Malan Noodles 马兰拉面
Manchu Nationality 满族
Mapo Tofu 麻婆豆腐
Mauna Loa 夏威夷的活火山的火山口
Mehmed 穆罕默德
Meilanfang 梅兰芳
Meili 梅里雪山
Miluo River 汨罗江
Ming Tombs 十三陵
Mogao Caves 莫高窟
Mount Lu 庐山
Mount Putuo 普陀山
Mount Song 嵩山
Mt. Huang 黄山
Mt. Junshan 君山
Mt. Lushan 庐山
Mt. Songshan 嵩山
Mu Family 木府

Namtso Lake 纳木错湖（天湖）
Nan Luogu Xiang Lane 南锣鼓巷胡同
Niagara Falls 尼亚加拉瀑布
Northern Styles 北派
Nuorilang Waterfall 诺日朗瀑布
Nvzhen tribes 女真族
Old Faithful 老忠实间歇泉
Onguiaahra 印第安语中意为"雷神之水"
Ottoman Empire 奥斯曼帝国
Pagoda of Bowls 顶碗
Pan County 潘县
Peking Man 北京猿人
Plate Spinning 转碟
Pu'er Tea 普洱茶
Purple palace 紫霄宫
Putian, Fujian Province 福建省莆田
Qi Hong 祁红
Qiao Family Compound 乔家大院
Qin Qiang 秦腔
Quick-Fried Tripe 爆肚
Red Theater 红剧场
Rongbaozhai 荣宝斋
Sakyamuni 释迦牟尼
Sanlitun Bar Street 三里屯酒吧一条街
Sea Cucumber in Brown Sauce 红烧海参
Shang Xiaoyun 尚小云
Shangri-la 香格里拉
Shaolin Temple 少林寺
Shark's Fin with Egg White 雪花鱼翅
Shichahai 什刹海
Shitazhenhai 石塔镇海
Shu Embroidery 蜀绣
Simuwu Ding 后母戊鼎
Songzanlin Lamsery 西藏的松赞林寺庙

Southern Styles 南派
Stir-Fried Shrimps 清炒虾仁
Streamer Balancing 耍中幡
Su Embroidery 苏绣
Suona 唢呐
Taichi 太极
Tang Xuanzang 唐玄奘
Tanzhe Temple 潭柘寺
the Big Dipper 北斗七星
the Buddha Fragrance Chamber 佛香阁
The Eagle 老鹰酒吧
the Eight Banners System 八旗制度
The Great Court 大中庭
the Hall of Central Harmony 中和殿
the Hall of Preserving Harmony 保和殿
the Hall of Supreme Harmony 太和殿
the Hall of Union 交泰殿
the Heavenly King 玉皇大帝
the Imperial Garden 御花园
the Jade Buddha Temple 玉佛寺
the Lakers 湖人队
the Lama Temple 雍和宫
the Lion Dance 耍狮子
the Naxi Ethnic Minority 纳西少数民族
the Oriental Pearl TV Tower 东方明珠电视塔
the Palace of Earthly Tranquility 坤宁宫
the Palace of Heavenly Purity 乾清宫
the Potala Palace 布达拉宫
Tianchi 天池
Turpan 吐鲁番
Twice cooked pork 回锅肉
Ultraman 奥特曼
Victoria Falls 维多利亚瀑布

Warlords《投名状》
West Lake Fish in Vinegar Gravy 西湖醋鱼
White Cloud Taoist Temple 白云观
White Horse Temple 白马寺
Wolongwan 卧龙湾
Xiang Embroidery 湘绣
Xilamuren Grassland 内蒙古希拉穆仁草原
Xuan Zong 玄宗
Xun Huisheng 荀慧生
Yang Xie Zi 羊蝎子
Yangwei 杨威
Yaze Lake 鸭泽湾
Ying Hong 英红

Yu Garden 豫园
Yuanshazhou 圆沙洲
Yuantong Sheng Jing 圆通胜景
Yuantong Temple 圆通寺
Yue Embroidery 粤绣
Yueliangwan 月亮湾
Yueqin 月琴
Yunwu 云雾
Zhenhe 政和大白茶
Zhongdian 中甸
Zhonghe Peak 中和峰
Zhongyue 中岳(五岳之一)

附录二

明清两朝皇帝

Emperors of Ming Dynasty (1368—1644)
明朝历代皇帝 (1368—1644)

Reign Title 年号		Name of the Emperor 在位皇帝		Reigning Time 在位时间
Hongwu	洪武	Zhu Yuanzhang	朱元璋	1368—1398
Jianwen	建文	Zhu Yunwen	朱允炆	1399—1402
Yongle	永乐	Zhu Di	朱棣	1403—1424
Hongxi	洪熙	Zhu Gaochi	朱高炽	1425
Xuande	宣德	Zhu Zhanji	朱瞻基	1426—1435
Zhengtong	正统	Zhu Qizhen	朱祁镇	1436—1449
Jingtai	景泰	Zhu Qiyu	朱祁钰	1450—1456
Tianshun	天顺	Zhu Qizhen	朱祁镇	1457—1464
Chenghua	成化	Zhu Jianshen	朱见深	1465—1487
Hongzhi	弘治	Zhu Youcheng	朱佑樘	1488—1505
Zhengde	正德	Zhu Houzhao	朱厚照	1506—1521
Jiajing	嘉靖	Zhu Houzong	朱厚熜	1522—1566
Longqing	隆庆	Zhu Zaihou	朱载垕	1567—1572
Wanli	万历	Zhu Yijun	朱翊钧	1573—1620
Taichang	泰昌	Zhu Changluo	朱常洛	1620 (29 days)
Tianqi	天启	Zhu Youxiao	朱由校	1621—1627
Chongzhen	崇祯	Zhu Youjian	朱由检	1628—1644

Emperors of Qing Dynasty (1644—1911)
清朝历代皇帝(1644—1911)

Reign Title 年号		Name of the Emperor 在位皇帝		Reigning Time 在位时间
Shunzhi	顺治	Fu Lin	福临	1644—1661
Kangxi	康熙	Xuan Ye	玄烨	1662—1722
Yongzheng	雍正	Yin Zhen	胤禛	1723—1735
Qianlong	乾隆	Hong Li	弘历	1736—1795
Jiaqing	嘉庆	Yong Yan	颙琰	1796—1820
Daoguang	道光	Min Ning	旻宁	1821—1850
Xianfeng	咸丰	Yi Zhu	奕詝	1851—1861
Tongzhi	同治	Zai Chun	载淳	1862—1874
Guangxu	光绪	Zai Tian	载湉	1875—1908
Xuantong	宣统	Pu Yi	溥仪	1909—1911

附录三

东西方主要节日

西方国家主要节日

New Year's Day 元旦	January 1
Memorial Day 阵亡将士纪念日	the last Monday in May
Independence Day 美国独立日	July 4
Thanksgiving Day 感恩节	the last Thursday in November
Christmas Day 圣诞节	December 25
Martin Luther King Day 马丁·路得金纪念日	the second Monday in January
Columbus Day 哥伦布纪念日	the first Monday after October 12
Christmas Eve 平安夜	December 24
New Year's Eve 除夕	December 31
Valentine's Day 情人节	February 14
Halloween 万圣节	October 31
Easter 复活节	the first Sunday after the paschal full moon

中国主要节日

春节(农历一月一日)	the Spring Festival (Chinese New Year)
元宵节(农历一月十五日)	the Lantern Festival
清明节(4月5日)	the Tomb-Sweeping Festival
中国青年节(5月4日)	Chinese Youth Day
端午节(农历五月初五)	the Dragon Boat Festival

中国共产党成立纪念日(7月1日)　the Party's Birthday
建军节(8月1日)　　　　　　　Army's Day
中秋节(农历八月十五)　　　　the Mid-Autumn Festival
教师节(9月10日)　　　　　　Teachers' Day
重阳节(农历九月九日)　　　　Double-ninth Day
国庆节(10月1日)　　　　　　National Day
除夕(农历十二月三十日)　　　New Year's Eve

附录四

应用文样本

1. 索取旅行社宣传手册

Dear Sir or Madam:

My friend and I would like very much to visit Cambridge and Oxford this summer when we have a holiday. We know you are the biggest tourist agency in the town, so we want you to arrange the tour for us.

We would be appreciated if you could send a brochure with prices, schedules, entertainment, etc. to us.

Thank you,
Daniel Black

2. 写信给旅行社要求取消行程

July 12, 2005

Dear Mr. Johnson:

My fiancée Linda and I booked a package tour through your agency. We planned to travel to Florida, from July 15 through 26, 2005.

Unfortunately, Linda suddenly fell ill this morning and her doctor told her that she would be having minor surgery, so we will not be able to go on the trip. According to the terms of our travel contract, we are entitled to cancel the trip and receive a full refund of our advance payment because of a medical condition. I have attached a copy of a letter from her doctor Ms. Anne Brick, confirming the surgery.

Please send a check to me at the address I left you. After my fiancée recovers, we'll call you to schedule a new trip.

Sincerely,
Bruce Miller

3. 邀请函样本

Invitation 1

You're Invited!

Yedong Company is having its 20th anniversary. Please join us for the celebration on Monday, May 12.

Anytime between 9 a.m. and 4 p.m

Yedong Company

156 Xingye Street

Luwan District 200023

Invitation 2

Dear Lucy and Alan:

We hope you'll join us on New Year's Eve for a special party—the first one since we got married.

We'll serve dinner and drinks starting at 8 p.m. and toast the new year at Midnight.

Please let us know if you can attend.

Sincerely,

Molly and Bruce Wang

Invitation 3

The pleasure of your company is requested by

Mr. Williams Lee

for cocktails

to meet

Maggie Q

international movie star

Friday, October 15

At 6:30 p.m.

In the Swan Hall

Garden Hotel

Invitation 4

Dear Rebecca:

On Sunday August 26 we will be hosting a small dinner party, and we would like to have you and your husband Alex join us.

Joe's sister Angela has become a famous Hollywood actress. She will be visiting us for a few days with her boyfriend Brian, who is also a movie star. We would like to introduce them to some of our special friends.

Please join us at our house for cocktails at 7 p.m. We look forward to seeing you both.

Please let us know if you are going to come.

Sincerely,

Catherine Luddy

4. 简历样本

Bruce Thompson

45 Century City, Chaoyang District, Beijing 100025, China

Tel: 010 6772 5588; 13681995858

E-mail: Bthompson@hotmail.com

PROFILE

- A competent and highly experienced sales manager with proven marketing skills.

PERSIBAL DETAILS

- Male
- Date of Birth: March 5, 1970

TRAINING AND QUALIFICATIONS

1976—1982 Beijing Experimental Primary School, Beijing

1982—1988 Beijing No.8 Secondary School, Beijing

1988—1992 Fudan University, Shanghai. BA Honours in Marketing

1992—1995 Beijing University, Beijing. MBA

EXPERIENCE

2003—present Sales Manager, Microsoft China

1998—2002 Representative of Sales Department, Shanghai 21st Century Real Estate company

1995—1998 Sales Majordomo, Nokia China

ACHIEVEMENT

- Has successfully doubled the sales of software for Microsoft China.

- Increased the sales and profit by 46 percent for Shanghai 21st Century Real Estate company.
- Successfully have the share of Nokia cell phones reach 39 percent in Shanghai.

PROFESSIONAL QUALITIES
- Skilful at organizing and motivating sales teams to achieve their objectives.
- Excellent communication and coordination skills.
- Good at prediction and decision making.
- Has a good eye for detail

OTHER SKILLS AND INTERESTS
- Mastery of English and French, oral and written.
- Computer Level 3 Certificate.
- Interested in mountain climbing and skiing.
- Fond of driving helicopters

REFERENCES

Mrs. Alison Bricks
Microsoft China
PO Box 28
Beijing 100058
AlisonBrks@Yahoo.com.cn

Mr. Liu Haiyang
Nokia China
30, Avenue Road,
Beijing 100035
010 83676969

附录五

世界七大奇迹

远古时代的世界七大奇迹

1. The Pyramids of Egypt
   埃及金字塔
2. The Hanging Gardens of Babylon
   巴比伦空中花园
3. The Tomb of Mausolus at Halicarnassus
   哈利卡纳苏摩索拉斯陵墓
4. The Temple of Diana at Ephesus
   希腊阿苔密斯神殿
5. The Colossus at Rhodes
   罗得港太阳神巨像
6. The Statue of Jupiter at Olympus
   奥林匹亚宙斯神像
7. The Pharos Lighthouse at Alexandria
   亚历山大城法洛斯灯塔

(以上所列的远古时代世界七大奇迹,只有埃及的金字塔依然存在。)

中世纪时代的七大奇迹

1. The Colosseum of Rome
   罗马圆形剧场(意大利)
2. The Leaning Tower of Pisa
   比萨斜塔(意大利)
3. The Catacombs of Alexandria

亚历山大陵墓(埃及)
4. The Great Wall of China
   万里长城(中国)
5. Stonehenge
   巨石阵(英国)
6. The Porcelain Tower of Nanjing
   南京琉璃塔(中国)
7. The Mosque of St. Sophia at Constantinople
   君士坦丁堡的索菲亚大教堂(土耳其)

(以上所列中世纪时代的世界七大奇迹,除君士坦丁堡的索菲亚大教堂外,仍存在于世或人们可以看到残址。)

附录六

十二属相与十二星宿表

十二属相表

rat	ox	tiger	rabbit	dragon	snake
鼠	牛	虎	兔	龙	蛇
horse	sheep	monkey	rooster	dog	pig
马	羊	猴	鸡	狗	猪

十二星宿表

星座(Sign)	出生日期(Date of birth)
Aquarius 水瓶座	Jan. 20—Feb. 19
Pisces 双鱼座	Feb. 20—Mar. 20
Aries 白羊座	Mar. 21—Apr. 20
Taurus 金牛座	Apr. 21—May. 20
Gemini 双子座	May. 21—Jun. 21
Cancer 巨蟹座	Jun. 22—Jul. 22
Leo 狮子座	Jul. 23—Aug. 22
Virgo 处女座	Aug. 23—Sep. 22
Libra 天秤座	Sep. 23—Oct. 22
Scorpio 天蝎座	Oct. 23—Nov. 21
Sagittarius 射手座	Nov. 22—Dec. 21
Capricorn 摩羯座	Dec. 22—Jan. 19

附录七

肢体语言

1. Cross one's fingers—Good luck.
   交叉手指——表示祝你好运。
2. Give me five—To celebrate something.
   击掌——表示祝贺某事顺利完成。
3. Kiss someone on the cheek—Nice to see you again.
   亲别人的面颊——表示问候。
4. Make the V sign with your middle and index finger—Victory.
   用食指和中指做出 V 的形状——表示胜利。
5. Move one's feet up and down—Fed up.
   上下颠脚——表示厌烦。
6. Pat someone on the back—Well done.
   轻拍某人的背——干得不错!
7. Pout—Unhappy.
   噘嘴——表示不高兴。
8. Pull a long face—Sad.
   拉长脸——不高兴。
9. Raise one's eyebrows—Surprised.
   扬眉——表示惊讶。
10. Roll one's eyes—Impatient and annoyed.
    翻白眼——表示生气或不耐烦。
11. Shake hands—Hello, glad to meet you.
    握手——你好,见到你很高兴。
12. Move one's head from side to side—No.
    摇头——表示不赞同。

13. Move one's head up and down—Yes.
    点头——表示赞同。
14. Shrug one's shoulders—One doesn't know.
    耸肩——表示不知道。
15. Slap one's forehead—One has forgotten something.
    在额头上打一下——表示忘掉了重要的事情。
16. Snap one's fingers—Get someone's attention.
    打响指——表示引起别人注意。
17. Thumbs down—Bad.
    大拇指朝下——不好。
18. Thumbs up—Good.
    竖起大拇指——好。
19. Wave—Goodbye.
    挥手——表示再见。
20. Wink—I'm joking.
    有意眨眼——我在开玩笑。

附录八

出入境检疫检验申明卡

英文版：

**ENTRY-EXIT INSPECTION AND QUARANTINE
THE PEOPLE'S REPUBLIC OF CHINA
HEALTH AND QUARANTINE DECLARATION
FORM ENTRY** ↑

☆☆This is machine-read card. Please do not knead or fold the card For affecting your pass. Please Mark ● before the items selected.

Name：_____ Sex：○ Male ○ Female

Birth Date：____ mm ____ yy Nationality (Region)：_____

Passport No.：_____ Vehicle/Ship/Flight No.：_____

1. The contact address and telephone number in the next 14 days：
   _____

2. Please mark ● before the items of following symptoms or illness if you have any now.
   - ○ Fever
   - ○ Cough
   - ○ Psychosis
   - ○ Diarrhea
   - ○ Vomitting
   - ○ Difficulty breathing
   - ○ Venereal disease
   - ○ AIDS/HIV
   - ○ Active pulmonary tuberculosis

3. Have you had close contact with any probable or suspected SARS case in the past 14 days?
   ○ Yes ○ No

4. Please mark ● before the items of following articles if you bring any of them.

○ Animal   ○ Animal carcasses and specimen
○ Animal products   ○ Human tissues
○ Microbes   ○ Biological products
○ Plant   ○ Blood and blood products
○ Soil   ○ Plant propagating materials
○ Plant products

I hear by declare that all the information given above is true and correct.

Date：_____ Signature：_____

_____

Body temperature (Quarantine official use only)：_____ ℃

中文版：

中华人民共和国出入境检疫检验
入 境 健 康 检 疫 申 明 卡 ↑

_____

☆☆本申明为机读卡片,请勿揉折,以免影响您正常通关。请您将选中项的 ○ 涂黑 ●

姓名：_____ 性别：○ 男   ○ 女
出生日期：_____年_____月 国籍(地区)：_____
护照号码：_____ 车(船)次、航班号：_____

1. 此后14天内的联系地址和电话：_____
_____

2. 如您有以下症状或疾病,请选项申报。
    ○ 发烧   ○ 呼吸困难
    ○ 咳嗽   ○ 性传播疾病
    ○ 精神病   ○ 艾滋病
    ○ 腹泻   ○ 开放性肺结核
    ○ 呕吐

3. 过去14天内是否与传染性非典型肺炎患者或疑似患者有过密切接触?
    ○ 是   ○ 否

4. 如您携带有以下物品,请选项申报。

○ 动物	○ 动物尸体、标本
○ 动物产品	○ 人体组织
○ 微生物	○ 生物制品
○ 植物繁殖材料	○ 血液或血液制品
○ 土壤	○ 植物
○ 植物产品	

我已阅知本申明卡所列事项,并保证以上申明内容正确属实。

日期：_____   旅客签名：_____

_____

体温(检验人员填写)：_____℃

参 考 文 献

1. 朱宝琛.最新汉英旅游辞典[M].北京：旅游教育出版社,1992.
2. 陈克成.旅游交际英语通[M].上海：华东师范大学出版社,1992.
3. 王逢鑫.汉英旅游文化词典[M].北京：北京大学出版社,2001.
4. 关肇远.导游英语口语[M].北京：高等教育出版社,2004.
5. 段开成.旅游英语[M].天津：南开大学出版社,2004.
6. 当代高级英语辞典[M].英国培生教育出版公司.北京：外语教学与研究出版社,2004.
7. 邹晓燕.旅游专业英语实用教程[M].北京：清华大学出版社,2005.
8. 理查德·艾·斯皮尔斯.美国英语口语辞典[M].上海：上海译文出版社,2005.
9. 金锦.旅游英语[M].北京：科学出版社,2006.
10. 刘泽彭.中国文化常识[M].北京：高等教育出版社,2007.
11. 吴云.旅游实践英语[M].北京：旅游教育出版社,2007.
12. 魏国富.实用旅游英语教程[M].上海：复旦大学出版社,2007.
13. 刘倩.旅游英语[M].北京：北京理工大学出版社,2007.
14. 黄中军.疯狂英语口语王基础会话[M].北京：京华出版社,2008.
15. 朱华.英语导游实务教程[M].北京：北京大学出版社,2009.
16. 谢关平.旅游英语[M].合肥：中国科学技术大学出版社,2009.
17. 赵丽.新编饭店实用英语听说教程[M].北京.清华大学出版社,2009.
18. 黄万武,刘加英.旅游英语[M].武汉：武汉理工大学出版社,2009.
19. 陈欣.导游英语情景口语[M].北京：北京大学出版社,2009.
20. 姜丽.旅游英语[M].北京：对外经济贸易大学出版社,2009.
21. 史爱华,顾宝珠.旅游英语[M].北京：机械工业出版社,2009.
22. 黄中军.实用旅游英语[M].旅游英语[M].北京：清华大学出版社,2010.
23. 林群.旅游服务英语[M].北京：清华大学出版社,2010.
24. 杨义德,李斌.旅游英语教程[M].北京：北京大学出版社,2012.
25. 李燕,徐静.旅游英语[M].北京：清华大学出版社,2013.
26. 莫红英.旅游英语[M].北京：旅游教育出版社,2013.

教师服务

感谢您选用清华大学出版社的教材！为了更好地服务教学，我们为授课教师提供本书的教学辅助资源，以及本学科重点教材信息。请您扫码获取。

❯❯ 教辅获取

本书教辅资源，授课教师扫码获取

❯❯ 样书赠送

旅游管理类重点教材，教师扫码获取样书

 清华大学出版社

E-mail: tupfuwu@163.com
电话: 010-83470332 / 83470142
地址: 北京市海淀区双清路学研大厦 B 座 509
网址: https://www.tup.com.cn/
传真: 8610-83470107
邮编: 100084